CROSS AND SCEPTER

CROSS & SCEPTER

The Rise of the Scandinavian Kingdoms from
the Vikings to the Reformation

SVERRE BAGGE

PRINCETON UNIVERSITY PRESS

PRINCETON AND OXFORD

Second printing, and first paperback printing, 2016
Paperback ISBN: 978-0-691-16908-8

The Library of Congress has cataloged the cloth edition as follows:

Bagge, Sverre, 1942–
Cross and scepter : the rise of the Scandinavian kingdoms from the Vikings to
the Reformation / Sverre Bagge.
pages cm
Includes bibliographical references and index.
ISBN 978-0-691-16150-1 (hardcover : acid-free paper) 1. Scandinavia—
History. 2. Middle Ages. 3. Scandinavia—Kings and rulers—
History. 4. Scandinavia—Politics and government. 5. Christianity—
Scandinavia—History—To 1500. 6. Monarchy—Scandinavia—History—To
1500. 7. Aristocracy (Political science)—Scandinavia—History—To
1500. 8. Scandinavia—Social conditions. 9. Social change—Europe—Case
studies. I. Title.
DL49.B34 2014
948'.023—dc23   2013040063

British Library Cataloging-in-Publication Data is available

This book has been composed in Garamond Premier Pro

Printed on acid-free paper.

Printed in the United States of America

3 5 7 9 10 8 6 4 2

⇥ CONTENTS ⇤

⚜ ACKNOWLEDGMENTS ⚜

THIS BOOK HAS ITS BACKGROUND in my period as the director of two research centers, the Centre for Medieval Studies at the University of Bergen (2002–12) and the Nordic Centre for Medieval Studies at the Universities of Bergen, Gothenburg, Odense, and Helsinki (2005–10), funded by grants respectively from the Norwegian Research Council and the Joint Committee for Nordic Research Councils for the Humanities and the Social Sciences. I thank my many colleagues in these milieus for pleasant company and a stimulating exchange of ideas. I am particularly grateful to Thomas Lindkvist, Bjørn Poulsen, and Jørn Øyrehagen Sunde, and to two anonymous readers who have read the manuscript and given useful suggestions, and to Ola Søndenå for his work with the illustrations. I also want to thank Patrick Geary for his interest in the book while acting as a board member of the Nordic Centre and for bringing me in touch with Princeton University Press. Once that contact was established, it was a pleasure to work with Brigitta van Rheinberg and her colleagues, who have combined enthusiasm, speed, and thoroughness in a most impressive way. I also thank the Oxford University Press for permission to use extracts from the *Oxford History of Historical Writing*, volume 2: 400–1400, edited by Sarah Foot and Chase F. Robinson (2012), Stanford University Press for permission to use the translation from Ljósvetninga Saga on p. 1, and the Museum Tusculanum Press, Copenhagen, for permission to use material published in my book *From Viking Stronghold to Christian Kingdom: State Formation in Norway, c. 900–1350* (Copenhagen, 2010).

Sverre Bagge
Bergen, September 2013

CROSS AND SCEPTER

⤝⇒ INTRODUCTION ⇐⤟

And when the tables were set, Ofeig put his fist on the table and
said, "How big does that fist seem to you, Gudmund?"
"Big enough," he said.
"Do you suppose there is any strength in it?" asked Ofeig.
"I certainly do," said Gudmund.
"Do you think it would deliver much of a blow?" asked Ofeig.
"Quite a blow," Gudmund replied.
"Do you think it might do any damage?" continued Ofeig.
"Broken bones or a deathblow," Gudmund answered.
"How would such an end appeal to you?" asked Ofeig.
"Not much at all, and I wouldn't choose it," said Gudmund.
Ofeig said, "Then don't sit in my place."

IN THIS STORY FROM the Icelandic *Ljósvetninga Saga,* power is
concentrated in a big fist in a way that recalls Hobbes's character-
ization of primitive man, whose life is "solitary, poor, nasty, brut-
ish, and short." There is constant competition and the physically
strongest is likely to win, as in the competition for leadership
among animals.

With increasing institutionalization, physical power is replaced by legitimate birth, specific qualifications, or formal election, and the fist by symbols of authority. Such symbols no doubt existed in Scandinavia from early on, but they assumed particular importance with the introduction of Christianity and the formation of kingdoms; in other words, with the introduction of the cross and the scepter. Bishops and archbishops were elected and consecrated and wore miters, staffs, rings, and crosses as signs of their dignity. Kingship eventually followed a similar path, the office being filled according to formal rules and by an incumbent who wore a crown and scepter. These leaders in turn had representatives of lower rank, who were supposed to carry out their commands. In theory, although not necessarily in practice, open competition was replaced by a formal hierarchy that was believed to have been instituted by God. Thus, from the tenth century onwards, a new concept of government and public authority was introduced to Scandinavia.

Can we use the term "state formation" when speaking of the Middle Ages? The term "state" is used in a different sense in different disciplines. While social scientists, particularly social anthropologists, are inclined to use the term when referring to any kind of lordship over larger areas or numbers of people, in some cases qualifying it as an "early state," historians often have stricter criteria. One of these has been the word itself. The Latin *status* ("condition," "state") derived from the combination *status rei publicae,* which was current in the Middle Ages, began to be used from the late sixteenth and early seventeenth century on as a technical term, meaning "state" in the modern sense. This terminological change is understood as expressing a new understanding of the state as an institution existing independently of the person or persons governing it, an understanding that incorporates the classical definitions of the state as a monopoly on violence or an impersonal and bureaucratic government. Although the importance of such a terminological change should not be underestimated, it can hardly be regarded as decisive; a new name does not mean that the phenomenon in question cannot have existed before. In practice, *res publica* in the Middle Ages may have had at least some of the impersonal connotations associated with the early-modern *status*.

In the present context, I regard the terminological question mainly as a practical one. The great divide in Scandinavian history was the formation of the three kingdoms, two of which have continued to exist until the present, while the third, Norway, preserved enough of its identity under Danish dominance to reemerge as an independent unit in 1814. It would thus seem natural to use the term "state" for these kingdoms from this date on, despite the rudimentary character of their political institutions. The most important concept in the following, however, is "state formation," which is a relative concept, implying centralization, bureaucratization, the development of jurisdiction, a monopoly or near monopoly on violence, and so forth, for it is more critical to decide whether a process is heading in this direction than to decide exactly how many of these criteria must be present before it is allowable to use the word "state." The following discussion will deal with the changes that took place in Scandinavia from the formation of the kingdoms in the tenth century until the end of the Kalmar Union and the introduction of the Reformation in the early sixteenth century, and with how the three Scandinavian kingdoms compared with other countries at the time in terms of "stateness."

Reflecting the strong link between historical scholarship and the nation state from the early nineteenth century onwards, state formation has been a central theme in Scandinavian historiography, as well as in that of other countries. The idea of the medieval state was further developed in the English-speaking world in the twentieth century by scholars like F. W. Maitland, Charles Homer Haskins, Joseph Strayer, and R. W. Southern. In contrast to nineteenth-century scholarship which, for the most part, regarded the Middle Ages as dominated by Church and Empire, and by ideas of hierarchy and the supernatural rather than rational thought, this tradition—Southern was to some extent an exception—emphasized the rational and secular aspect of the period and regarded the development of law and administration as an attempt to solve the practical problems of government and the distribution of power. Thus, it was the Middle Ages rather than Classical Antiquity or even the Renaissance, that laid the foundations for the modern state, a view expressed most succinctly in Strayer's short but important book on the medieval origins of the state.

During the second half of the twentieth century, notably from around 1970 on, this view has been challenged from two directions. One is the historical sociology, which has generally sought the origins of the modern state in the Early Modern Period rather than the Middle Ages. This view turns on the importance attached to the military element in state formation, and a negative judgment of the state as mainly an instrument of oppression; in Charles Tilly's words: "War made the state and the state made war." Real states were created in the period of standing armies, guns and cannons, elaborate fortifications, and heavily armed warships, which were costlier and necessitated a larger and more complex administration than the simpler military equipment of the Middle Ages. The other challenge came from the medievalists themselves, partly from the French Annales School and partly from German historians of the interwar period who regarded medieval kingdoms and principalities as antitheses to the modern state rather than as its forerunners. This approach was revived in the late twentieth century under the influence of social anthropological research on stateless societies and has resulted in a series of successful studies of early-medieval society. However, there have also been reactions against these impulses. One is Susan Reynolds's rejection of the concept of feudalism, which she replaces with the notion that a society not very different in kind from the modern one that was in place already in the early Middle Ages. Another is R. I. Moore's "First European Revolution," which sees the years between 975 and 1215 as crucial to the evolution of European society and to global history in general, a period when new and more intensive forms of government were established by the Church as well as the state. The gradual formation of the nation state in the Middle Ages is also a central theme in Michael Mann's analysis of social power.

The challenges from the early medievalists and the early modernists serve as a starting-point for the following discussion. Without denying the importance of the early-modern military revolution or of military matters in general, the emphasis in the following will be on alternative paths to state formation and on the specifically medieval contribution to this process. The new ideas about personal relationships, rituals, feuds, and mediation will to a greater extent serve as a source of inspiration for this study. However, they have mainly been applied to the early Middle Ages and been based on the study of narrative sources. It is now time to apply them to the following period and to reexamine the question of change or continuity against this background.

In the late 1070s, Pope Gregory VII addressed the kings of Denmark, Norway, and Sweden with advice and admonitions in a series of letters that form some of the earliest examples of papal correspondence with the Scandinavian countries. One of his concerns was to prevent the king of Norway from meddling in the conflict over the succession to the Danish throne. The pope sternly warns the king of disasters that may follow from such a course of action, quoting Christ's words in the Bible about the division of a kingdom leading to its destruction (*Omne regnum in seipsum divisum desolabitur*, Luke 11:17). The saga of King Håkon of Norway records that more than 150 years later, in 1247, during a period of frequent contact between the papacy and Scandinavia, Cardinal William of Sabina told the king that it was unheard of that a country should be without a king, thus allowing him to take steps to bring Iceland under his rule.

These two statements express what had by now become established orthodoxy at the papal curia and in fact throughout most of Western Christendom, namely that the world was supposed to consist of a number of separate territories, each governed by a king, and that these kings should respect each other's rights and not interfere in the realms of their neighbors. This was a radical change from the situation that prevailed both at the time when the Christian Church was founded and when it became the official religion of the Roman Empire, which according to many contemporaries embraced the whole inhabited world (Luke 2:1). The breakdown of the Roman Empire and its Carolingian successor forced the Church to adapt to political division and gradually made it a force in upholding this division, which has proved one of the distinctive features of Europe compared to other civilizations, and which is still with us today, despite the increasing importance of the European Union. Exactly when this division was finally established is disputed and shall not concern us here, but an important stage in the process was no doubt the expansion of Western Christendom from the ninth century onwards to include Scandinavia and East Central Europe, whereby the idea of separate kingdoms spread to these regions.

A discussion of Scandinavian state formation is not only about more or less "stateness" in a comparative perspective, but also about the changing map of Western Christendom in the High Middle Ages. From the tenth century onwards, the European state—in the elementary sense of larger territories ruled by independent kings or princes—was exported to new areas, notably to the north and east. Western Christendom expanded greatly in the Mediterranean, in Scandinavia, and in East Central Europe, an expansion that marks the beginning of the European conquest of the rest of the world. The process partly took the form of conquest and even colonization, parallel to what happened during the Great Discoveries from the sixteenth century onwards, but it also led to the formation of independent kingdoms and principalities, which is its most interesting feature from our point of view. Whereas the southeastern shore of the Baltic Sea was for the most part an object of conquest and colonization, independent kingdoms were established to either side of this region, namely the three Scandinavian kingdoms in the North and West, and Poland, Bohemia, and Hungary in the East.

If we regard a multiplicity of centers of political power as an essential feature of Europe, in contrast for instance to China and the Islamic world (as is commonly done), the expansion becomes as important as the internal changes. Whereas most of Western Christendom had been united under one ruler in the Carolingian period and a substantial part of it under the Ottonian and Salian emperors, the expansion, combined with the weakening of central power in Germany, made the territorial principality the normal unit of political organization of Western Christendom. In addition to the three kingdoms of East Central Europe and Denmark on Germany's border, territorial principalities like Brandenburg, Mecklenburg, and Pomerania made themselves independent of the emperor in most respects. Most of these entities would remain in existence until the great changes in the nineteenth century, under Napoleon and Bismarck. The expansion thus established the combination of cultural unity with stable political division that characterized Europe until the formation of the European Union in the second half of the twentieth century.

The following account of the three Scandinavian kingdoms can therefore be regarded as a kind of European history in miniature, showing the rise of kingdoms from their very beginning and how the borders originally established by military conquest became part of the right order of the world. In addition to extending the geographical area normally covered in overviews of European medieval history, it may also contribute to the understanding of the European state system as such. Although of course no thorough-going comparison with other areas will be attempted, a study of one area may contribute to an understanding of the export of state formation from the old to the new areas of Western Christendom, of the relationship between the imported and indigenous elements of this process, and of the general relationship between the old and the new regions. It is my hope in this way to stimulate further research into these questions.

Living in a secularized society, we tend to identify the state with the monarchy, particularly in the Scandinavian countries with their long Protestant tradition. If we are interested in government, however, there is no reason to focus exclusively on the monarchy. The later state was a descendant not only of the monarchy but also of the Church, a point that is particularly obvious in Scandinavia, where at the Reformation the king took over most of the Church's lands and administration. From the point of view of the common people, it hardly mattered very much whether they were subject to the king, the Church, or a local lord, and the administrative and judicial systems employed by these power holders were not necessarily very different. Admittedly, rivalry within the governing elite might have serious consequences and might even lead to the dissolution of the country in question, or to its conquest by stronger and more centralized neighbors. As we shall see, however, Scandinavian, as well as European state formation was in general characterized by a certain balance between the various elements that made up the governing elite.

CHAPTER ONE

The Origins of the Scandinavian Kingdoms

Early Scandinavian Society

Although most histories of Scandinavia, including the present one, focus on the period from the formation of the kingdoms in the tenth and eleventh centuries, the area as a whole has a long history going back to the first settlements which date to the end of the last glacial age around 10,000 BC. The earliest inhabitants were hunters and gatherers. Agriculture was introduced gradually from around 4000 BC, first in the form of slash and burn cultivation, later with the establishment of permanent settlement. Already during the last centuries BC, a largely homogenous agricultural zone had developed in Denmark, southern Sweden, the coastal regions of Norway up to Trøndelag, and southern and western Finland. The rest of Scandinavia was dominated by low-intensive agriculture, hunting and gathering, or pastoral nomadism (the Sami in northern Norway, Sweden, and Finland). The high-intensive agricultural zone gradually expanded until the demographic crisis caused by the Black Death in the mid-fourteenth century, after which a new expansion of the zone of intensive agriculture followed in the sixteenth and seventeenth centuries. In parts of the north, however, nomadic or half-nomadic life continued until the twentieth century.

Because of its climate and terrain, large parts of Scandinavia pose problems for agriculture. The Scandinavian countries are situated between around 54 and 70 degrees north, thus forming the northernmost part of Western Christendom. In addition to being far north, large parts of Scandinavia are also highland, particularly in Norway, and to some extent also in northern Sweden. However, because of the Gulf Stream, the climate is far warmer than in any other part of the world at this latitude—by as much as 5 to 7 degrees C. Thus, it is possible to grow grain at around 70 degrees north in Norway.

As the southernmost of the three kingdoms, with no elevations greater than 200 meters above sea level, Denmark is clearly best suited for agriculture. In the Middle Ages, this country was both the most populous and the most densely settled, its population equal to or perhaps even larger than Sweden and Norway combined. In absolute numbers, the population of Denmark has been estimated at more than 1 million, perhaps nearly 2 million in the early fourteenth century, that of Norway at between 350,00 and 500,000, and the Swedish population at somewhere between 500,000 and 650,000.

But even in Denmark there are local variations. The islands and eastern Jutland were the richest agricultural areas in the Middle Ages, while heath and more marginal land prevailed in western and northern Jutland. Sweden, the largest of the three countries, also had significantly less highland than Norway and correspondingly larger agricultural areas. The latter were mainly concentrated in two parts of the country, in the Mälar valley west of present-day Stockholm and around the large lakes further west, Vänern and Vättern. The southern coast of Finland also has good agricultural land. It eventually became densely settled and formed an important part of the kingdom of Sweden. The remaining part of Sweden and Finland are more hilly and have less productive soil. Taken together the main agricultural areas in Norway, the area around Lake Mjøsa in the east, Jæren in the southwest, and the large valley north of present-day Trondheim in the north, cover a far smaller area than the corresponding districts in Sweden. However, the more marginal areas of this country have other assets, which make them suitable for human habitation. The coast of Norway, as well as its rivers and lakes, have rich fisheries, and the forests and mountains abound in game (elk, deer, and various smaller animals), and provide pasture. Although it is not particularly well suited to agriculture, the western coast of Norway has a mild climate, which protects the grain from frost and, together with the fisheries and wide areas suited for pasture, creates conditions conducive to relatively dense settlements. By contrast, eastern Norway and the more marginal parts of Sweden have the same advantages when it comes to hunting and pasture, and fish are plentiful in the lakes and rivers, but crops are more exposed to frost.

Iceland is by far the most marginal of the Scandinavian countries, not because it is so far north—at 63–67 degrees, it is just south of the Arctic Circle—but because it is situated far out in the Atlantic and its soil is mostly ill-suited to agriculture. When the immigrants arrived, mostly in the period between 870 and 930, the pastures and fisheries were extremely rich. It was also possible to grow grain there until around 1100, when the climate became colder. Eventually, the pastures deteriorated because of too much grazing, the forest was cut down or destroyed by the animals, and the soil became poorer because of erosion. Iceland became a marginal country with very difficult living conditions.

The natural conditions largely explain settlement and to some extent also social organization. Village settlement, which was the normal form of habitation in most of England and large parts of the Continent, was only to be found in Denmark and the best agricultural parts of Sweden. Settlement in the rest of Scandinavia was dominated by individual farms, although, particularly in western Norway, such farms, at least in later periods, are known to have been divided between several families whose houses were joined around a common courtyard.

The written sources give the impression that the Scandinavians suddenly came into contact with Europe around 800, with the expansion of the Carolingian Empire and the Viking expeditions, and that Scandinavia was then transformed as the result of the introduction of the monarchy and the conversion to Christianity. In addition, earlier scholarship has often depicted Scandinavian society in the previous period as relatively egalitarian, a society of free and independent farmers organized in extended families. This society was then gradually transformed, as a result of demographic growth and the new impulses from Europe, into the hierarchical and aristocratic society we know from the following period.

More recent research has revised this picture. There is archaeological evidence dating back to the first centuries AD of contacts with Europe as well as social stratification. A number of graves excavated in various parts of Scandinavia contain exquisite objects of Roman origin: drinking-horns and cups of glass, silver plates with reliefs of warriors and deer, and arm-rings used as indications of rank. Even a drinking-cup of silver has been found, showing two scenes from Homer: King Priam of Troy humbly asking Achilles for the body of his son Hector and Odysseus stealing Hercules's bow from Philoctetes.

Some of these objects may of course just be booty from plundering expeditions in parts of the Roman world, but their number and the context in which they have been found suggest something more. They may be the result of gift exchanges or rewards for war services rendered to the Romans, and they certainly form evidence of powerful rulers already at this time. The sacrifices of thousands of conquered arms, dating from the beginning of the Christian era until around 500, found in swamps in Denmark,

Figure 1. Drinking-cup from Hoby (Denmark), Roman, ca.
first century AD. Priam, to the left, kneels before Achilles,
asking to have his son Hector's body returned to him for burial.
From *Nordiske Fortidsminder*, vol. 2, ed. Det Kgl. Nordiske
Oldtidsselskab (The Royal Nordic Society of Antiquities)
(Copenhagen, 1911), plate 9. Photo: Pacht & Crone Eftf.
Fotoyp. Avdeling for Spesialsamlinger, Universitetsbiblioteket
i Bergen (Department of Special Collections, University of
Bergen Library).

complete the picture. The arms come from various parts of Europe, but most are from Germany and the other Scandinavian countries. It is likely that they indicate victories over people in these areas. They may even form a kind of parallel to the Roman triumph; the fact that only arms and not men were sacrificed makes it most likely that the arms were captured abroad. Did the Danish chieftains stage a procession similar to the Roman triumph but then destroy the arms as a sacrifice instead of retooling them for use by their own army, as the Romans did?

There is also evidence from the Roman period of principalities in various parts of Scandinavia, first in Denmark, southern Sweden and southern Norway, and the Baltic islands of Gotland and Öland; later from northern Sweden, and parts of Finland and Norway as far north as Lofoten in northern Norway.

A reduction of the quantity of grave-goods in finds from the seventh century was earlier interpreted as evidence of an agrarian crisis, similar to the one that took place in the fourteenth century, and was explained in the same way, namely as a consequence of the plague, which we know hit the Mediterranean region from the sixth century onwards. Later archaeologists found evidence of continued population growth and attribute the shortfall of grave-goods to cultural change rather than poverty. There thus seems to be a greater continuity between the wealth of the powerful chieftains of the Roman and Merovingian periods and the Scandinavian chieftains we meet in Carolingian sources from the eighth and ninth centuries and during the Viking expansion.

Taken together, the evidence suggests the existence of kingdoms and principalities in Scandinavia from the first centuries of the Christian Era onwards, possibly covering quite extensive areas, although it is impossible to trace exact borders. Large territorial units and strong rulers are therefore not necessarily a novelty resulting from the formation of the three kingdoms in the tenth and eleventh centuries. However, there is little to suggest that the earlier units corresponded to the later ones; most probably, we are dealing with various entities in mutual competition and with considerable changes in the centers of power over time.

Although there is no sure way to quantify the distribution of landownership or to delineate the social structure in the early Middle Ages, it is reasonable to imagine a wider distribution of land and less social stratification than in the following period. Most important institutions were local, with the king's position depending on his ability to gain adherents and satisfy them, failing which he might easily be deposed or killed. The Eddic poem *Rigsthula* may provide some clues. Here society is depicted as consisting of three classes, represented by three individuals: the slave, the commoner, and the earl. The commoner represents a kind of middle class, living respectably in contrast to the slave but not in luxury, in contrast to the earl. Although the date of *Rigsthula* is uncertain and disputed, there are good reasons to believe that it dates from the Viking Age. Moreover, we can point to other evidence confirming its picture. Archaeological material as well as foreign sources suggest the existence of large armies, in contrast to the elite forces that dominated from the twelfth century onwards, and place names point in the same direction.

This does not mean that early-medieval society mostly consisted of small, independent farmers owning their own land. Instead, we should probably imagine landownership as less strictly defined than in later times. Examinations of early-medieval agrarian structures in Norway based on place names and archaeological evidence suggest a combination of larger farms, probably owned by local magnates, and smaller ones dependent on them, but probably in a kind of patron-client rather than owner-tenant relationship. As in the rest of Europe in the early Middle Ages, land was not particularly valuable in itself. What was most important was control over the people who worked the land. Moreover, chieftains needed subordinates not only to cultivate the land, but also to serve them as warriors, both as participants in Viking expeditions and in conflicts with other chieftains. Thus, even if early-medieval society was neither democratic nor egalitarian, there are reasons to believe that it was less hierarchical than it later became. The magnates were more numerous and less wealthy and the social distance between them and the rest of the people was not as great.

Earlier scholarship imagined early-medieval society as stateless and dominated by large clans headed by elders, and regarded kinship solidarity as the main source of security. Some passages in the laws, as well as evidence from the sagas seem to point in this direction. However, there is little support for the idea of a "society of kindred" in recent research. A closer examination of the Scandinavian kinship system has shown that it was bilateral, as was the case in most of Western Europe. Nor is there any evidence that this system replaced an earlier one of large clans, as is to be found in many other parts of the world. When descent is reckoned in the cognatic as well as the agnatic line, families overlap and there will be a tendency for relatives either to mediate conflicts or to take a stand based on considerations other than kinship. It has also been claimed that the often-elaborate kinship system we meet in some of the laws is actually a late inventions, influenced by the Church (below, pp. 98–101). Nevertheless, the "anti-kinship trend" can easily be taken too far. Even if there were no large clans, kinship was clearly important in the early Middle Ages. Norwegian provincial laws, which are the oldest in Scandinavia, suggest the existence of a relatively strong kindred group, based on male descendants from a common agnatic grandfather. In addition, marriage created strong links and, more generally, links between people, tended to be personal rather than institutional, either between people of equal status or between patrons and clients of higher and lower status, respectively. Relatives were important, though the ties between them were not automatic but depended on choice.

In his *Heimskringla*, Snorri Sturluson tells the story of the local chieftain Asbjørn in northern Norway, who at the age of eighteen inherited his father Sigurd's farm and position in local society. Sigurd had been a highly respected man, known for his generosity and for the lavish parties he gave in honor of the gods in the pagan period and then of Christ after the conversion to Christianity. Asbjørn followed in his father's footsteps. Eventually, however, the harvests deteriorated and it became more difficult to continue the hospitality. His mother suggested that he reduce it, but Asbjørn refused and scoured the surrounding countryside to buy the foods he needed for entertaining his neighbors. After another bad year, however, even this was not possible, and Asbjørn decided to go south to buy grain from his maternal uncle, Erling Skjalgsson, at Sola, south of present-day Stavanger. Erling had plenty of grain, but there was a problem. King Olav Haraldsson had forbidden exports from southern Norway to ensure that there would be sufficient provisions for his own visit to the area the following summer. Erling had just made peace with the king and did not want to provoke him. On the other hand, it would be a great shame for him to let down his nephew, so he allowed Asbjørn to buy grain from his slaves, hoping that this would not be considered a direct breach of the king's command.

However, Asbjørn was caught by the king's local representative, had his cargo confiscated, and had to return empty handed. He could afford no Christmas party, found it humiliating to accept the invitation of his paternal uncle, Tore Hund (Dog), and suffered ridicule from Tore and from his neighbors. Next spring, he went south to take revenge. He cut off the head of the royal representative in the king's presence, so that it landed in the king's lap. Asbjørn was detained and immediately condemned to death, but he was saved at the last moment by Erling, who arrived with a large army and forced the king to accept a settlement. When Asbjørn later broke the settlement, he was killed by one of the king's men. This brought Tore Hund into the conflict. On a visit to Asbjørn's mother, Tore received the spear that had pierced Asbjørn as a parting gift with the words:

> Here is the spear that pierced my son Asbjørn, and there is still blood on it.... Now you would perform a brave deed if you thrust it out of your hands in such a way that it stood in the breast of King Olav. And now I say ... that you will be considered a coward by every man if you do not avenge Asbjørn. (Heimskringla, *The Saga of St. Olav*, ch. 123)

The story is only known from thirteenth-century sources and its trustworthiness is doubtful. Nevertheless, its picture of norms and behavior is confirmed by a number of other sources and has a realistic ring. There is extensive archaeological evidence of great sacrificial parties from the pre-Christian period, including large halls that were evidently used for such purposes, such as the one in Lejre in Denmark (Zealand). Around thirty to forty such halls dating from the first millennium AD have been excavated in various places in Scandinavia, from Lofoten in the north to southern Jutland in the south. In a runic inscription from Blekinge in Denmark (now in Sweden), dated to 550–700, a man called Haduwolf boasts that he has sacrificed nine stallions and nine bucks for a good year. The sacrifice as well as the inscription show the same aim as motivated Asbjørn, a chieftain wanting to defend or extend his leadership through lavish hospitality. Nor did the opportunity to do this disappear with the conversion to Christianity; for, like the story of Asbjørn, Norwegian provincial laws emphasize continuity, decreeing that three great drinking parties should be held each year in honor of Christ and the Virgin.

The story of Asbjørn provides evidence of a highly competitive society, where generosity in the form of hospitality or gifts is a means to winning adherents. Asbjørn acts as the typical "big man" described by social anthropologists. He cannot command his subordinates, but has to attract them by largesse. Without grain to brew beer and give parties, Asbjørn is nothing. Admittedly, people like Asbjørn probably had slaves and tenants whom they could command, but to become leaders of larger areas, they had to win adherents by generosity and by offering protection. The sagas, those of the Norwegian kings as well as the Icelandic family sagas, are full of examples of this. Snorri has to admit that St. Olav became unpopular among the chieftains, but exonerates him from the accusation that he was stingy. Another king in *Heimskringla,* Øystein Haraldsson who was killed in 1157 during a battle with his brother, apparently was guilty of this vice. When mobilizing his men to fight for him during the conflict, he received the following answer from one of them: "Let your gold chests fight for you and defend your kingdom." Then they all left him.

Asbjørn's story gives a somewhat ambiguous picture of kindred solidarity. Asbjørn and Tore lived close to each other, and there was some rivalry between them. According to Snorri, Tore was the more esteemed of the two because he was the king's retainer. Asbjørn's frantic effort at hospitality would seem to be a means to challenge Tore's standing. Tore's sarcasm after Asbjørn's disastrous journey to Sola may suggest that he was not too unhappy to see his relative humiliated. Tore is also unwilling to lose the king's friendship by avenging Asbjørn, but the gift of the spear in public forces his hand; it would be too great a humiliation not to accept the challenge. Although not Asbjørn's rival, Erling has a similar problem, but he stands by his nephew and goes to extreme lengths to save his life. In the bilateral system, the obligations of maternal and paternal relatives are equivalent, at least when the kinship is as close as between uncle and nephew. It is also interesting to see that Asbjørn's mother turns to her brother-in-law rather than her brother to get revenge for her son. The obvious reason for this is that Tore was closer by, but it also says something about the links created by marriage, not only between the spouses themselves but also between their relatives. Here it may be objected that many scholars have regarded the woman urging her male relatives to take revenge as a literary rather than a historical figure, but such a practice is well attested in many societies where revenge is practiced, and there is also contemporary Icelandic evidence of it.

Although the king plays a central part in the drama, there is no clear idea of royal authority. The king's local representative is a thoroughly unpleasant character and a man of low rank, descended from slaves. Characteristically, when Asbjørn has killed him and the king gets furious, Erling Skjalgsson's son and Asbjørn's cousin, who has become a royal retainer, comments: "It is unfortunate, sire, that the deed seems hateful to you, for otherwise a good piece of work has been done." The reason for the king's fury is not that Asbjørn killed a royal official, but that the killing took place at Easter and in the king's presence and "that he used my feet as the chopping block."

The picture in this story is confirmed by other sources. Divisions between factions during the internal struggles in Denmark and Norway in the twelfth century were based on personal loyalty that derived from friendship, kinship, and marriage or other links based on the exchange of women. There is no evidence that the factions formed in the 1150s were regularly based on preexisting divisions between magnate families. They are more likely to have rested on individual magnates' personal relationships to individual kings. Once a choice had been made, however, it typically became permanent and was passed on to the magnate's descendants. Admittedly, there are many exceptions to this, but not so many as to form an argument against the importance of family ties. Friendship should be added to kinship as a basis for faction formation, although the two categories tended to overlap. Despite the fact that there was no automatic solidarity with kindred, friends were often chosen from among relatives. Additionally, personal relationships were deliberately used to link prominent adherents more closely to their leaders. As in earlier times, the kings gave daughters and other female relatives in marriage to their most trusted adherents. The kings themselves normally married foreign princesses, if they married at all, but they had mistresses from prominent Norwegian families who served to form alliances, in addition to fulfilling the sexual and emotional needs of such relationships.

The previous examples point to some continuity in the nature of Scandinavian society before and after the rise of the kingdoms and the introduction of Christianity. There were, however, significant changes, and these will be dealt with in the following discussion. A first step in this direction was the greater involvement in Christian Europe through the Viking expeditions.

Scandinavian Expansion: The Viking Expeditions

Under the year 793, the Canterbury manuscript of the *Anglo-Saxon Chronicle* contains the following entry:

> Here terrible portents came about over the land of Northumbria … these were immense flashes of lightning, and fiery dragons were seen flying in the air, and there immediately followed a great famine, and after that in the same year the raiding of the heathen miserably devastated God's church in Lindisfarne island by looting and slaughter. (*The Anglo-Saxon Chronicle*, trans. M. Swanton [London: Dent, 1996], 54–56)

This is the first recorded example of a Viking raid, but it was followed by several others, in England as well as in other countries.

Many narrative sources give dramatic accounts of bands of robbers rising out of the high seas, killing, raping, burning, and carrying off gold, silver, sacred objects, and men and women to be used or sold as slaves. Monasteries and ecclesiastical institutions were particularly exposed, as they were wealthy and often unprotected, but there were also attacks on towns. England and the Carolingian Empire largely managed to fend off the Vikings until around 830, so Ireland, where a number of kings were fighting one another, became the main target during this period. From the 830s onwards, a series of large-scale attacks were directed against many parts of Western Europe. The Vikings exploited internal conflicts in the Carolingian Empire between Louis the Pious and his sons, as well as the later conflicts between the latter, and directed a series of attacks, particularly against France, including two sieges of Paris (855 and 885) and attacks on various other towns. At the same time, they interfered in conflicts between the various English kingdoms to plunder as well as to gain a foothold in this country, which they achieved with the conquest of Northumbria. In 844, a fleet of fifty-two Viking ships attacked Galicia and later Lisbon and Seville. Gradually there was a change from plundering to regular conquest. Viking kingdoms were founded in Ireland and northern England, and in 911 King Charles III granted the Duchy of Normandy to Scandinavian Vikings in order to protect the area against other Vikings. This seems to have worked; there is little evidence of Viking attacks on France in the tenth century. Around the same time the Vikings were also defeated in England, first by King Alfred (870–899) and then by his successors who in 952 or 954 conquered the Viking realm of Northumbria.

One reason for these setbacks may be that the East offered better opportunities for the Vikings during this period. There is evidence of settlements of Scandinavians, called "Rus," around the Ladoga Sea from the late eighth century. The term *Rus* is derived from the Finnish name for *Svear* (Swedes). Archaeological evidence suggests a marked increase in these settlements in the tenth century, which is clearly connected to an increase in trade along Russian rivers with Byzantium and the Arab world. The Scandinavians were well placed to act as intermediaries on the trade routes between Russia and Byzantium and Western Europe, a trade that apparently yielded a substantial surplus, as is evident from the large hoards of silvers found in the Scandinavian settlements. Their merchandise was attractive in the East as well as in the West: the furs of northern Norway and the Kola Peninsula, for example, as well as captives from various raids to be sold as slaves. The Swedish historian Sture Bolin claimed that the trade route via Russia and the Baltic replaced the Mediterranean as the main link connecting Western Europe and the Arab and Byzantine worlds. Although this is an exaggeration, the northern trade route must still be regarded as important. Trade was thus relatively more important than plundering in the East, and the Scandinavian settlements often seem to have been the result of peaceful cooperation with the local population rather than of conquest. Nevertheless, the Scandinavians were able to found a dynasty with a center in Kiev, which, however, gradually became Slavicized. Igor (=Ingvar) married Olga (=Helga) and was succeeded by his son Svjatoslav, who in turn was succeeded by Vladimir who converted to Christianity in 988.

The rise of Kievan Rus may have limited Scandinavian expansion in this area from the late tenth century, which in turn may explain the last phase of Viking expansion in the West, the Danish conquest of England. Another explanation of this is provided, however, by the unification of Denmark under Harald Bluetooth from the middle of the century. The first major raid on England in 991 was led by Harald's son Sven Forkbeard, who in the following years led several expeditions against this country, as did also several other Scandinavian warriors. Finally, in the summer of 1013, Sven arrived with a large fleet and chased King Ethelred out of the country. He was acclaimed king shortly before Christmas, but died six weeks later. His son Cnut (Danish: Knud) returned a few years later, conquered the country, and ruled England from 1017 until his death in 1035.

In addition to their plundering expeditions, the Scandinavians also settled on islands in the North Sea and the Atlantic. There were contacts between Norway and the Orkneys already in the seventh century and a number of Norwegians settled there, as well as on Shetland and the Hebrides in the mid-ninth century, after having suppressed the indigenous inhabitants. According to the oldest written account, by Ari the Wise, the first settlers arrived in Iceland in 870 and found the island empty, apart from some Irish monks. During the following sixty years, a number of new settlers arrived, mostly from Norway but possibly also from other countries, after which all the available land had been taken. Greenland was discovered in the late tenth century and settled in the following period. Despite its cold climate—which was probably warmer a thousand years ago—the country was rich in pasture, fish, and game and thus attractive to settlers. Some expeditions from Iceland and Greenland also arrived in North America—remains of their houses have been found on Newfoundland—but there is no evidence of permanent settlement. According to the sagas, the Native Americans made this too difficult.

Various explanations have been suggested for this expansion. One of them is population pressure, leading people to seek new opportunities abroad. There is evidence of demographic growth at the time, expressed in a proliferation of new settlements. Population pressure may also explain why hitherto uninhabited countries, like Iceland and Greenland, were settled during this period. However, it is difficult to explain the Viking expeditions in general in this way. A warlike population does not require population pressure to turn to plundering abroad; military strength and a knowledge of the wealth to be gained are sufficient motivation. Wealthy and undefended monasteries must have posed a particularly strong temptation. In so far as population increase was a factor, it serves to explain the presence of sufficient manpower, not the incentive for the expeditions.

Rather than seeking an explanation in poverty and need, it seems reasonable to seek it in the awareness of new opportunities. A significant factor must have been the development of seafaring technology.

The Viking ship was fully developed around 800, when it was equipped with sails, although at the same time it remained admirably suited to the use of oars. It was one of the most advanced vessels of its time, easy to maneuver and well able to cross the open sea, whereas European ships kept closely to the coast. Another factor in the Vikings' favor was their familiarity with European countries as the result of increased trade in the previous period. The first Norwegian mentioned by name in history was actually engaged in the fur trade. This was Ottar of Hålogaland, whose narrative of his journey from northern Norway to King Alfred's court in Wessex was recorded in Anglo-Saxon as a preface to a translation of Orosius (below, pp. 131–32.)

The conquests in the later phase of the Viking Age show that the Scandinavians were able not only to organize raiding expeditions, but also to create their own kingdoms and principalities. There is also some evidence of increasing political organization in Scandinavia itself. Rimbert's *Life of Ansgar* and other Carolingian sources from the ninth century mention kings in Denmark and Sweden. A Danish king, Harald Klak, was baptized in Mainz in 826, but was deposed soon after his return to his home country. Although the Swedish kings mentioned in these sources are clearly local chieftains, we cannot exclude the possibility that the Danish kings ruled over larger territories; there is even some

Figure 2. A Viking ship from a burial mound on the Oseberg farm near Tønsberg in Vestfold (Norway). Built 834, excavated 1904, now in the Viking Ship Museum, Bygdøy, Oslo. The Oseberg burial is one of the most important and well preserved finds from Viking Age Scandinavia, containing a fully seaworthy ship with all kinds of equipment for the burial of a high-ranking woman. The shape of the ship and the details of its construction show its advantages over other contemporary vessels. The Viking ship is light, easy to maneuver and elastic, so that it bends rather than cracks in heavy sea. Photo: Dalbera.

evidence that they controlled parts of southern Norway. On the other hand, the use of the title "king" in Carolingian sources need not imply any knowledge of Scandinavian conditions but may simply be a convention for referring to foreign rulers. In any case, we have little evidence either of the size of the territories these rulers commanded and to what extent these territories were regarded as permanent entities. Only from the mid-tenth century onwards is there evidence of a Danish kingdom ruled by one dynasty. This marks the beginning of a major change, the division of Scandinavia into three kingdoms and the introduction of Christianity, which brought them into the European family of kingdoms.

The Division of Scandinavia into Three Kingdoms

In the year 1000, a battle was fought between the kings of the three Nordic countries, celebrated in skaldic poetry as well as by later saga writers. The former depict showers of arrows, streams of blood, and eagles and wolves being fed, while the latter gradually prepare their readers for the final tragedy, the disappearance and probable death of the hero, the Norwegian King Olav Tryggvason. His enemies have prepared an ambush for him and are waiting on shore for Olav's enormous ship, Ormen Lange (=the Long Serpent), believing that one after the other of the large ships passing by is the right one, until it finally arrives and they attack with an overwhelmingly superior force. Spotting his enemies, Olav refuses to flee. He speaks with contempt of the Danes and the Swedes but recognizes his Norwegian adversary, Earl Eirik, as a brave man and a dangerous foe. Olav is proved right; the Danes and the Swedes try to board, but are driven back, while Eirik and his men finally manage to swarm onto Olav's ship and after hard fighting defeat his exhausted and decimated crew. Olav jumps overboard and is killed—or, as some of the versions have it—escapes and spends the rest of his life as a monk in the Holy Land. Nearly 200 years later, King Sverre of Norway (r. 1177–1202) is said to have mentioned him as the only man standing on the poop of his ship throughout a battle.

The many accounts of the battle in the sagas present the now familiar picture of a Scandinavia consisting of three kingdoms. Although it is doubtful whether we can really reckon with this as early as the year 1000, there is little doubt that the battle was actually fought and that the kings mentioned in the skaldic poetry and the sagas were real persons. It is usually referred to as the battle of Svold or Svolder, an otherwise unknown island off Rügen in northern Germany, where it took place according to the later sagas, but the most likely site is Øresund, where the earliest sources place it. The battle was thus fought near the later border between the three kingdoms, which is significant, giving a glimpse of an important stage in the formation of the three Scandinavian kingdoms.

The origin of institutions and territorial units is a central problem in historical writings. Consequently, the formation of the three kingdoms occupies a prominent part in the Scandinavian national historiography that developed from the early nineteenth century onwards. Typically, historians dealt with the formation of each kingdom separately, explaining when, how, and why the country was "unified." The previous sketch has indicated that the formation of larger territorial units may have been less novel than is often imagined. On the other hand, the fact that the previous units seem to have been unstable points to the novelty of what happened in the tenth and eleventh centuries, the formation of the kingdoms of Denmark, Norway, and Sweden. This raises three questions: First, why was Scandinavia divided into these three units only? Second, why did this happen just at this time? And, finally, why did this division become permanent?

The battle of Svolder points to one part of the explanation. It took place at sea, like most important battles of the period, a fact that highlights the importance of sea power. The elegant, well-built Viking ships could move quickly over great distances. And they could carry provisions for considerably longer periods than an army moving over land, which was usually limited to a three-days' march. The Scandinavians could therefore plunder as well as build principalities over the entire area around the North and the Baltic Seas and were in frequent contact with its kings and princes. If we consider the fact that the sea linked localities together, while forests, mountains, and uninhabited land divided them from one another, the division between the three Scandinavian countries becomes quite logical. Jutland, the islands around it, and the low, cultivated land across Øresund became Denmark, whereas the long coast from the arctic regions to the lands around Oslofjorden became Norway. Sweden could not be controlled from the coast, but instead developed around the great lakes, Vänern and Vättern in the west and Mälaren in the east. Sweden was then separated from Denmark by forest and thinly inhabited land north of Scania. Typically, the most contested area was the coastline between present-day Oslo and Øresund, the meeting-place between all three countries.

The exact borders of each country of course also depended on its relative strength and on luck, energy, and the degree of dynastic continuity of its sovereigns. Denmark was clearly the strongest of the three, in the Viking Age as well as later. As we have seen, a Danish kingdom may possibly be traced back to the late eighth century. There then seems to have been an eclipse for about a hundred years (c. 850–950), either because the kingdom dissolved or because the decline of the Carolingian Empire put an end to attempts to Christianize and subordinate the Danish rulers, and thus to information about Denmark in Carolingian sources. A revival then occurred with Harald Bluetooth, who in

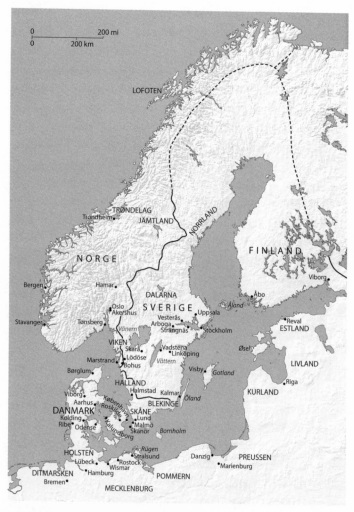

The Scandinavian Kingdoms in the Middle Ages. Map by Poul Pedersen, from *Danmarks Nationalmuseum: Unionsdrottningen. Margreta I och Kalmarunionen* (Copenhagen, 1996), p. 425.

the inscription on a Jelling Stone boasts of conquering the whole of Denmark and Norway and making the Danes Christian.

Harald Bluetooth was the father of the King Sven who fought at Svolder. The same Sven was a great warrior and Viking chieftain who later conquered England and who hardly conformed to the scornful picture of him that we get in the sagas, where he is the instrument of his wife Sigrid who wants revenge because Olav has slapped her face, and the leader of the "soft" Danes who preferred to lick their bowls during pagan sacrifices rather than expose themselves to danger in battles. Against the background of the Jelling inscription (see illustration in chapter 3), as well as the following story of Sven's son and successor Cnut the Great conquering Norway, the battle of Svolder forms evidence of the power of Denmark at the time, a power that increased further as a consequence of the Danish victory, which replaced Olav with the earls Eirik and Svein, both clients of the Danish king.

According to the sagas, the kingdom of Norway was as old as that of Denmark, being the result of Harald Finehair's conquests in the late ninth century and later ruled by his descendants. Nevertheless, the sagas admit that the kingdom was divided after Harald's death (c. 930) and that various pretenders, including the Danish kings, fought over the country in the following period. Actually, the dynasty was probably less and the Danish influence more important than the sagas suggest. The Danish kings continuously intervened in Norway, using Norwegian pretenders as their clients and deposing them or trying to do so when they became too independent. This seems to have been the case with the last of Harald's descendants, the sons of his eldest son Eirik, who came to power with Danish aid but were replaced by Earl Håkon of Lade in Trøndelag, who was in turn succeeded by Olav Tryggvason. It is known from English sources that Olav fought on the Danish side against the English in the 990s, but he was baptized and confirmed with the English King Aethelred as his godfather and may have received aid from him when returning to Norway. The site of his last battle, Øresund, well within what must have been the Danish realm, suggests that he was the attacker. Considering the relative strength of the parties, it was probably a preemptive strike or just a raid, not an attempt to conquer Denmark.

Olav's namesake and successor, Olav Haraldsson, another Viking chieftain, presents a largely similar case. He managed to conquer Norway in 1015, at a time when Sven's son and successor, Cnut the Great, was busy conquering England, and ruled for thirteen years (1015–1028). Despite an alliance with Sweden against Cnut the Great, the ruler of Denmark and England, he was defeated and exiled and at his return in 1030 was killed in battle against his Norwegian adversaries. This time, however, the Danes introduced direct rule, which backfired. A rebellion brought Olav's son Magnus on the throne. At about the same time, Cnut the Great died in Winchester (November 1035), after which his empire was divided among his sons. Ten years later, they were all dead.

When Cnut's last son, Harthacnut, died in 1042 without leaving a descendant, he was succeeded by King Magnus of Norway. According to the sagas, this was because of an agreement between the two kings that the one of them who lived longer should succeed the other. However, there is no contemporary evidence of this, and it seems more likely that when Harthacnut had left for England to become king there (in 1040), Magnus simply used the opportunity to take over the Danish throne and then kept it at his rival's death. Nevertheless, Magnus was soon challenged by Sven Estridsen, who belonged to a sideline of the old dynasty and succeeded in establishing himself after a prolonged struggle with Magnus and his successor Harald. The result was a settlement in 1065 that became the basis for the permanent division between the two countries.

We know less of the third kingdom, Sweden. Most probably, the real unification of Sweden did not take place until around 1250, although there may have been moves in this direction earlier. The Swedish king who participated in the Battle of Svolder, Olof Skotkonung, is probably a historical person, but we know neither how far his kingdom extended nor what relationship he had to King Sven of Denmark. Whereas Olof, possibly because of personal links to King Sven, supported the Danes in the battle of Svolder, his successor, Anund Jakob, took the attitude that later became normal for Swedish rulers of seeking a balance of power between the two neighboring countries, thus supporting Norway against Denmark. On the other hand, the importance of sea power meant that Sweden was a less attractive target for Danish expansion than Norway and thus played a less prominent part in the inter-Nordic struggles in the early period.

Although hardly regarded as a decisive shift at the time, the events of the mid-eleventh century settled the division between the three countries, thus confirming the trends that had begun to make themselves felt in connection with the Battle of Svolder. The borders between them would not change in their basic outlines until the great shifts of the mid-seventeenth century. The Oslofjord area was contested between Norway and Denmark as late as in the second half of the twelfth century, but eventually came to belong to Norway. There was no geopolitical inevitability in this outcome, but it may be explained by the fact that the king of Norway likely gave higher priority to this aim than his Danish counterpart, who had other fields of expansion, in England, Northern Germany, and the Baltic area.

The Viking expeditions were an obvious factor in the radical change that took place around this time. They contributed to military specialization, as well as to the creation of an economic base for stronger principalities by providing chieftains with the gold, silver, and luxury items that they needed to gain followers. Gift exchange was an important political and economic factor in the Viking age and beyond, and both royal generosity and the precious objects that changed hands are celebrated in the skaldic poetry. Wealth from the Viking expeditions made it possible for chieftains to attach more men to their service than was possible in earlier times, and the added manpower could then be used to procure further wealth. The mobilization of large fleets in the later phases of the Viking Age may have had important internal consequences, too, providing lessons in political organization, and foreign conquest may have worked in the same direction, giving Scandinavians familiarity with administrative practice in other countries as well as experience in local government. Finally, the Viking expeditions increased the Scandinavians' contact with Christianity. Those who settled abroad normally converted, and some of them, notably the Norwegian Viking kings, tried to introduce the new religion in their home country.

However, there were some differences between the countries in this regard. As we know so little about Denmark in the period between about 850 and 950 and of the origins of the Bluetooth dynasty, it is difficult to give a precise account of the importance to this country of the Viking expeditions. Though there can hardly be any doubt about the profitability of raiding expeditions from the late eighth century onwards, the climax of the Viking Age in Denmark, the conquest of England, was a consequence of, rather than a precondition for the unification of the country. Thus, there was no abrupt break but rather a smooth and gradual transition from the Viking Age to the period of an established monarchy in Denmark. From early on, the Danish king had a firm base in cultivated land, as well as in the trading center of Haithabu, near present-day Schleswig, and, by combining these resources with surplus from Viking expeditions, was able to embark on ambitious projects of foreign conquest, beginning in the late tenth century.

Denmark's relations with Germany were another important factor. The conquest of Saxony by Charlemagne made the Carolingian Empire Denmark's neighbor to the south and exposed the country to Carolingian conquest or penetration, while at the same time presenting a model for an ambitious conquering king. In a similar way, the final conversion of the country to Christianity around 965 is clearly connected to the rise of Ottonian power to the south, coming just after Otto I's victory over the Hungarians at Lech in 955 and his invasion of Italy and imperial coronation in 962. It also coincides with the conversion of Poland, traditionally dated to 966, and was preceded by the conversion of Bohemia some decades earlier and followed by that of Hungary some decades later. After Otto I's death in 973, war broke out between Harald and Otto II. First Harald attacked Saxony. Otto made a counterattack in the following year and conquered Dannevirke and possibly larger parts of Jutland, which, however, Harald was able to regain after the Saracens defeated Otto in 983. The Christianization of Germany's neighbors, about which we have very little information, may alternatively be regarded as the result of increasing German influence or as a countermeasure to avoid being absorbed by German power, thus in both cases as provoked by increasing German strength. The unification may be regarded in a similar way. Germany may have served as a model for the conquering king, who could then use German pressure to gain support for himself; the magnates and petty kings being forced to choose between submitting to the Germans or to a national conqueror.

Viking surplus probably also played a part in the rise of the kingdom of Sweden, although, given the inland character of this country, the degree of its importance is more doubtful. Norway, on the other hand, is the Viking kingdom *par excellence,* as all of its rulers between around 930 and 1066 had a Viking or mercenary background, and most of them came directly from abroad to take power in the country. The two Olavs as well as Harald Hardrada are the preeminent examples. However, Viking wealth likely increased the number of chieftains as well as the number of their followers and consequently did not necessarily lead to larger political units. Nor did the surplus have to be spent on creating national kingdoms. Many chieftains preferred to establish themselves abroad in the British Isles, Normandy, or Russia. Moreover, as long as it was easy to profit from Viking expeditions, the principalities that emerged were likely to be unstable: new chieftains with fresh resources might easily expel the old ones. This pattern seems to apply to the series of Viking kings taking power in Norway, whereas the Danish king eventually managed to monopolize the Viking expeditions by conquering England.

Consequently, it would seem that in Norway and to some extent in Sweden, the Viking expeditions made a greater surplus available to be invested in lordship, created greater ambitions among the chieftains, and led to more intense struggles between them, but did not directly lead to consolidated kingdoms. The latter appear rather as a result of the *end* of the Viking expeditions. When the strengthening of feudal Europe in the eleventh century had put an end to the Viking exploits, the only place for ambitious chieftains to gain wealth and power was within Scandinavia. In the case of Norway, this period coincided with large parts of the aristocracy and the people rallying around indigenous kings who resisted Danish dominance. In this respect, Norway resembles the kingdoms of East Central Europe whose emergence also coincides with the end of the raiding expeditions against Germany and other parts of Western Christendom: the Slavs were defeated by Henry I in 929 and 933, and a Polish duchy emerged a few decades later. The Hungarians were defeated by Otto I in 955, and the principality (or kingdom, from 1000 AD) of Hungary was established towards the end of the century.

However, we also have to take into account the internal relationship between the countries. Denmark, by far the strongest of them, is likely to have influenced the consolidation of the two others. As we know so little about the early history of Sweden, it is difficult to assess the importance of Denmark for this country, but there is clear evidence of it in the case of Norway. Here, as we have seen, the final consolidation of the kingdom was a direct consequence of the rebellion against Danish rule in the 1030s. There is evidence from Carolingian sources of Danish control of southwestern Norway already in the early ninth century, and it has also been suggested that Harald Finehair's conquest was a reaction against previous Danish dominance. The importance of Denmark in turn points to the importance of Germany; we can imagine a chain reaction in the form of German pressure leading to the consolidation of Denmark, which in turn resulted in the consolidation of Norway and possibly Sweden.

The main factors in the formation of the Scandinavian kingdoms were, first, the Viking and trading expeditions, the surplus from which was invested in clients and political power at home. Second, the pressure from Germany contributed to the unification of Denmark and thus indirectly influenced the two other kingdoms. Third, the competition between the centers of power in Scandinavia eventually led to the division into three kingdoms with borders determined by the fact that the conquests were carried out by sea power. Finally, Christianity served as an instrument in the monopolization of power. As in East Central Europe, conversion to Christianity coincided with the formation of kingdoms in Scandinavia, but a causal relationship between the two phenomena is not easy to ascertain. Most likely, there was coalescence between the two factors, rather than a distinct cause and effect. Moreover, the greatest impact of Christianity probably came in the following period, partly in its contribution to the continued existence of the kingdoms, partly in its role in their further development.

As we have seen, the formation of the Scandinavian kingdoms parallels developments in East Central Europe at about the same time. The three new kingdoms there were also neighbors of Germany, which served as a model as well as a threat, stimulating unification under one ruler. In contrast to Denmark, however, the Eastern principalities had no sea power and lacked the natural borders that made the division of Scandinavia relatively uncomplicated. Although the three East European kingdoms continued to exist for several centuries, until they were conquered or entered into unions with neighboring kingdoms, their borders changed significantly more than the ones between the Scandinavian kingdoms.

The Continued Division of Scandinavia: Foreign Policy until around 1300

From the mid-eleventh century onwards, historians normally regard Scandinavia as consisting of three kingdoms, discuss the relationships between them, and distinguish between internal and foreign policy. Indeed, the approximate borders that were established at the time remained basically the same until the mid-seventeenth century. Nevertheless, there is little to suggest that those borders were regarded as final, nor is there evidence of any distinction between internal and foreign policy. The three kings who fought one another at Svolder certainly made no such distinction, and it is impossible to point to an exact date when it might have become relevant. Politically, the most important factor was that the strongest of the three kingdoms, Denmark, largely abstained from interfering in the two others. Admittedly, a Danish prince tried to become king of Sweden in the early twelfth century, and the Danes tried to get hold of Viken, the part of Norway to the east of the Oslofjord, in the mid-twelfth century and interfered in the internal conflicts in the country in the following period. However, none of these interventions had any lasting effect. And conversely, neither of the two other countries would normally have been in a position to interfere in Denmark. As the long border between Norway and Sweden mostly consisted of mountains and uninhabited land, both countries were also likely to give priority to expansion in other directions. There were as well internal conflicts in all three countries in this period, although these were not attempts to form independent principalities in opposition to the king, but instead concerned the succession to the throne of the country as a whole. Thus, from the mid-eleventh century onwards, we can begin to distinguish between internal and foreign policy and discuss the relationship between the Scandinavian kingdoms and the surrounding area.

During the eleventh century, England ceased to be a target for Scandinavian expansion. The Norwegian king Harald Hardrada attempted to gain the English throne when Edward the Confessor died without issue in 1066, but he was defeated by Harold Godwinson at Stanford Bridge. Three weeks later, William the Conqueror defeated Harold at Hastings and founded the Norman dynasty in England. King Sven of Denmark remained at home in 1066, but his successors made several unsuccessful attempts to regain control of England. The last of them was St. Knud's mobilization in 1086, which came to nothing because of the rebellion that cost the king his life (below, p. 40).

In the following period, the Danish kings turned towards Germany and the Baltic. One of the highlights of Saxo Grammaticus' great work about the deeds of the Danes is the siege and conquest of Arkona on Rügen in 1169. Saxo celebrates the courage and skill of his compatriots and above all their leaders, King

Valdemar I and Bishop (later Archbishop) Absalon, while also describing in detail the barbarity and superstition of the Wends, the Slavonic population of the Baltic area. The king orders his men to build siege engines to destroy the fortifications of Arkona, but then changes his mind. He is convinced that the pagan town can be brought down without the use of any such equipment, as Charlemagne had once converted the population of Rügen and ordered them to pay tax to St. Vitus. Therefore, they only have to wait for St. Vitus's day, when the saint will destroy the walls of the town in revenge. The king's prophecy proves true, a fire breaks out in the town and the inhabitants surrender and convert to Christianity.

Saxo pays great attention to the conquests in the Baltic region, emphasizing the close connection between warfare and the spread of Christianity. Not all conquests were as easy as Arkona; often the Danes had to fight bloody battles and sustain long sieges in order to overcome the opposition of the natives. The crusader ideology had been introduced in Western Christendom, first in the expeditions to the Holy Land that began in the 1090s and then extended to the remaining pagan areas, while at the same time Western Europe had become superior in military technology and organization.

Saxo and his contemporaries depict the Wends not only as pagans but as robbers who plundered the Danish coasts, behaving much as the Danes themselves had behaved a century or two earlier. Although Saxo does not explicitly point to this parallel, the continuity does not seem to have escaped him. In addition to Valdemar and Absalon, Cnut the Great is one of his heroes and his conquest of England duly celebrated, although described in less detail than the struggles against the Wends. Saxo is also full of praise for Cnut's namesake on the throne, St. Knud, who was planning a new conquest of England when he was murdered by his disobedient and lazy people, who refused to take part in the hardships of war. Thus, there is certain continuity between the Viking expeditions and the territorial conquests in their wake and the crusades in the twelfth and following centuries. The great advantage of the latter was that there were ecclesiastical privileges attached to them, spiritual blessings as well as the opportunity to tax the Church to finance the expeditions. Politically, there was booty to be gained and land that might be colonized. Thus, forays to the Baltic could offer some of the same advantages as did the Viking expeditions.

Although the Baltic expeditions did not take the place of conflicts with other Christian countries, they played an important part in the following century, for Denmark as well as for Sweden. Norway was too distant from the Baltic to be involved. The expansion towards the Baltic began in the early twelfth century and reached a climax in the conquest of Estonia (1219). It was undertaken partly in alliance and partly in competition with the Germans. At the same time, the relationship with Scandinavia's mighty neighbor to the south, the German emperor, was problematic. Valdemar I had to do homage to Frederick Barbarossa, while Northern Germany was dominated by Henry the Lion, duke of Saxony and Bavaria, who was a sometime ally, sometime rival in the Baltic crusades. Henry's fall in 1180 changed this and made the Danish king the strongest force in Northern Germany. Knud VI (1182–1202), and above all his brother and successor Valdemar II (1202–41), exploited this opportunity to intervene in conflicts between the various princes in the area. Several of them had to do homage to the king of Denmark, who in 1201 also became the lord of the wealthy towns of Lübeck and Hamburg. This lordship was particularly important, as the profit from it came in the form of ready money, which could be spent wherever the king wanted. Most of his other income was in kind, which either entailed considerable transport costs or had to be sold to be converted into money.

After his brother's death, King Valdemar continued the expansion into Germany and the crusades in the Baltic. In 1214, the new emperor, Frederick II—who at the time had to make concessions in order to overcome his rival Otto IV—transferred to Valdemar imperial power over all the territories he had conquered in Northern Germany. Valdemar suffered a setback when he was taken captive in a surprise attack by his vassal, Count Henry of Schwerin (in 1223). He was released in exchange for a huge ransom, tried to regain his power in Germany, but was defeated in the battle of Bornhøved in 1227 and gave up any further attempts at expansion, although he retained part of his influence in Northern Germany. In the following period, internal struggles prevented further adventures abroad. On the contrary, Germans were more likely to interfere in Denmark than vice versa. This period also saw the beginning of a problem that has vexed Danish-German relations into the twentieth century: Southern Jutland was granted as a fief to Abel, a younger son of Valdemar II, and developed into a semi-independent duchy.

In 1301, the young King Erik VI Menved had Frederick II's privilege transcribed, and in the following period set out to put its conditions into practice. For nearly two decades he intervened in Germany in various ways and with considerable success. To finance his conquests, he had to mortgage castles and territories in his own kingdom, which were redeemed when he had achieved his aims. Unfortunately, however, he died suddenly in 1319 at a time when most of his kingdom had been mortgaged and was succeeded by his brother Christoffer with whom he had been in almost continuous conflict throughout his reign. This introduced a period of chaos, which included eight years when Denmark was without a king. At his succession (1340), Christoffer's son Valdemar IV had to redeem the mortgaged areas before he could embark on an independent foreign policy, which, as we shall see, involved new challenges and opportunities as a consequence of major changes in the relationship between the Nordic countries.

Given Norway's orientation towards the coast, the islands in the North Sea and Atlantic were the natural field for its expansion, the more so as the people of these islands were mostly emigrants from Norway and spoke the same language. Some of the sagas state that Harald Finehair made an expedition to the Orkneys, and although this is most probably a later invention, it may be an expression of the idea, apparently current in the thirteenth century, that the kingdom of Norway should include all peoples of Norwegian origin and speaking the Norwegian language and that such expeditions were, consequently, natural extensions of the original conquest of mainland Norway. Olav Tryggvason and St. Olav, both former Viking leaders and mercenaries, also seem to have sought influence in this area, as did Harald Hardrada with his failed attack on England. Around the turn of the next century, Magnus Barelegs (1093–1103) spent most of his reign pursuing victories in the West. He gained control over the Orkneys, the Hebrides, and Man, and fought to establish a foothold in Ireland, where he was killed. His successors gave up Ireland, but upheld the claim on the islands. The rulers there had to recognize the king of Norway as their overlord, and in certain periods, the Norwegian king was also able to assert some real control over them. This claim was strengthened through the foundation of the Norwegian archdiocese in 1152/53, in which all of these islands were included. They also played some part in the Norwegian civil wars; one of the frequent rebellions against King Sverre (1177–1202) started in the Orkneys. After it was put down, Earl Harald Maddadson had to accept Sverre as his direct overlord, and, at least for some time, the islands became more strongly linked to the king of Norway.

After the end of the civil wars (below, p. 56), Sverre's grandson King Håkon Håkonsson (1217–63) spent the last twenty-three years of his long reign engaged in various foreign enterprises, partly offensive, partly defensive. He sought to strengthen Norwegian control of the islands in the West and was partly successful. However, the Norwegian revival in this area coincided with a similar one in Scotland, directed at the Hebrides and Man, which were just off the western coast of Scotland and of course much closer to that country than to Norway. The war between the two countries (1263–1266) ended with Norway ceding the islands against an annual money payment and Scottish recognition of the Norwegian possession of the Orkneys and Shetland (the Treaty of Perth, 1266). Relations with England and Scotland remained important to Norwegian foreign policy in the following period. King Eirik Magnusson twice married a Scottish princess, and his daughter was recognized as heir to the throne of Scotland after King Alexander III's death in 1286, but she died before she could ascend to the throne. Throughout this and the following period, the Norwegians repeatedly tried to make the Scots pay the sum of money they had promised in the treaty of Perth, but with little success.

The loss of the Hebrides and Man was to some extent compensated by Greenland and Iceland submitting to the Norwegian king, the former in 1261 and the latter in 1262–64. Iceland and Greenland were thus brought into the proper world order as enunciated by Cardinal William of Sabina. Both now had a king. Iceland had until then been kingless, with no centralized government, though it was not without political institutions. The island was from early on divided between thirty-nine chieftains called *godar*, and in addition it had a central assembly, called the Allting (ON Allþingi = general assembly), where decisions of general interest were made—regarding, for instance the introduction of Christianity—and where conflicts were adjudicated. A law was allegedly issued in 930, based on the Norwegian Law of Gulating and revised and written down in 1117–1118. A later version of this law, preserved in manuscripts of the late thirteenth century, is extant. It is very detailed and highly sophisticated, but it is doubtful to what extent it was actually applied, as there was no executive power. During the first centuries after settlement, political power was divided between a considerable number of local chieftains, probably more than the thirty-nine *godar*. From the late twelfth century onwards, and particularly from around 1220, power became increasingly concentrated in a few magnate families, who got hold of most of the *godord*. The explanation of this must be sought in the combination of increased population and reduced resources, which made the common people more dependent on the chieftains. An important factor is also the development of the Church, which led to a concentration of wealth, partly through ecclesiastical landownership and partly through the introduction of the tithe, both of which served the interests of the chieftains who controlled the churches.

This concentration of power gave rise to intense competition between the chieftains, which provided an opportunity for the Norwegian king to interfere. He commissioned one after the other of them to work for his interests in Iceland, in the beginning with limited success; but eventually, he managed to make most of them members of his body of retainers (the *hird*). Though the king of Norway was not particularly wealthy, he was far wealthier than the Icelandic chieftains and his friendship was thus very attractive to them. The final agreement of 1262–1264, when the Icelanders submitted to the king of Norway (on certain conditions), was a logical consequence of this.

From a purely political point of view, medieval Iceland was a poor and distant island whose development had little influence on the rest of Scandinavia. From a cultural point of view, however, its importance was enormous. More evidence of pre-Christian religion and culture is preserved in Icelandic manuscripts than exists for any other Scandinavian country. Icelanders also wrote the majority of the sagas about Norwegian kings, in addition to a rich literature dealing with a number of other subjects, as will be dealt with later (Chapter 4). Because of this literature, combined with the lack of a central government, Icelandic evidence is often used to illustrate pre-state society in other parts of Scandinavia, notably Norway. Although this has its dangers, Icelandic material can at least be used to gain a more complete picture of phenomena of which there is some evidence in the other countries.

In the following period, the king sought to integrate the possessions in the North Sea and the Atlantic as far as possible into the kingdom of Norway, through legislation and the appointment of Norwegian officials, although the distances between the islands and the mainland were an obstacle to such a policy. The kingdom of Norway also expanded towards the north, partly through missions to the Sami, partly through attempts to control the lucrative fur trade in this area, and partly through Norwegian settlement in the north. This brought the Norwegians into contact with the Russians, who were expanding westward towards the same area, a confluence that led to several altercations in the fourteenth century. The relationship to England and Scotland continued to play an important part in Norwegian foreign policy as well, until the early fourteenth century.

Swedish expansion across the Baltic Sea can be traced back to before the formation of the kingdoms; there were Swedish settlements in Southern Finland before the year 800, although most of them date from the eleventh and twelfth centuries onwards. Sweden's national saint, King Erik (d. 1160), is said to have led the first crusade to Finland in the 1150s. Although this is disputed, we know that the Swedish settlements in Finland were extended and the population in the new areas converted at that time. From the 1220s, a permanent episcopal see existed in Finland, which from around 1290 at the latest was located in Åbo (Turku in Finnish). Both the diocese and the *len* were important parts of the kingdom of Sweden; the latter was often held by prominent member of the aristocracy. A new crusade took place in the mid-thirteenth century as the result of a pagan uprising. The expansion in Finland led to conflicts with the Russian principality of Novgorod. The Russians, who belonged to the Orthodox Church, were for a long time regarded as fellow Christians, even after the schism of 1054. Eventually, however, they were stamped as schismatic and an appropriate target for crusades. During two expeditions in the 1290s, the Swedes moved into Karelia and conquered most of the southern shore of Finland. In 1292 they built Viborg castle and later defended it against Russian attacks. A peace treaty was concluded with Novgorod in 1323, which was supposed to settle the borders between the two countries. It gave the Swedes Southern Finland and most of the Karelian Peninsula, whereas exact borders were probably not drawn in the thinly inhabited areas in the north. The treaty did not lead to permanent peace—there were several wars in the following period—but it was often cited in later negotiations.

Geography is certainly an important factor in explaining the direction of the conquests. It would be difficult to imagine Swedish attempts to conquer the Orkneys or Southern Finland as a target for Norwegian expansion, but geography was not the only determining factor. An important motivation for conquering an area was to convert its inhabitants to Christianity. The crusading ideology was strong in Scandinavia from early on. The kings of Denmark and Norway were among the first to conduct expeditions to the Holy Land, the former in 1103 (he died on Cyprus on his way to Jerusalem), the latter in 1108–1111. Later crusades were mostly directed at the Baltic area, where pagan peoples lived close to the frontier of the Christian kingdoms of Denmark, Sweden, and Germany. Denmark and later Sweden played an important part in the movement that eventually made the southern shore of the Baltic Sea part of Western Christendom.

Norway played a smaller role in this respect, but Norwegian kings worked for the conversion of the Sami, while pushing the frontiers of their kingdom further north. Expansion at the cost of pagan peoples implied great advantages. The kings and their men received papal privileges, were often allowed to tax the Church to finance their expeditions, and did not need to worry about justifying their aggression.

Attacks on Christian countries risked raising legal and moral objections and required special justification. Magnus Bareleg's arguments for his expeditions to the West (1098–1103) may be difficult to discern, but his thirteenth-century successor, Håkon Håkonsson, claimed that he had a legal right when he went to war against Scotland, and he could point to historical arguments in support of this claim. Danish expansion in northern Germany was supported by diplomatic negotiations and legal arguments, in particular after the Danish king had received the imperial privilege of 1214, which would still serve as an incentive and a justification nearly a hundred years later, when Erik Menved revived his great-grandfather's policy.

It would be an exaggeration to claim that the tender conscience of medieval kings prevented them from going to war without a watertight legal justification, but it would nevertheless be rash to dismiss such arguments as irrelevant. Arguments about legality might influence the amount of support a king could expect to get from the aristocracy, as well as the attitude of potential rivals. This may serve to explain some of the choices made by medieval kings in their foreign policy. Around 1260, when Denmark was in a deep crisis, it would probably have been more profitable for King Håkon Håkonsson to join the Danish king's enemies in conquering the wealthy region of Halland, just across the border, than to cross the North Sea with a large fleet in order to defend the Hebrides and Man. The latter expedition had little chance of success and, even if successful, would hardly add much to King

Håkon's wealth. For Håkon, however, the difference between the two areas was that he had a right to the latter but not to the former. In a similar way, King Erik of Pomerania in the fifteenth century spent most of his reign fighting to conquer the duchy of Schleswig, which had been joined with that of Holstein, an ambition that eventually led to his deposition. When his successor Christian I gained both duchies in 1460, he did not use them for further expansion into northern Germany, but instead tried to regain Sweden, a policy that was continued by his successors. The Danish king had not attempted to conquer Sweden before the Kalmar Union. After 1448, this aim became top priority, because from now on the Danish kings had a legal claim.

Thus, the various fields of expansion of the three kingdoms, to a great extent determined by geopolitical factors, served also to cement the apparently coincidental division between them that was established in the mid-eleventh century. However, it is difficult to imagine such clear divisions without a considerable amount of internal consolidation. That subject will form the theme of the following chapter.

CHAPTER TWO

The Consolidation of the Scandinavian Kingdoms, c. 1050–1350

The Dynasty and the Royal Office

On the morning of November 22, 1286, King Erik V Klipping of Denmark was found dead in his bed with fifty-six wounds in his body. "The king was killed by his own men, those whom he loved so much," says a contemporary chronicler. The way Erik was killed constitutes clear evidence of a conspiracy. Each of the conspirators had dealt the king one or more wounds, all of which were above the waist, suggesting an "honorable" killing by men of rank, not an attack by a band of robbers. Who the murderers were has remained unknown to this day, but there were a number of suspects. Erik had been involved in frequent conflicts both with his relative, the duke of Southern Jutland, and with members of the aristocracy. The regency for his son Erik VI Menved, led by the dowager queen, suspected the latter and half a year later accused a number of Danish magnates of the crime and forced them to leave the country. This mysterious murder and its consequences for inter-Danish and inter-Scandinavian relationship in the following years have frequently been discussed by scholars, most of whom believe that those who were convicted were actually innocent. More interesting than the identity of the murderers, however, is the fact that they are unknown.

King Erik Klipping's was the last instance of the murder of a Danish king and the second to the last of a ruling king in Scandinavia as a whole—the last being that of Gustaf III of Sweden in 1792. By contrast, there are plenty of examples from the previous period of kings being killed either by rivals or as the result of popular rebellions. This happened to all three royal saints: Olav, Knud, and Erik. Although the detailed accounts of the killing of the two former lament their deaths, they do not contain any reference to a ban against killing a king. Quite the contrary, the Norwegian Law of Frostating even had a paragraph demanding that the people in a district gather and kill royal officials, or even the king himself, if they have acted unjustly against a member of the community. The paragraph was not abolished until the introduction of the Code of the Realm in the 1270s.

By contrast, the men who killed Erik Klipping were clearly aware that they had committed a crime; otherwise, they would have come forward to replace Erik with another king. There were actually candidates. These included Erik's son, who succeeded his father at the age of twelve, but also other descendants of Erik's grandfather Valdemar II (d. 1241), among them Duke Valdemar of Southern Jutland, who has been regarded as the prime suspect by modern historians. However, the conspirators must have been aware that the days were gone when it was possible to murder a king with impunity and replace him with someone else. They had to commit a crime that was in fact, according to the old laws, more serious than just killing another man, namely killing in secret.

Whereas the way in which the murder was committed clearly points in the direction of a new understanding of the monarchy, the punishment seems surprisingly mild compared to what happened to such criminals in later ages. (They were most often tortured to death.) This may partly be explained by the power and status of the accused and partly by the fact that the evidence against them was only circumstantial; if they had been caught red-handed, they would probably have been killed. When one of them was caught later, he was broken on the wheel. Despite this reservation, the 1286 murder forms clear evidence of a change in the relationship between the king and his subjects. There were now rules for appointing a king, either through hereditary succession or election or, usually, a combination of the two, and once in his office, he was protected from being killed by rivals or as the result of popular rebellions. In this respect, Scandinavia conforms to the prevailing pattern in Western Europe, except that the change had taken place earlier in most other countries. The king had become qualitatively different from his subjects, an idea of dynastic continuity had emerged, and there was at least some sense of the royal office as an entity distinct from the king's person.

Characteristically, dynastic continuity is a central element in the rich historical literature that emerged in Scandinavia in the twelfth and thirteenth centuries. Although the genealogies in these sources are often later constructions, they are nevertheless significant evidence of the importance of dynastic continuity at the time when they were composed, probably in the twelfth century. A Danish dynasty had developed already in the mid-tenth century, whose members ruled the country for around a hundred years, until the death of Cnut the Great's last son, Harthacnut, who was succeeded by King Magnus of Norway. Thus, dynastic succession seems not to have been sufficiently firmly established to prevent the election of a foreign king. However, Magnus was soon replaced by Sven Estridsen who belonged to a sideline of the old dynasty. His descendants ruled Denmark until the death of Valdemar IV, the last in the male line, in 1375.

Exactly when the idea of dynastic succession became permanently recognized in Denmark is difficult to say; the early sources are too meager to allow us to distinguish between succession due to personal virtues or physical strength and a universally recognized hereditary succession. However, Danish kings in the tenth and eleventh centuries seem to have been strong enough to have their sons accepted as their successors, which probably led to the development of the idea of a dynasty. Individual succession also seems to have been introduced at an early stage; the five sons of Sven Estridsen ruled one after the other, not jointly (1074–1134). Legitimate birth—however this may have been defined at the time—seems to have been of no importance, whereas there was a preference for the eldest. Successions were not always peaceful, but there were no prolonged struggles within this generation, in contrast to the next, possibly because most of these kings reigned only for a short time. In 1131, Duke Knud Lavard, son of the late King Erik, was murdered by his cousin Magnus, son of the ruling King Niels. This led to the death of Niels and Magnus in the battle of Fodevig (1134) and to struggles between various members of the dynasty until the final victory of Knud Lavard's son Valdemar I in 1157. In the following, more peaceful period, there was a strong move in the direction of a purely hereditary succession, which, however, came to an end when a new series of internal conflicts erupted between the sons of Valdemar II (d. 1241) and their successors. In the early fourteenth century, kingship in Denmark was formally defined as elective, although in fact the eldest surviving son of the previous king was always elected, if there was one. Elective monarchy in practice meant the opportunity for the electors to pose conditions for accepting the king. The new king had to issue an election charter (*håndfæstning,* see p. 149).

The Norwegian dynasty originated later, although the sagas claim that all Norwegian kings were the descendants of the first king supposed to have ruled the whole country, Harald Finehair. Most probably, however, Harald's line became extinct with his grandsons, after which there was open competition for the throne until the mid-eleventh century, when Harald Hardrada (1046–1066) and his descendants ruled in relative peace for four generations. The change must be understood partly as a reaction to the period of Danish rule 1030–1035 and partly as the result of the canonization of Olav Haraldsson (1031), from whom later kings derived their right to the throne. Olav was succeeded first by his son Magnus (1035–1047) and then by his half-brother Harald. The rules of succession were vague, but seem to have favored agnatic descendants, whether born in wedlock or not. There was no rule of individual succession; if there was more than one candidate, which was often the case, they either had to share the power between them or fight over it. During the following series of inner struggles, only members—or alleged members—of the dynasty were allowed to compete, which is evident from the fact that many of the pretenders were only boys. Formal rules of succession were laid down in the Law of Succession of 1163/64, which introduced individual succession with preference for the late king's eldest legitimate son, although it also established an element of election by prescribing an elective body dominated by the bishops.

The Law of 1163/64 may be regarded as an attempt to assure peaceful succession to the throne, but it was first and foremost intended to protect the ruling king, Magnus Erlingsson, against his rivals, by defining their claims as illegal and stamping them as rebels and heretics. Magnus was only seven years old and related to the dynasty through his mother, but he had the advantage from point of view of the Church that he was born in marriage. The real ruler during Magnus's minority, and even longer, was his father, the Earl Erling Ormsson, nick-named Skakke (the Wry-neck). However, far from protecting Magnus against rivals, the law occasioned a most intense period of internal conflicts. Magnus was challenged by a queue of rivals, the most important of whom was Sverre Sigurdsson, allegedly an illegitimate son of a previous king. During a series of campaigns, Sverre managed to defeat and kill first Erling (1179) and then Magnus (1184), rule until his death in 1202, and leave the kingdom to his descendants, although he had to spend most of his reign fighting rebellions. His grandson Håkon Håkonsson put an end to the internal struggles and consolidated the kingdom during his long reign (1217–1263). During his and his successors' reigns, the principle of individual succession by the king's eldest son was laid down in the Law of 1260, revised in 1274 and 1302. These laws were based exclusively on the principle of hereditary succession. They decreed that an assembly should meet after the death of a king, but that its duty was only to acclaim the next in the line of succession. An election would only take place in case the dynasty had become extinct.

The first king of Sweden of whom we have any concrete knowledge is Olof Skotkonung ("the Tax King," so called either because he taxed his people or because he had to pay tribute to King Cnut the Great), who fought at Svolder. He issued coins, some of which are extant. Olof may have been recognized as king of most of present-day Sweden, but his main area seems to have been in the west. We know the names of his successors until the thirteenth century, but very few details about them. Medieval Sweden was divided into three main parts, from west to east: Västergötland, Östergötland, and Svealand. Lake Vättern forms the line of division between the two former, whereas Svealand is the fertile area around Lake Mälaren. From the late eleventh century onwards, there were almost continuous struggles over the throne between two dynasties, the one of Erik and the one of Sverker—both named after the most frequent names of their kings, most of whom were either murdered or killed in battle. The former dynasty had its main base in Västergötland, the latter in Östergötland, but both tried to control as much as possible of the country. No real unification of the country seems to have happened, however, until the mid-thirteenth century. The Sverker dynasty became extinct in 1222, which left Erik Eriksson (1222–1250) on the throne. He was succeeded by his sister's son Valdemar, son of the mighty Earl Birger, who was the real ruler until his death (1266), as he had also been during the latter part of Erik's reign. Birger's descendants continued to rule Sweden until the second half of the fourteenth century. Primogeniture and individual succession were introduced here as well, but, at least in the beginning, with limited success. There was a strong tradition of elective kingship, and after the election, the king had to travel around in the country to receive popular acclamation in the various provinces (*Eriksgata*). The Code of the Realm of 1350 explicitly stated that kingship in Sweden was elective and not hereditary.

The regulation of the succession took place during periods of frequent struggles between pretenders to the throne, in Denmark between 1131 and 1170, in Norway from 1130 to 1240, and in Sweden more or less continuously until the mid-thirteenth century. Although to some extent a symptom of incomplete state formation, these struggles actually led to increased centralization. They were not struggles between the central power and magnates attempting to carve out independent territories; the contending parties all aimed at securing the central power for themselves. In contrast to some suggestions, particularly from Norwegian historians, there is also little to suggest a conflict between an emerging aristocracy and the rest of the population. Although there is clear evidence of a strong aristocracy in all three countries even before this time, the divisions are more likely to have been between various aristocratic factions than between social strata. Nor did the struggles usually transcend established borders. Admittedly, pretenders in one country often received aid from supporters in another—in particular, the king of Denmark often intervened in this way in the other countries and may indeed have had territorial gain as one of his aims. In the 1160s, he tried to annex the Oslofjord area, but in the end had to confine himself to letting the earl Erling Skakke rule it on his behalf. In most cases, however, the pretenders and factions were specific to each country. The attempts to achieve final victory and secure it led to military and administrative reforms, which were continued by the victors of the struggles, Valdemar I and his successors from 1157 in Denmark, Håkon Håkonsson and his successors from 1240 in Norway, and Earl Birger and his successors from 1250 in Sweden (as kings from 1266).

The formation of a dynasty, combined with rules about individual succession, gave the monarchy a legal foundation. One particular person had a birthright to rule the country, which was in this sense his property, in the same way as a farmer had the right to his land. This was most clearly set forth in Norway, where the monarchy was defined as hereditary and where this analogy actually occurs in the mid-thirteenth-century *King's Mirror*, but the principle of individual succession and thus of one individual's exclusive right to the realm was equally strong in the two other countries, where the monarchy was elective. The idea of lawful succession and the king's right to rule the country was developed in charters, historiography, and didactic works, and served to defend the monarchy against internal as well as external rivals. To this was added the ecclesiastical ideology of kingship as an office and the king as God's representative on earth, expressed in the ritual of coronation, introduced in Norway in 1163/64, in Denmark in 1170, and in Sweden—where it never had the same importance as in the other countries—in 1210. During the coronation, the king received the symbols of his power: crown, scepter, globe, and sword, which served to distinguish him from other people and appeared in pictures, statues, and seals to represent the royal dignity. He also had a special seat, the throne, to which he was led or lifted during the acclamation and coronation, showing that it was his by right and general consent.

The new ideology is expressed particularly clearly in *The King's Mirror*, composed in Norway, probably in the 1250s. This work deals directly with the problem of regicide. Discussing God's different judgments of the evil King Saul and the good King David, the author points out that despite Saul's evil character and God's rejection of him, David saved his life when he had the opportunity to kill him, adding that he was not allowed to kill the Lord's anointed. At the end of the work, the author shows the king before God's seat of judgment, and declares that an evil king will get his punishment from God, not from his subjects. In another passage the author accordingly states that the king represents God on earth where, like God, he is the lord of life and death: it is only he and his representatives who are allowed to kill other humans. This last passage should not be understood as an expression of the king's arbitrary power but as the introduction of the idea of a public power with rights and duties different from those of ordinary people, in other words as an explicit expression of the ideas that brought an end to the practice of regicide.

However, protection against murder was not the same as protection against opposition or even deposition. Kings during the following period potentially faced two problems. One was younger brothers, who were now excluded from the throne as long as their elder brother lived, but had to be provided for in accordance with their status, normally with a part of the country held as a fief. The other was opposition from the Church and/or the aristocracy, which rested on the idea that a king should rule in accordance with the interests of the people, in practice mainly the aristocracy. However, this opposition increasingly took legal forms. It might be violent, but not until peaceful means had been exhausted. Violence had to be preceded by a formal declaration of war or a renunciation of obedience, and its use normally preceded by prolonged negotiations. Above all, resistance to the king was increasingly formalized; it had to be carried out by an organized body, eventually the council of the realm. This combination of lawful resistance and kingship by the grace of God may at first seem paradoxical, but there is a connection between the two. The doctrine of the divine origin of kingship was the same in Byzantium and the Muslim world, but there the murder of rulers and coups d'état were commonplace. This was not the case in the West, and the explanation seems to be that here there was a lawful way of opposing the ruler. As these conflicts are particularly characteristic of the period of the Kalmar Union, however, they will be dealt with later.

Eventually, members of the aristocracy received protection similar to that of the king. The saga of King Sverre lists sixteen members of the top aristocracy who were killed, together with King Magnus Erlingsson, in the 1184 battle of Fimreite in Norway. Captive aristocrats were frequently executed in internal conflicts in all three countries, and if they were not, the reason should probably be sought in tactical considerations rather than rules of chivalry. In the later Middle Ages, however, aristocrats profited from similar rules as the king. Although without covering up the tricks and stratagems of the dukes, the early-fourteenth century *Chronicle of Erik* is full of references to the chivalrous treatment of captives and honorable burials of fallen enemies. The common European rules of chivalrous behavior towards aristocratic enemies seem in most cases to have been followed in internal as well as external wars. Thus, in contrast to England, where from the late thirteenth century onwards increased respect for the king led to stricter punishments for treason or rebellion, even for aristocratic prisoners, the rules were similar for the treatment of kings and aristocrats in Scandinavia.

The changes resulting from this stabilization of the monarchy can be summarized in the terms "centralization" and "bureaucratization." The formation of dynasties and the change in the status of rulers was accompanied by the development of royal and ecclesiastical administrations, which replaced personal and patronal rulership with a government that was in some degree bureaucratic; or that at least exhibited some elements of bureaucracy. The rise of the Scandinavian kingdoms is thus an example of the export of some central features of the civilization that was forming at the time in Western Christendom, notably a royal and an ecclesiastical organization, which entailed the centralization of important social functions such as religion, law, and warfare.

Religion: The Introduction of Christianity

The old royal center at Jelling in Jutland stands as a visual monument of the transition from paganism to Christianity in Denmark. It comprises two burial mounds, two rune stones, and a Christian church. One of the mounds contains a pagan grave, probably that of King Gorm (d. c. 950), who raised a monument to his wife, Queen Tyra, in one of the rune stones. The other mound, possibly intended for Gorm's son Harald Bluetooth (d. 986), is empty, but Harald is present on the other rune stone, which celebrates his conquest of Denmark and Norway and his conversion of Denmark, underneath a carving of Christ. The inscription runs: "King Harald let carve these runes after Gorm his father and Tyra his mother, Harald who won all Denmark and Norway and made the Danes Christian."

The Jelling monument is one of the most important testimonies to the Christianization of Scandinavia and its inscription one of the relatively few contemporary sources for it. What does it mean that Harald "made the Danes Christian"? Another contemporary source, the German chronicler Widukind of Corvey (c. 967/68), attributes their final conversion to a German cleric and later bishop, Poppo. Although the Danes had been Christian for a long time, they continued to practice pagan rituals. During

Figure 3. Jelling Stone (Denmark). The picture shows the victorious Christ, surrounded by ornaments interpreted as the Tree of Life or possibly the cross. This style ornamentation was current in Scandinavia ca. 880–1000 and is referred to as the Jelling style. The stone has three sides; the two not depicted here show, respectively, a lion (a Biblical symbol of Christ), and the inscription quoted in the text. Photo: P. Thomsen. Dept. of Special Collections, University of Bergen Library.

a discussion at a party at the king's court, some of those present claimed that although Christ was a god, there were also other and mightier gods, who were able to produce greater signs and miracles. To this Poppo answered that Christ was the only God and that the pagan gods were without power. King Harald then asked Poppo if he could prove the truth of his faith. Poppo accepted the challenge and successfully carried hot iron as evidence, which convinced the king to convert, to honor the Church, and to forbid pagan cult.

Two main questions have dominated scholarly discussions about the Christianization of Scandinavia: (1) Was the process sudden or gradual? (2) Was it mainly carried out by indigenous kings or leaders or were the main players foreign missionaries? The idea of a gradual Christianization predominated in the second half of the twentieth century, based in part on the experience of modern conversions, which typically require a long process of missionary activity before success is achieved; in part from a tendency to reduce the importance of the kings; and in part from archaeological evidence of prolonged contact between Scandinavia and the rest of Europe, which led to the reception of various external impulses, Christianity among them. Gradual Christianization thus centers on a religious understanding of the process, linked to the work of missionaries, though political forces were not excluded from the explanation: Scandinavian chieftains formed links with kings and nobles abroad and brought Christian rites and objects home with them.

Concerning the first question, most sources, including the two contemporary ones on the conversion of Denmark, point either to one decisive event or to a short period of confrontation between the two religions, although Widukind refers to a prehistory of gradual Christian infiltration. By contrast, they give different answers to the second question. The foreign sources that deal with the mission to Scandinavia, notably Rimbert's *Life of*

Ansgar (c. 875) and Adam of Bremen's *History of the Archbishops of Hamburg* (c. 1070), attribute the conversion to German missionaries, beginning with Ebo's and Ansgar's missions (823 and 829), whereas the indigenous ones tend to emphasize the importance of the kings. Although Saxo accepts Poppo's miracle as the decisive event, he also points to the Danes' own contribution. At King Gorm's orders, Thorkel sets out on an expedition to the northern edge of the world, where, in great danger, he invokes the God of the universe and is saved, after which he goes to Germany, which had recently converted to Christianity, and is instructed in the basic elements of Christian doctrine. The emphasis on the role of indigenous kings or chieftains is even stronger in the Old Norse sagas, where the conversion of Norway is mainly attributed to the two missionary kings, Olav Tryggvason (995–1000) and St. Olav Haraldsson (1015–1030), while the clerical missionaries play a subordinate part. The earliest of these sources, Ari's account of the conversion of Iceland in the year 1000, dating from the 1120s, regards the whole process as political. According to Ari, several leading men had converted to Christianity, whereas others were strongly opposed. The Icelanders were under pressure as well from the Norwegian King Olav Tryggvason, who was introducing Christianity into Norway. On the advice of a highly respected pagan, Thorgeir Thorkellsson, the Icelanders agreed to convert to Christianity, in return for some concessions to the pagans. This was done entirely for pragmatic reasons, in order to maintain the unity of the people. Neither doctrines nor miracles were involved. There are very few written sources for the conversion of Sweden, but a thirteenth century source, *Gutasagan* (the "History of the Gotlanders") describes the conversion of the island of Gotland as a pragmatic decision, not unlike what happened in Iceland.

None of these sources is completely trustworthy. The missionary sources are chronologically closer to the events or, in the case of Adam, at least partly based on earlier written sources, but they are likely to exaggerate the importance of the missionaries. The indigenous sources, which are later, are also biased but in the opposite direction. Both the sagas and Saxo contain in addition a number of stories that are clearly legendary. Nevertheless, our general knowledge of early Scandinavian society clearly points in the direction of a political explanation of the conversion, a conclusion that gains support from the oldest indigenous account, that of Ari.

To some extent, this discussion is about definitions. If we understand Christianization as a fundamental transformation of a people's beliefs and religious practices, it obviously requires a prolonged process, one that is impossible to date through the available source material. By contrast, if by "Christianization," we mean the formal decree making Christianity the only lawful religion, we can in most cases narrow it down to a precise date, or at least to within a few decades. This still leaves the question of the relationship between the official conversion and previous Christian influence. It is difficult to imagine a royal decree introducing a new and completely unknown religion, at least if such a decree is to have any effect, but it is an open question how much preparation would have been needed. Depending on the strength of the monarchy and the status of those supporting Christianity, the formal introduction may well have come at a stage when only a minority of the population were Christians. On the other hand, a majority of Christians would not necessarily translate into a religious monopoly for Christianity.

The relevance of the parallel to modern missions is also doubtful. Medieval accounts show that what the missionaries tried to achieve was a formal, collective conversion. Their efforts were directed at influencing the kings or other leaders of society with the aim of bringing about the establishment of an ecclesiastical hierarchy and the baptism of the population. Some individual conversions might be a means to achieve this, but, unlike modern missionaries, their medieval counterparts were not concerned with deep personal convictions. From this point of view, the missionary and the indigenous sources agree.

There may be stronger arguments in favor of a more secular version of gradual conversion. Increasing contact with Christian Europe might have led to familiarity with Christianity, as well as to personal links between Scandinavian chieftains and their foreign counterparts, which might have entailed baptism. Baptism and the acceptance of Christian missionaries were clearly means by which Scandinavian kings or chieftains might gain the friendship of their counterparts abroad, as did the two Olavs, who were baptized respectively in England and in Normandy, and Harald Bluetooth, whose conversion to Christianity may have been calculated to win the friendship of Otto the Great.

However, it is difficult to imagine that these means, either missionary or secular, would lead to the decisive step from accepting a certain Christian influence to actively rejecting paganism. From the point of view of traditional Scandinavian religion, the acceptance of new gods did not mean the rejection of the old ones, as is evident from Widukind's account.

If we are to explain this, we have to consider the kings. Religion and political power were closely connected in the pagan period. There was apparently no professional priesthood; the chieftains acted as cultic and religious leaders. We can assume that the position of chieftain was unstable; there was typically competition between several leading men for local power. Although it would not have been impossible for one of these chieftains to achieve domination over his competitors, the pagan religion did not give the same support to this kind of lordship, and to a newcomer, the lack of firmly rooted political and religious leadership over a given area was clearly a handicap. This would apply both to a ruler like Harald Bluetooth, who, from a base probably in southern Jutland, tried to conquer the whole of Denmark, and even more to the Norwegian kings, who returned with men and booty from Viking expeditions abroad. By contrast, Christianity was a unitary religion, with one cult, one God, and a professional cult organization that immediately abolished the religious importance of local chieftains. The sources occasionally draw a parallel between the rule of one king and the belief in one God, thus suggesting that there is a logical connection between the new religion and larger political entities: just as one God rules the world, so there must be one king in a country. Snorri lets Harald Finehair swear by the Almighty God that he will conquer Norway and states that he disliked the pagan magic, *seiðr*.

Although the king was not necessarily the head of the ecclesiastical organization, he had considerable control over it in the early Middle Ages, notably in countries where Christianity was a new religion. Admittedly, this organization must in the beginning have been too weak to add very much to the king's power. Nevertheless, Christianity had a centralizing effect by virtue of being a new religion. The struggle for this religion, including the destruction of pagan cult sites, of which there is archaeological evidence, gave the king an opportunity to replace old chieftains with his own adherents. Thus, the conversion is likely to have strengthened the position of the king, although this did not mean a general decline of the aristocracy. The magnates who converted could maintain their position in local society by building churches and appointing priests, but, at least in the beginning, the new religion attached them more closely to the king. Finally, Christianity also gave the king an incentive to conquer new areas in order to propagate the new religion. Admittedly, we cannot exclude the possibility that other chieftains besides the kings acted in the same way; for in fact there was hardly a sharp distinction between kings and other leaders at this time. The important point is that

Christianity was a means to centralization, whether carried out by men who were already regarded as kings or not.

On these matters, Harald Bluetooth and the sagas probably give an accurate account, although the latter exaggerate the importance of the two main missionary kings, Olav Tryggvason (995–1000) and St. Olav Haraldsson (1015–1030). In any event, after the death of Harald Finehair in the 930s, all rulers of Norway except one were Christian and probably contributed in various ways to the final outcome. In a similar way, Saxo is wrong in contrasting the Christian Harald with his successor Sven, who allegedly returned to paganism and was brought back to Christianity only through God's punishment; most probably, Harald's conversion of the country became permanent. It also seems that the towns worked as bridgeheads of a kind for the conversion of the surrounding countryside, to the extent that we can talk of "ports of faith" in analogy with "ports of trade" (Sæbjørg Nordeide). Nidaros (now: Trondheim), founded by King Olav Tryggvason in the 990s, is an example, as is Sigtuna in Sweden at around the same time. Moreover, although the archaeological evidence from Norway shows that conversions took place at different times in different parts of the country, there is nothing to indicate the coexistence of Christianity and paganism within any particular area. Thus, while not ignoring the importance of other contacts with Christian Europe, via Viking and trading expeditions for example, we have to conclude that the decisive step was taken by the kings, who established the Church and banned pagan cult.

The main pattern of Christianization is the same throughout Scandinavia, but we may point to some differences between Denmark and Norway (we know too little about Sweden to draw conclusions about this country). In the case of Denmark, its conversion is clearly influenced by its powerful neighbor to the south, Ottonian Germany. In 965, when Poppo allegedly performed his miracle, Otto the Great was at the height of his power and his friendship must have been very attractive to Harald, both as a source of prestige and to diminish the threat from a mighty neighbor. Otto may also have served as a model for Harald of a powerful ruler with stronger control of his subjects than Harald and his predecessors had managed to achieve in Denmark. Finally, Germany was actively engaged in missionary activities, and a separate ecclesiastical organization devoted to this enterprise, the archbishopric of Hamburg-Bremen, had existed for around a hundred years.

By contrast, the English kings were less able to intervene in Scandinavia. King Ethelred (979–1016), the contemporary of Sven Forkbeard and the two Olavs, was an unsuccessful ruler who was repeatedly defeated by Scandinavian Vikings and was eventually succeeded by the Danish Cnut the Great. Nevertheless, Anglo-Saxon England was a wealthy and highly centralized country with a monarchy that might well have served as a model for the Scandinavian kings. Moreover, in contrast to their Danish counterparts, the Norwegian kings lacked a firm local base, which gave them an even stronger incentive to introduce a new religion, and, above all, to suppress the old one, on which the power of their rivals was based.

It may be objected that this explanation completely ignores religious and cultural factors and regards people in that time as acting solely out of rational self-interest. The best response to this accusation is that such considerations are fully compatible with a religious attitude. There was no sharp distinction between the religious and the secular spheres in the early Middle Ages, certainly not in paganism, and considerably less in Christianity than in later ages. Consequently, success in the secular field might easily translate to a religious advantage. Nor was contemporary religion an objective system of dogma. It was instead, and intensely, a matter of personal relationships, so that there was a strong connection between allegiance to a leader and allegiance to his gods.

The Christianization of Scandinavia formed part of a greater wave of conversions that brought most of Northern and Eastern Europe into Western Christendom. Bohemia converted in the early tenth century, Poland in 966, and Hungary in 1000, whereas Russia converted to Eastern Christendom in 988. In all these cases, we witness voluntary conversions by local rulers—conversions that differ in character from those of previous and subsequent periods. The closest parallel is the conversion of England in the early seventh century, which was carried out by missionaries from Rome without any military or political pressure, although there was probably a stronger presence of Christianity in seventh-century England than in Scandinavia and East Central Europe three hundred years later. The subsequent conversion of the Netherlands and northern Germany also shows some resemblance to the Scandinavian experience, but these areas were at least nominally under the control of the Carolingians who supported the missionaries. By contrast, the conversion of Saxony, previously outside the Carolingian Empire, was the result of a prolonged and bloody war, as was also the conversion of the lands on the southern shore of the Baltic Sea from the twelfth century onwards.

It seems that the tenth-century conversions took place in a period when there was a relative balance of power between the old and the new parts of Europe. The old monarchies, Anglo-Saxon England and imperial Germany, were strong enough to serve as important models for rulers of the new kingdoms, but not to conquer them. By contrast, the increased strength of the Christian kingdoms in the following period, which now also included previously pagan areas like Denmark and Poland, shifted the balance of power and made pagan areas targets for conquest, a trend that was stimulated by the growth of the crusading ideology, which mobilized the secular aristocracy for the cause of Christianity. Thus, early and voluntary Christianization was an important asset for the six kingdoms, whereas those that remained pagan until the mid-twelfth century became the victims of conquest. This in turn points to the importance of Christianity for state formation, not only for the development of the internal organization of the countries but also for the formation of territorial kingdoms and principalities.

The Development of the Ecclesiastical Organization

The political centralization that resulted from conversion was furthered through the establishment of an ecclesiastical organization. Christianity in its medieval Catholic form featured an elaborate cult and an equally elaborate doctrine, both of which required the services of a professional priesthood. Whereas pagan cult observances consisted in the main of sacrificial parties, apparently not too unlike ordinary meals presided over by the ordinary leaders of the community, the main Christian cult, the mass, although originally based on a meal, had in the Middle Ages developed into a highly specialized ceremony. It could only be celebrated by a priest and normally took place in a special building. The original meal had been reduced to a thin wafer and a drop of wine (normally consumed only by the priest). In 1215 the Fourth Lateran Council decided that the laity should receive this meal, termed Holy Communion, once a year, and this was normally the only time they did so. At around the same period, it also became the practice that the laity received the sacrament in the form of bread only, not wine. In addition to Holy Communion or the Sacrament of the Eucharist, there were six other sacraments, given at important stages in life, from birth to death, most of which also had to be administered by the priests. The exception was marriage, which the partners gave to each other, and baptism, which any Christian could administer if no priest were available. Thus, priests and churches became essential if people were to conduct a Christian life and reach salvation after death.

In addition, the priests had to teach Christian doctrine to new converts and see to it that they lived according to the rules of the Church. In contrast to modern Protestantism—and largely also to modern Catholicism, where Christian ethics is basically an appeal to the individual conscience—medieval Catholicism consisted of a panoply of detailed rules, whose observance was monitored by priests and other ecclesiastical authorities. Every four days, on average, there was an ecclesiastical holiday when it was forbidden to work. Every Friday was a day of abstinence, when it was forbidden to eat meat or to have sexual intercourse. These prohibitions were also in effect at various other times, the most important of which were the four weeks before Christmas and the seven weeks before Easter. Characteristically, the Icelandic historian Snorri Sturluson (1179–1241) summarized the pagans' objections to Christianity in the statement that people were forbidden to work and to eat. Transgressions of these rules were punished by fines, and the priest or the bishop's local representative was responsible for bringing the culprit to justice. In addition, the Church introduced new rules governing marriage, defining it as a voluntary agreement between a man and a woman, not, as previously, a contract between two kindred. The church also prohibited divorce and incest, the latter originally defined as marriage between partners related in the seventh degree, but in 1215 reduced to the fourth. Most of these provisions were established by law, and breaches were prosecuted at the local assemblies or, eventually, at separate ecclesiastical courts. The same applied to the use of magic, pagan cult, or doctrines opposed to that of the Church. Thus, there was a sliding transition between cult and doctrine on the one hand and government and the administration of justice on the other. Functions of both kinds necessitated a considerable bureaucracy.

Of the Scandinavian countries, Denmark was the first to have an ecclesiastical organization that conformed to European norms. Its precedence was due partly to the early introduction of Christianity in this country, partly to the greater influence there of the German mission, which was more concerned with organizational issues than was the English mission. Despite the formal division of Denmark into dioceses as early as 948, the Danish diocesan organization with eight dioceses in practice dates from around 1060. Regular dioceses were established in Norway in the late eleventh century, but the organization was not fully developed until the mid-twelfth century, when there were five dioceses. In addition, six dioceses on the Atlantic isles belonged to the Church province of Nidaros. In Sweden, the first diocese, that of Skara, was founded in 1015. The country was later divided into seven. In 1104, Scandinavia became an independent church province with its archbishop's see at Lund in Denmark (now in Sweden).

The province was further divided in 1152/53, when Norway got its own archbishop in Nidaros, and in 1164 with the establishment of a Swedish archbishopric, centered in Uppsala. Cathedral chapters developed in the three kingdoms around the time of the foundation of the church provinces, but not in Iceland or in some of the smaller dioceses on the Atlantic isles. Beginning in the twelfth and above all in the thirteenth century, diocesan organization was further elaborated, with a growing array of provosts, archdeacons, and other officials engaged in administrative and judicial duties. There were, however, considerable differences between dioceses, commensurate with their relative wealth and size. The first Benedictine monasteries were founded in Denmark in the late eleventh century and in Norway in the early twelfth. The earliest monasteries in Sweden were the Cistercian foundations of Alvastra and Nydala, both dating from 1143. At the same

Figure 4. Lund Cathedral (Denmark), now in Sweden. Built in a German-influenced Romanesque style. The cathedral was consecrated in 1145 and dedicated to St Lawrence. It was restored 1860–80. Photo: Anton Holmquist. Wikimedia Commons.

time, Cistercian monasteries were founded in the other countries as well. The clerical orders that became popular in the rest of Europe during the twelfth century, the Augustinians and Premonstratensians, were also introduced to Scandinavia around this time. The mendicants arrived relatively early. The first Dominicans settled in Lund in Denmark under the patronage of Archbishop Anders Sunesen in 1223 and established their Scandinavian province (Dacia) in 1228. The Franciscans came from Germany to Denmark in 1232 and established their province of Dacia in 1239. Twenty of their thirty-one Scandinavian houses were established before 1250.

Parish organization took shape gradually. In Denmark, a period of intense church building began in the eleventh century, mostly under the direction of kings and magnates, and eventually resulted in the division of the country into parishes. The introduction of the tithe from around 1100 was an important factor in this development. In Norway, an organization of churches for large districts is found in the provincial laws from the late eleventh or early twelfth century on, but it is doubtful to what extent this represented actual organization. In any case, the parish organization we meet in the thirteenth century and later is largely based on the numerous churches built by local magnates who wanted to have a church in the vicinity of their estates. As in Denmark, the introduction of the tithe is regarded as an important factor in the development of parish organization. According to the sagas, the tithe was introduced by King Sigurd in the 1120s, but it most likely did not become a regular contribution until the second half of the century. A large number of churches seem to have been built over a short period, although somewhat later than in Denmark, in the late twelfth and early thirteenth century. Swedish parish organization developed in a similar way as in the neighboring countries, but at a somewhat later date.

The development of the Scandinavian churches from modest beginnings to wealthy and powerful institutions can to some extent be traced in the sources. A paragraph in the Norwegian Law of Gulating, probably from the first half of the twelfth century, states that priests should no longer be beaten when they have offended but should instead pay fines, which was the normal pun-

Figure 5. The Dominican House in Ribe (Denmark). Fifteenth century. The building complex is almost completely preserved. The Dominicans normally settled in towns. They were active as preachers and confessors and were often well educated. Unknown photographer.

ishment for free men. The paragraph adds that they have now become respectable men to whom members of the local communities might marry their daughters—clerical celibacy was still unknown at this date. In Denmark, some papal letters from the 1070s complained that priests were blamed for natural disasters

Figure 6. Two local churches of the Middle Ages. **A.** The tiny stave church in the mountain community of Uvdal (Norway). The construction of the church can be dated to 1168 through dendrochronology. It was extended in the eighteenth and early nineteenth century. Photo: Linn Marie Krogsrud. Middelaldernett. **B.** The monumental Öja stone church on the wealthy island of Gotland (Sweden). Its oldest parts date from the early thirteenth century. Around a hundred stone churches of the Middle Ages are still preserved on the island, often referred to as "parish cathedrals." Öja is one of the largest, and in addition is richly decorated. Photo: Therese Foldvik. Middelaldernett.

and severely persecuted, which again points to their low status, although we do not know whether this refers to their customary treatment or only to some individual cases. Whereas priests and bishops were in the beginning often foreigners, these offices were gradually taken over by indigenous candidates from the twelfth century onwards. It is particularly significant that members of the high aristocracy became bishops, a sure sign that the office had become a prestigious one, that the Church had become wealthy, and that its most prominent servants played a powerful role in society. Ecclesiastical wealth also increased as the result of gifts from the king and the aristocracy, including the bishops themselves, who often gave a part of their fortunes to their churches.

Compared to the other new countries of Western Christendom, Poland, Hungary, and Bohemia, the organization of dioceses came late to Scandinavia; in the three eastern countries, they were introduced very soon after conversion. The greater emphasis placed on formal ecclesiastical organization by the German Church in contrast to the English was in part responsible, but a strong wish by the rulers of the converted countries to establish their equality to and independence of the strong German Empire was also a factor. The latter also explains why Poland and Hungary became independent church provinces already in the early eleventh century, whereas Bohemia, closer to Germany and more dependent on this country, had to wait until 1344. Scotland had to wait even longer; the Scottish church was under the Archbishop of York until 1472. The Scandinavian church provinces came earlier than this but later than those of Poland and Hungary. They might have been even further postponed were it not for the Investiture Contest and the conflicts that followed it between the pope and the emperor. The province of Lund was erected in 1103, when the Archbishop of Hamburg-Bremen sided with the emperor against the pope. Nidaros in 1152/53 came at a time when the Archbishop of Hamburg-Bremen tried to reassert his superiority over the Scandinavian churches, and although there was at the time no open conflict between the emperor and the pope, the latter may have judged a division of the province of Lund to be a useful precaution. Finally, the Swedish province came during the papal schism, when the Danish king sided with the anti-pope Victor IV.

Although the medieval Church was far from a Weberian bureaucracy, its introduction to Scandinavia marked a decisive step in the direction of bureaucratization. The Church, particularly the post-Gregorian Church, introduced the ideas of office and hierarchy. The ecclesiastical organization consisted of officers, from the local priest to the pope at top, who were supposed to act not on their own behalf but on behalf of the organization to which they belonged. Through common rules of behavior and of rights and duties, education, and from the eleventh century, celibacy, the Church tried and at least partly succeeded in introducing an *esprit de corps* among its servants. In its capacity as an organized hierarchy, the Church could insist on obedience from inferiors to superiors in a way that might serve as a model for secular organization as well. Even as late as the mid-thirteenth century, the Norwegian treatise *The King's Mirror* uses the ecclesiastical hierarchy as a model when teaching the king's men the importance of obedience: if the priest disobeys his bishop or the bishop his superior, they are removed from their offices. Comparing Saul's sin, which led to his deposition, to David's sin, for which he was punished but forgiven, the author states that the reason behind their different treatments was not that the act Saul had committed was in itself worse than David's sin. Saul had been ordered by God to kill all the captive Amalekites, whereas David had committed adultery with the wife of one of his officers and then killed the officer in order to cover up the sin. Like most of his readers, the author of the treatise might have found it difficult to deny that David's was actually the worse of the two acts, but he insists that it was nonetheless outweighed by Saul's sin because Saul had disobeyed a direct order from God.

The twelfth century has often been viewed as the heroic age of the Scandinavian Churches, even by historians with little sympathy for the Catholic Church. It was the age of great, visionary churchmen with international connections and a program for fundamental reform of the Scandinavian kingdoms in accordance with the ideas of ecclesiastical liberty (*libertas ecclesiae*). Their program was the familiar one promoted by the contemporary papacy all over Europe. They wanted ecclesiastical control of the appointment of clerics and of ecclesiastical property; independent ecclesiastical jurisdiction, notably in judgments of clerics; and they wanted to secure the economy of the Church through the introduction of the tithe and by abolishing or reducing restrictions against donations to the Church that had been imposed in order to protect the interests of the donor's heirs.

Evidence from two great reforming archbishops of the twelfth century, Eystein in Norway (1161–88) and Eskil in Denmark (1137–77), both members of aristocratic families, gives some idea of the status of the Scandinavian churches at this time and of the attempts taken to bring their two church provinces into conformity with international standards. Eystein's efforts in this direction are most easily discernible in the collection usually referred to as the *Canones Nidrosienses,* which most scholars nowadays attribute to him. The collection, probably issued in 1163/64, shows the clear influence of Gratian's *Decretum,* which Eystein may have encountered already on his journey to Rome to receive the symbol of his dignity, the *pallium.* The collection shows a good grasp of its source and an ability to apply its regulations to Norwegian conditions. In Canon 1, Eystein applies the essence of Gratian's reasoning and his sources to his ordinance about the rights of the founders of churches (the *ius patronatus*). In the canons dealing with the most sensitive and controversial issues of the day, ecclesiastical elections and celibacy, Eystein shows an awareness of the limits on what could be achieved under twelfth-century Norwegian conditions. Whereas the contemporary trend was to reserve episcopal elections for the cathedral chapters, Eystein describes an assembly made up of a broader range of clerics, suggesting that the cathedral chapters were probably still weak at the time. He does not exclude some lay influence, although he omits to mention the king. He points to the ideal of purity and sexual abstinence for clerics, but only forbids marriage for canons and for ordinary priests wishing to marry widows or divorced women. Thus, celibacy was not yet the rule in Norway, almost a century after Pope Gregory VII had forbidden priests to marry. As late as 1237, Pope Gregory IX expressed his surprise that Norwegian priests continued to be married and forbade the practice. In the following period, celibacy was introduced in the sense that priests did not contract formal marriages. They continued to live with women, however, as they probably did in most other countries as well. The difference was that it in Norway it was comparatively easier for them to have their children made legitimate and eligible to inherit than in the other countries.

A series of letters from Pope Alexander III (1159–81) to Eystein with answers to questions posed by him show his contacts with the curia and the international Church. In 1169, he asked about the criteria determining the legality of a marriage—a topic hotly discussed by contemporary canonists. He received an answer from Alexander III that settled this issue in canon law: consent was the decisive criterion and not sexual intercourse, which was the alternative point of view. Eystein also asked about concrete issues, such as the proper penance for a man who has committed homicide and the actions that should be taken against a cleric guilty of sexual intercourse with a nun.

The pope's answer to a question about royal influence on episcopal elections shows some pragmatism on the part of both

Eystein and Pope Alexander. The pope states the principle of free ecclesiastical elections, but does not forbid the archbishop to consult the king beforehand. Some questions of this kind may also have their origin in Eystein's work on ecclesiastical legislation and preparing liturgical books. Eystein was thus a conscientious prelate who wanted his church to conform to the international Church. From the point of view of the papacy, the distant north was also of some importance at the time, because of the schism. Eystein was a staunch supporter of Alexander III, whereas King Valdemar I of Denmark in periods belonged in the opposite camp. The foundation of a Norwegian Church province had clearly increased the pope's influence in the north, and Eystein's appointment as papal legate (*apostolice sedis legatus*) may be understood as an appreciation of this fact.

Eystein's greatest political success came in the form of privileges issued in connection with King Magnus Erlingsson's coronation in 1163 or 1164 (the first in Scandinavia): the Law of Succession (1163/64), the coronation oath (1163/64), and Magnus Erlingsson's privilege to the Church (c. 1170). All three documents express the ecclesiastical doctrine of kingship as instituted by God and emphasize the king's duty to rule justly and in accordance with ecclesiastical doctrine and the guidance given by the Church hierarchy, in addition to his responsibility to defend the rights and privileges of the Church. However, when Magnus was deposed and killed, his successor Sverre refused to recognize these privileges, which led to a major conflict between the monarchy and the Church. Both Eystein and his successor Eirik (1188–1205) had to go into exile for a period, but both eventually returned and agreed to some kind of compromise with the king; Eirik admittedly only after Sverre's death.

In Denmark, Archbishop Eskil displayed an attitude similar to Eystein's and, like Eystein, also ran into conflicts with the kings, including Valdemar I (1157–82), particularly when the latter—

under the influence of Frederick Barbarossa—recognized the anti-popes against Alexander III during the 1159–1177 schism. Eskil's relationship to Valdemar may, however, also have been influenced by the fact that he belonged to a kindred in Jutland with ties of loyalty in other directions. By contrast, his successors Absalon (1177–1201) and Anders Sunesen (1201–1222) from the Hvide kindred, whose links to Valdemar and his successors were strong, had an excellent relationship to the king, despite the fact that they belonged to the same highly educated and internationally oriented clerical elite as Eskil.

In hindsight, it is easy to see that the medieval Church was a competitor to the state. This is evident from the great increase in the state's wealth and power that followed on the Reformation, when the king took over most of the lands of the Church and its personnel became directly subordinate to him. In the twelfth century, however, the situation was different. Then the expansion of the Church meant an expansion of public authority that also benefited the monarchy, and although a large part of the lands belonging to the Church were gifts from the king, he would probably have had to give it to secular aristocrats if the Church had not existed. If we consider the conflict in the two countries in a broad perspective, the picture of a head-on clash between the monarchy and the Church is considerably modified. The support Erling and Magnus received from the Church was well worth their concessions, and the conflict in the following period can largely be explained as the result of the change of dynasty. An alliance had been concluded, not primarily between the Church and the monarchy, but between the Church and a particular faction. Eystein as well as his successor Eirik had family and personal links to this faction, which at least to some extent explain their support for Magnus and their sour relations with Sverre.

Thus, the difference between Eskil and Eystein on the one hand and Absalon on the other cannot be explained simply by different attitudes towards ecclesiastical reform and the relationship between monarchy and Church, but must also be understood in the light of their family and political loyalties. This does not mean that the ecclesiastical loyalties of these prelates and their embrace of the Gregorian reform should not be taken seriously, but it must be kept in mind that they had to maneuver between sometimes conflicting loyalties. Contrary to Melchisedech, who having no father or mother was the ideal priest, medieval prelates did not burn the bridges that linked them to their families and social networks. Wealth, interests, a common culture, and common education linked the clerics to one another, but they still had divided loyalties, which means that the individual prelate's political and ideological choices have to be determined in each separate case, not taken for granted because of his position within the Church.

Despite the fact that the expansion of the Church was no unmixed blessing for the monarchy, it is difficult to imagine a similar bureaucratization of any function other than the religious under contemporary conditions. Thus, the Church contributed greatly to social change and to the formation of a society that was significantly more structured than that of the previous period. The rise of the ecclesiastical organization therefore forms an important part of the explanation for the stability of the three kingdoms. The fact that the borders of three Church provinces corresponded to the national borders (with one exception, namely that a part of Norway, Jämtland, which belonged to the Swedish church province) obviously favored stability. However, this coincidence of state and Church was an exception internationally, and the medieval Church played a similar part in other countries. It is often understood as primarily an international organization under the leadership of the pope, whose ability to interfere in the affairs of the national churches was no doubt impressive. Nevertheless, the Church also held to a doctrine of obedience to secular authorities derived from the New Testament and transferred from the Roman emperor to national kings. The bishops depended on the king for internal peace and quiet and were normally interested in maintaining a good relationship to him. Many of them held *len* from the king or served as chancellors or members of his council. Other prelates had similar offices in the royal bureaucracy.

The aid the Church could offer a king with whom it had a good relationship can be illustrated by a passage in Archbishop Eystein's *Canones Nidrosienses*. The text notes that clerics are forbidden from taking part in war and exempted from the tax collected for this purpose, but then continues:

> But we want the bishops, the abbots and the other clerics … to exhort the people … to fight bravely against excommunicates and disturbers of the peace, reminding them that if they die in the faith for the protection of the peace and the salvation of the fatherland, they shall win the kingdom of heaven.

This is the international crusading ideology transferred to domestic conflicts. We know, too, that the precept was followed; Eystein as well as other bishops preached against Sverre and his men, and Sverre in a speech after a victory parodied their propaganda, urging the audience to rejoice at all his fallen enemies who have now entered heaven. The Church had introduced an ideological element to struggles over power and resources, where loyalties had so far been based on personal connections. In the long run, the new faction that came to power with Sverre would exploit a similar ideology and eventually get the Church to support the ruling dynasty and admonish the people to obey the king as the Lord's Anointed. Both in Scandinavia and in other areas, there are many examples of bishops supporting the king in conflicts with the papacy.

An even stronger link between the monarchy and the Church was established in Denmark under Eskil's successor Absalon (archbishop 1177–1201). Absalon is the great hero in Saxo's chronicle, fighting together with King Valdemar against the pagans. He acts as a general, bringing his own troops into the battle, making tactical and strategic decisions, and even fighting in person and killing several enemies, despite the ban on clerics shedding blood. When Valdemar falters, Absalon urges him to stand firm. Thus, when Valdemar is reluctant to risk the lives of many brave men by engaging in battle, Absalon asks whether he would prefer to lead cowardly ones. Absalon also acts as a diplomat, as bishops often did, in negotiations with pagan enemies as well as with the German emperor. As a cleric in Absalon's service, Saxo no doubt exaggerates the virtues and importance of his master, but the relationship between Absalon and the king, first Valdemar and then his son Knud, nevertheless illustrates the value of the Church and its leaders for the development of the monarchy.

From the king's point of view, bishops and prelates were desirable officers as they had administrative skills and legal learning, as well as the advantage that their offices were not hereditary. If the king could influence their elections, as was often the case, he might thus gain subordinates who owed their office to him and who could be replaced by others equally beholden to him. The prospect of a bishopric would also serve to make royal service more attractive. With such links to the king, the prelates also had the same interest as their counterparts in the secular aristocracy in national independence; for there was no guarantee that they would receive similar favors from the king of the neighboring country. This does not mean that bishops and archbishops never opposed the national king or allied with other kings against him, but such cases were the exception rather than the rule.

Figure 7. Illustration after the tombstone of Niels Jakobsen Ulfeldt, Bishop of Roskilde, d. January 18, 1395. The bishop wears full liturgical clothes and episcopal insignia: a miter, a staff, and the gloves with the ring, while the chalice, symbolizing the Eucharist, appears on his breast. Drawing: Søren Abildgaard, 1764. Lithograph by R. Hartnack, from J. B. Løffler, *Gravstenene i Roskilde Kjøbstad* (Copenhagen, 1885). Photo: Dept. of Special Collections, University of Bergen Library.

Justice: Royal and Ecclesiastical Legislation and Courts of Law

In the saga of Egil Skallagrimsson, composed in the first half of the thirteenth century, the protagonist Egil goes to Norway to take possession of the inheritance of his wife Asgjerd, whose father has just died. To achieve his aim, Egil has to challenge his brother-in-law, Berg-Onund, who claims that Asgjerd has no right to inherit, because she descends from slaves and was not born in legitimate marriage. The two parties meet at Gulating, the legal assembly (*thing*) in Western Norway. They present their case before the judges, thirty-six altogether ($=12 \times 3$), who are seated in the middle of the plain where the *thing* is assembled, surrounded by sacred ropes. Egil seems to have a good chance, as his friend Arinbjørn controls two thirds of the judges. In accordance with the law, Egil presents twelve men willing to swear to his wife's legitimate birth. However, Egil is the king's enemy, while Berg-Onund is his friend, and the king is present at the *thing*. The king is reluctant to intervene, but his wife, Gunnhild—the classic wicked queen of the sagas—has her men attack the court, cutting the sacred ropes and chasing the judges away. A strong case and lawful witnesses are of no use; the king and the queen are able to prevent a settlement. We may in addition note a reference in the saga to Arinbjørn's control of the court. Would this have been a more important factor than Asgjerd's legitimate birth and Egil's oath-helpers if the king and queen had not been there? Was the problem from Egil's point of view not that the queen interrupted a legal proceeding, but that she cancelled the advantage Egil had because of his friendship with Arinbjørn?

The account in the saga is of course no unimpeachable record of what went on at the mid-tenth century Gulating. However, the thirteenth-century Icelandic family sagas and the contemporary *Sturlunga Saga* give ample evidence of legal practice in similar situations, before the submission to the king of Norway and the reception of Norwegian law. Although we cannot apply conclusions drawn from pre-state Iceland to the rest of Scandinavia in the early Middle Ages, the early laws from these countries indicate that legal practices there were in many respects similar in the early period, until around the mid-twelfth century.

First, the system was based on formal rules and procedures and relied on the testimony of formally appointed witnesses or oath-helpers. Thus, when sued, a defendant had to prove his case by compurgation, aided by between one and eleven co-jurors, the more jurors the more serious the accusation. In some particularly serious cases, he or she might also have to undergo an ordeal, by carrying or walking on hot iron or by fishing an object out of a boiling kettle (the latter ordeal was mostly used for women). Witnesses were widely used, though their function differed from that of witnesses as we know them in later courts. All contracts and agreements were entered in the presence of formally summoned witnesses who had the same function in an oral society as written documents in literate ones. Such witnesses would then be required to testify in court.

Secondly, justice was not administered by public authorities acting independently but always as a resolution of conflicts between private parties. There was no distinction between civil and public law. Thus, a murder case would be dealt with in the same way as a dispute over property and would be settled by the killer or his kinsmen paying compensation to an injured party. There was no police and no office of a public prosecutor; it was up to the individual to claim his or her rights.

Thirdly, there was a thin line between legal and extralegal disputes. Examples like the one in *Egils Saga* of the stronger party breaking off the proceedings by the use of violence abound. Sufficient manpower was therefore needed to win a court case. Moreover, at least in the Icelandic sagas, a court decision rarely constitutes the final solution to a conflict, but is rather a means to achieve an advantage over an adversary, which may eventually lead to a favorable settlement.

All this changed over the course of the twelfth and thirteenth centuries. The Church introduced the idea of crimes against God and society, and took steps to punish them, as is evident from passages in the oldest Norwegian laws about punishment for failing to respect the ecclesiastical holidays. For a long time, such prosecutions had to be conducted within the framework of the old judicial system, where the bishop or his representative acted like any other individual who felt himself wronged, but it led gradually to the development of ecclesiastical prosecution and courts of law. Public justice was based on the idea that certain acts were offenses against God, society, and the social order and had to be punished. It was not only damage done to an individual or a kindred that had to be repaired or compensated. Thus, a concept of crime evolved and, beyond that, the idea of subjective guilt, which meant that not only the act itself but its background and the criminal's intentions had to be taken into account. Crimes committed as the result of weakness, without knowledge of the seriousness of the act or under duress, should be punished mildly, whereas those done out of haughtiness or malice should be punished severely. This is not to suggest that the distinction between intentional and unintentional acts was unknown in the previous period, but such a distinction was more difficult to apply when there was no judge above the parties.

Ideas introduced by the Church were eventually adopted by the king. An early example is the peace legislation from Norway in the 1160s and Denmark around 1170, which identified acts that could not be atoned for by fines but instead rendered the criminal an outlaw. Outlawry in itself is probably older as a punishment for actions that affected the whole community, but these particular laws are so similar to decrees from the first three Lateran Councils and to German peace legislation that there can be no doubt about the influence. The crimes mentioned are killing under particularly aggravating circumstances, sorcery, highway robbery, rape, and the seduction of women. In practice, a criminal could atone for even such a crime by fines; but he would have to "buy his peace" from the king at a heavy price. (The expression indicates that he had lost his "peace" or right to remain in the country because of his crime, and would have to buy it back.) The king followed up by punishing killings, theft, violence, and other offenses against the public order. Although in the beginning, the king only demanded fines for offenses against himself, he eventually did so for most acts defined as crimes, although on the condition that the offended party had sued.

An important step in this direction was taken in Denmark with King Knud VI's 1200 ordinance against homicide. In his 1260 ordinance, King Håkon Håkonsson of Norway forbade revenge on any other than the killer himself, whereas earlier, his relatives had also been legitimate targets. Håkon also decreed that an offer of compensation had to be accepted, whereas earlier it had been up to the injured party to choose between revenge and compensation. Håkon's successor Magnus, nicknamed the Lawmender, went one step further and almost completely banned revenge.

A change in the field of evidence paralleled the new distinction between private and public law. The Church had long distrusted the compurgation oath, which was rarely used in canon law. A papal letter of 1218 to the archbishop of Lund denounces it as a pestilence and contrary to all justice. Nevertheless, compurgation continued to be widely used in Scandinavia throughout the Middle Ages, although it was to some extent supplemented by other forms of evidence. By contrast, ordeals were eventually abolished by a decision at the Fourth Lateran Council in 1215, which forbade the clergy to participate in them. In practice, they disappeared: in Denmark soon after 1215, in Norway in 1247, and in Sweden in the 1250s or 60s, though in Sweden the ban had to be repeated as late as the 1320s. Now, instead of a defendant proving his innocence by formal means, both parties had to present their evidence before the judge or judges who would decide on this basis which party was in the right. The new principles are expressed in Denmark in the Law of Jutland in 1241 and in Norway in the Code of the Realm of 1274, with some anticipation in previous legislation. Thus, in the latter, a defendant accused of murder has the opportunity to prove his innocence if he can produce twelve men who are willing to swear that they were present with him at a place so far away from the site of the crime that he could not have committed it. Here the compurgators are not only men of good reputation, but provide the necessary information to give the accused person an alibi, thus resembling witnesses rather than oath-helpers.

These changes in the understanding of crime and legal evidence necessitated changes in the administration of justice. Skill and education were needed both to evaluate the evidence presented in court when it was no longer formal, and to mete out punishment in accordance with motives and circumstances in criminal cases. A court of law also needed authority to intervene against powerful men in local society. Consequently, the administration of justice was professionalized. This applied above all to the ecclesiastical courts of law, where the bishop was the highest judge. He often had a university education in law and in addition often delegated his judicial powers to officers with a similar education, to his deputy (Lat. *officialis*) or to provosts or archdeacons. However, ecclesiastical courts continued to use local people, mostly as witnesses but to some extent also as judges.

Secular courts made greater use of ordinary non-professional people. Both in Denmark and Norway, the judges were normally committees of local men, similar to English juries, in Denmark either permanent committees or committees appointed by the plaintiff. Norwegian juries were selected from the local assemblies, probably by the lawman (*lagmann,* Old Norse *lǫgmaðr*), a royal judge appointed by the king. From the second half of the thirteenth century on, the country was divided into ten districts with one such judge in each. The lawman was originally a member of the local assembly who was well versed in the law, and who was supposed to quote the relevant passage from it for the assembly to use in its decisions. Later, he was appointed by the king. He might in some cases judge alone, but in cases of serious crimes normally acted together with a local jury; if the two disagreed, the case had to be appealed to the king. According to the Code of the Realm, only the king might set aside the lawman's decision, "for he is above the law." In this way, jurisdiction was governed by the king in a much more direct sense in Norway than in either Denmark or Sweden. Although local society played a prominent part in all three countries and most cases were probably decided either by local juries or local arbitration, there was a direct link from the king to the local courts in Norway, which was absent in the other Scandinavian countries.

In Denmark, the local assemblies (*herredsting*) formed the courts of law. These had originally been administered by the peasant landowners, but beginning in the thirteenth century they came increasingly under the control of the aristocracy, which during this period acquired ownership of most of the land, while the majority of the peasants became their tenants. The new landowners eventually became the patrons of their tenants, while at the same time they also received the fines their tenants paid when convicted in court. A tenant would thus have to face the court with the knowledge that his patron would profit from his conviction!

Nevertheless, there is evidence that the sway of royal justice also expanded during the second half of the thirteenth century and the first decades of the fourteenth, both in Denmark and Sweden. Special royal courts of law emerged with jurisdiction above the local courts. They served partly as courts of appeal and partly as courts of the first instance, though the latter mostly for the aristocracy and the upper classes. While in the 1282 statute of the diet of Nyborg, issued in favor of the aristocracy, the king promises to bring his cases before the ordinary local courts, the statute issued by King Christoffer II at his accession in 1320, which is equally aristocratic in its contents, takes a special royal court of law for granted. A royal court of law also developed in Sweden in connection with the peace legislation. As for Iceland, the main changes came with the island's submission to the king of Norway, which led to new legislation, based on similar principles to that enacted in Norway (in 1271–1273 and in 1281), and to a system of public justice administered by royal officials. There were however already detectable tendencies in this direction in the principalities formed by the great magnates in the first half of the century.

In all three countries, homicide was in principle punished by outlawry, which meant that the culprit had to leave the inhabited community; if not, the victim's relatives could kill him without incurring punishment. However, outlawry in Denmark and Sweden only applied to the law district where the crime had happened, whereas in Norway it applied to the entire country. In practice, therefore, feuds and revenge could continue more easily in the former countries, particularly among powerful men, and the resolution of such conflicts was more often the result of negotiation than of formal judicial procedure. Although the Danish and Swedish kings tried to restrict feuds, they were prevented by the strong aristocracy in these countries, who resented infringements on their freedom to uphold their honor. Feuds between nobles were not banned in Denmark until 1683. The sources give evidence of a number of feuds in Denmark in the later Middle Ages, particularly among the nobility. The king often tried to mediate between the parties and to regulate the conduct of the feud, but he had no power to prevent it.

In 1405 Queen Margrete personally intervened in a conflict between two noble families. The County Justice of Jutland, Lord Jens Nielsen (Løvenbalk) of Avnsbjerg had killed Jens Jensen Brok of Clausholm. Accompanied by two hundred noblemen, the killer knelt before the victim's widow and family and humbly asked the victim's father for forgiveness with the words, "If I were the noblest and most powerful knight in Denmark, I would also have entered such an agreement." He then transferred a substantial tract of land to found an altar on which a priest appointed by the deceased's descendants would say masses for his soul in perpetuity. The formula spoken by the killer illustrates the attitude that made it difficult to abolish feuds, particularly within the nobility. The only real compensation for the loss of a life was another life. Consequently, the man who accepted fines as compensation for a dead relative risked incurring shame. To avoid this, the one who paid the fine had to swear an oath that he, too, would have accepted a fine if he had been in the opposite situation. Such oaths are known from the Icelandic sagas, and they became a standard condition in settlements between nobles in the later Middle Ages. Although the killer in all likelihood paid a heavy fine to the victim's kinsmen, it is probably significant that this sum is left unmentioned, whereas there is a detailed account of the gifts given to the Church to purchase masses for the dead man's soul. In this way, any intimation that the receivers profited from the death of their relative or preferred material goods to revenge was avoided. Nor could the king or royal officials feel safe against attempts at revenge for actions they had taken in their official capacity. Consequently, the king also had his opponents issue letters of reconciliation. It must be added that Denmark was probably closer to the European average in this respect than Norway. Feuds and revenge were not prohibited in France, for example, until the first half of the fourteenth century and then only as a measure to unite the country against attacks from England during the Hundred Years' War. England forms an exception in this respect, for here a system of public justice and strict rules against feuds and revenge developed from the twelfth century onwards.

In order to prevent feuds in Norway, the king became directly involved in cases of homicide. To ensure that the crime was punished in the proper way, without setting off a series of feuds, the royal representative, the *sysselmann,* had to handle matters and send the offender off to the king with a letter explaining the circumstances of the crime. The king then normally would pardon the offender on the condition that he paid compensation to the victim's relatives and two heavy fines to the king himself, one as compensation for having killed the king's subject and one to buy his peace. A number of such letters have been preserved, from the early fourteenth century onwards, including some of the *sysselmann*'s reports, which often give a vivid picture of the event and of contemporary local society.

In the year 1501, a certain Jon Eiriksson killed one Olav Olavsson. We have the following account of the circumstances: Olav had wanted to buy a horse from Jon. Jon refused, because he had had trouble in earlier dealings with Olav and his father. A heated discussion broke out, which eventually touched on a horse Jon had bought from Olav's father and with which he was dissatisfied. Olav's reply to Jon's complaint was: "If you regret that horse, may you get it back again and in your arse and may you ride straight to the devil on it." Jon answered, "May God let no one ride there." Jon then left the house where the quarrel had taken place, intending to go home. As it was dark, however, and the host asked him, he returned and sat down, whereupon the quarrel started up again. Olav stood and stabbed Jon, who stabbed back and killed Olav. He then left the house and declared that he had killed Olav. The *sysselmann* ends his report by declaring that he has received trustworthy evidence of the event and that the culprit now needs God's and the king's grace. At this point in time, the king did not decide in person; from around 1400 at the latest, such decisions had been delegated to the chancellor.

Figure 8. The king hands over a letter of pardon, from the fourteenth-century Codex Hardenbergiensis. The Codex, named after its owner in the sixteenth century, is a collection of legal texts, written by altogether thirteen scribes at different dates. It includes a richly illuminated manuscript of King Magnus Håkonsson's Code of the Realm, dated to ca. 1325–1350. Facsimile from the Codex Hardenbergiensis, *Corpus codicum norvegicorum medii Aevi*, quarto series, vol. 7 (Oslo, 1983), facsimile 15v, page 66. Dept. of Special Collections, University of Bergen Library.

The letter is in many ways typical. It uses a standard terminology and some standard formulas, such as the final line about the need of grace. The killing is referred to euphemistically—the killer "happened to harm" the victim, which meant that the killing was not premeditated. (In some case documents, it is added that there had been no enmity between the parties beforehand, which was important, because killing in revenge was considered more serious than killing spontaneously.) As usual, there is no shortage of witnesses. Most killings took place in public, normally in connection with drinking, and this was the case here as well. The *sysselmann* names the witnesses and takes care to quote exactly what they have said. In contrast to ecclesiastical officials, however, he does not examine the witnesses separately; his report gives the impression of being the collective account agreed upon by the local community. It is a detailed and vivid narrative, which resembles similar episodes in the Icelandic sagas, but it is not told for the sake of the story. Rather, the details in the account are relevant testimony necessary to inform the king's decision. Its aim is to show that Jon had been seriously provoked; we may suspect that the witnesses and perhaps also the *sysselmann* have contrived to tell the story in such a way as to get Jon off as lightly as possible. Olav's words, quoted above, are highly insulting, while Jon's answer is a model of moderation and self-control. It is significant that Olav refers to the devil and Jon to God. Moreover, it speaks in Jon's favor that he wanted to leave the party in order to avoid further quarrelling, as he in fact did after the killing, when he went directly to the house next-door to report the crime, a report being absolutely essential if he was to gain the king's pardon. According to the law, a killing must be reported in the nearest house, unless it belongs to a relative of the victim. If the killing has not been reported, it no longer counts as "a harm that has happened," but as murder. Unfortunately, we do not know how this particular case was settled. We know from other cases, however, that the conditions for gaining the king's peace might vary, but there are no cases where both the report and the king's decision have been preserved, so we cannot weigh the importance of the various aggravating or attenuating circumstances for the outcome.

The idea of crime and subjective guilt would logically imply a focus on individual responsibility. Nevertheless, even in thirteenth-century laws, a large number of relatives have to contribute to paying one man's fine, while an equally large number are entitled to receive it, the amount for each depending on how closely they were related to the deceased. Traditionally, these rules have been considered evidence of extensive kindred solidarity in the old society, in accordance with the idea of a society of kindred. More recently, scholars have objected that the rules often give the impression of being learned constructions without any practical importance; thus, the rules of the Norwegian Law of Gulating from the eleventh or twelfth century seem so complicated that it difficult to imagine how they might have been put into effect. Moreover, as we have seen (above, p. 16), most scholars nowadays reject the idea of large family clans in Western Europe, including Scandinavia, in the Middle Ages and earlier. An alternative theory is therefore that these rules were new and may even have been introduced by the Church or under ecclesiastical influence, whereas, according to the old theory, the Church was the main opponent of kindred solidarity and a staunch proponent of individual responsibility. Arguments in favor of this view are that collective responsibility is not mentioned in the earliest Danish laws and that a passage in the Law of Jutland (1241) defines relatives within the fourth degree as liable to pay fines, which corresponds to the incest prohibitions introduced at the 1215 Lateran Council.

However, the fact that the degree of kinship is consonant with canonical rules is not evidence that kindred solidarity as such was invented by the Church. The absence of the rule in the earliest Danish laws is a more serious objection, but on the other hand, there are detailed rules about collective responsibility in the Norwegian Law of Gulating, which is older than the oldest Danish laws. Moreover, the evolution of the Norwegian laws corresponds perfectly with the traditional theory. They show a gradual reduction of the importance of kindred solidarity until the Code of the Realm is reached (1274–76), which only demands payment from the killer to the victim's nearest heir. The Swedish laws, which all date from the second half of the thirteenth century or later, are divided on the issue; some require collective payment, others do not.

From a practical point of view, collective payment has much to recommend it, as it increases the chance that the victim's relatives will get full compensation; not all killers would be able to pay a heavy fine alone. An objection might be that individual responsibility would be weakened and that people might kill more readily if they knew that they would not have to pay the full damages themselves. However, this argument may also be turned upside-down: collective payment would guarantee that responsible people within the kindred would control their young hotheads and thus prevent killings in the first place. Scholars who believe in ecclesiastical influence attribute arguments like this to the Church. If that were the case, however, kindred solidarity must already have been a factor; it is difficult to imagine the churchmen being so unrealistic as call upon nonexistent kindred solidarity to prevent killings. But if the solidarity was already operative, what prevents us from believing that collective fines might also have been customary before the Church intervened? The evidence from the Law of the Gulating is a strong argument in favor of this assumption. As for the oldest Danish laws, they can be read as suggesting either that collective responsibility existed in some places but not in others, or that the earliest laws left it to the parties themselves to arrange compensation. In this context, it may be pointed out that fines were by no means the only way of settling a murder case; as we have seen, there is evidence, even from the later Middle Ages, that taking revenge was considered a more satisfactory and honorable action than accepting a fine.

Finally, the collective payment must be considered in connection with collective revenge. There is ample evidence, both from the Icelandic sagas and the laws of the three Scandinavian kingdoms, that not only the killer himself but also his relatives could be killed in revenge. There is also a clear connection between the abolition of collective revenge and collective fines in the Norwegian laws. In his 1260 decree against manslaughter, Håkon Håkonsson restricts the number of relatives entitled to fines, while at the same time curtailing the right to revenge by forbidding the killing of others in the place of the killer himself. In the Code of the Realm, King Magnus completely bans revenge, while restricting the right to fines to the victim's direct heirs and abolishing the payment of fines by the killer's relatives. While it is possible that the Church introduced collective fines, it is inconceivable that it would also have introduced collective revenge. Consequently, both phenomena are likely to have their origins in the early period, although collective fines were clearly more acceptable to the king and to the Church than collective revenge. This does not mean that the exact rules found in the laws were of ancient origin, however. Kindred solidarity may well have been less extensive as well as less formalized in the early period. The numerous examples of revenge and conflict in the Icelandic sagas show people seeking support from relatives, but not according to specific rules about proximity. The rules found in the laws may therefore well be artificial, though not without some connection to actual links between people. The argument that the detailed rules are unrealistic and that people were unlikely to know their ancestors up to the seventh degree is not convincing, for there are examples of illiterate societies in other parts of the world where knowledge of kinship relations is equally exhaustive.

Regardless of the origin of collective payments, the practice was clearly handled differently in the different countries. Its abolishment in Norway already in the 1270s was exceptional. Danish provincial laws that included this provision were in force until 1683, when they were replaced by Christian V's Danish Law, the first code that applied to the whole of Denmark. The Swedish Code of the Realm of 1350 emphasized individual responsibility and made the punishment more severe. A killer caught on the spot or within twenty-four hours after the murder was liable to the death penalty, whereas afterwards, he could atone by paying fines. If he were to die before the full amount had been paid, however, his heirs would be responsible for the rest. Despite this provision, there is evidence of collective responsibility in Sweden as late as in the seventeenth century.

Royal legislation developed parallel to the expansion of royal justice. The earliest provincial laws of Norway were written down in the late eleventh or early twelfth century and the earliest Danish ones in the late twelfth or early thirteenth century, while in Sweden the earliest written laws are of the late thirteenth century and later. These laws are not codes issued by a legislature and organized in a systematic form, but rather records of what were believed to be the laws of a particular area. These Scandinavian laws have been the subject of much discussion. In the nineteenth and early twentieth century, the extant written laws were mostly believed to have been preserved orally over centuries and were used as sources for an alleged ancient, common Germanic law. This theory is now almost universally rejected and greater importance has instead attached to the king and the Church, although there is still disagreement about what is old and what is new. Influence from canon law can be traced already in the earliest extant laws, the late-eleventh- or early-twelfth-century Norwegian provincial laws, but these laws also contain elements that point to a traditional or popular origin. In particular, it would seem that the procedural rules in many cases reflect established practice. In a similar way, some provisions in thirteenth-century Swedish laws resemble statements in early-medieval runic inscriptions.

The royal legislation of the thirteenth and fourteenth centuries, the Danish Law of Jutland (1241), and the Norwegian and later the Swedish Code of the Realm (1274–77 and 1350, respectively) represent something new. They are codes issued by a legislative authority, they show greater influence from Roman and canon law, and they are composed in a systematic way. The Law of Jutland opens with a passage influenced by Gratian's *Decretum:*

> The country shall be built by law. If there were no law in the country, then the one who could grasp most would have most. Therefore, the law should be made according to the needs of everyone, so that those who are peaceful and innocent may enjoy their peace and the evil and unjust may fear what is written in the law (...). The law should not be written for the particular benefit of any man, but according to the needs of everyone who lives in the country.

In contrast to the provincial laws, the written law has now become an authoritative text, and there is some idea of a public authority with the right to define the norms of society, but at this date it is still an open question to what extent cases were settled according to the letter of the law. The king's authority to issue laws was disputed in the Middle Ages as well as among contemporary scholars. Early royal legislators, in Scandinavia as well as in the rest of Europe, often referred to an alleged old law or to general principles of justice to legitimate their decisions, as did Knud VI of Denmark and Håkon Håkonsson of Norway in their decrees about homicide.

This reasoning takes an even more explicit form in *The King's Mirror,* where the author warns the king as the highest judge against adhering too rigidly to the letter of the law. Instead, he should judge according to "the holy laws," namely God's own laws as laid down in the Bible and Christian doctrine—the Old Testament holds a particular importance here, as most of the examples set up for the king are taken from this source. Although *The King's Mirror* contains no explicit reference to the king as a legislator, its doctrine that the king's duty is to do what is just regardless of the existing laws, lays the intellectual foundations for royal legislation. This idea was developed further by Håkon's son Magnus in the Norwegian Code of the Realm, according to which the law in the final analysis is anchored in an absolute, objective justice—God's own justice, which supersedes the articles of the written law.

However, there were limits to how far this idea could serve to justify the various solutions to practical problems laid down in royal or even ecclesiastical law codes. God could hardly be made responsible for the change from two to three months of military service or changes in the terms of land lease. As in the early period, a certain idea of positive law was a necessary element, only now the question of the authority behind this law was posed more explicitly. When King Magnus issued the National Law, he first presented his plans to the provincial assemblies (*lagtings*) to get permission to carry them out. Having composed the lawbook, he presented it to the assemblies once more and had it formally promulgated by them in the years 1274–76 (as the *lagtings* met at approximately the same time in different parts of the country, the king could only be present at one of them each year). He was thus very diligent about seeking the consent of the people, but his actions seem to imply that in giving the king their consent the people had permanently delegated their legislative authority to him. In accordance with the exalted theory of *The King's Mirror*, the king may well have claimed to be the supreme legislator, and he certainly regarded himself and the legal experts in his circle as vastly superior in wisdom and knowledge of the laws. Another section in the law alludes to the well-known passages in the *Corpus iuris civilis*, according to which the emperor is not subject to the law and his decisions have the force of law.

Although most medieval jurists interpreted these passages in a narrow sense and the exact meaning of the allusion to them in the Code of the Realm is not quite clear, there is no doubt that the Norwegian king claimed considerable authority as a legislator. This is expressed in another statement in the code, which declares that only a fool confines himself to the letter of the law, whereas the wise man considers the background and circumstances in order to apply the law in the best way. Thus, the law has to be administered by the king and his legal experts who, unlike ordinary people, are qualified to adjust it in different ways.

By contrast, there were greater restrictions on the king's legislative power in Denmark and Sweden. In his 1282 charter, which became the model for later election charters, King Erik V Klipping had to promise not to change King Valdemar's law. Consent to or even active participation in legislation became a frequent provision in the later election charters. It is also significant that no law for the whole of Denmark was issued until the king had become absolute (in 1660) and issued the Danish law of 1683. However, the kings issued a series of ordinances, which in practice came to have a similar status to that of laws. Sweden did get a national law in 1350, but it was to a greater extent than the Norwegian one an expression of aristocratic interests.

The emergence of public justice, organized by the Church as well as the monarchy, was an important factor in political centralization and the emergence of an elite, for it created new officials and transferred economic resources and political power from the peasants to the upper classes. Should it then be regarded primarily as yet another means of exploiting the population, or was it a "service function"? Both points of view have had and have their adherents. Public justice clearly served the interests of the monarchy and the elite, who increased their power and profited from the fines paid by those convicted. From the point of view of the people, its main disadvantages derived from the corruption of royal officials and the fact that public justice was slow justice. In the case of Denmark, it has also been claimed that the new procedures, which would at first seem to us to represent progress, actually weakened the position of ordinary people. Whereas the old formal means of evidence gave a well-connected man in the local community a reasonable chance to acquit himself of an accusation by summoning his neighbors and relatives as co-jurors, the new juries, which could be bribed or manipulated by powerful landowners, made him dependent on an aristocratic patron. In the case of Norway, we have examples of abuses of the system, both from the sagas and from royal complaints, but we do not know how widespread they were. As for the advantages of public justice, it is important to note that the feuds were suppressed not primarily by prohibitions and punishment, but through alternative ways of resolving conflicts. The existence of public justice made it easier to settle legal questions, while at the same time making it possible to abstain from revenge without losing face. It is difficult, in fact, to know where to draw the line between exploitation and common interests. In any case, whether or not the evolution of public justice was consonant with the "objective" interests of the people, the reason for its progress must be sought in ideology more than in direct pressure from above, this in contrast to what happened in the field of military specialization. This is evident from the fact that not only royal but also ecclesiastical jurisdiction expanded during our period, and that the expansion of public justice took place mainly in periods of internal peace and stability.

Despite the fact that our knowledge of the earliest period is, as usual, limited, there can hardly be any doubt that considerable changes took place in the field of law and justice in Scandinavia from the twelfth century onwards. The oldest legal system can be reconstructed from provincial laws, at least in the field of procedure, while the extant laws must largely have been formulated at the time of writing and show the influence of the Church and the monarchy. We are dealing with a transition from a form of law and justice that regulated issues between equal parties according to formal rules, to public justice, exercised by the Church and the monarchy. This entailed an impartial judge operating above the parties and judging according to his own interpretation of written laws. These changes in law and justice are the clearest expression of how ideas about the right order of the world (discussed above) were applied in practice. Thus, the adaptation of common European law and jurisprudence, which began as early as in the twelfth century provincial laws and was greatly extended in the legislation from the second half of the thirteenth century, had far-reaching consequences. Viewed from an international perspective, the Scandinavian legal system may be regarded as a combination of the English and the Continental variants. As in England, the national legal tradition was largely retained, whereas the existence of law codes as well as influence from Roman and canon law point to continental parallels. The combination of professional judges and popular representatives may also seem to represent a blending of the two traditions, although on this point there are so many different solutions in England as well as on the Continent that it is difficult to make an exact classification. What is clear, however, is that Scandinavia was deeply influenced by the legal revolution that was underway in contemporary Europe. Although the king's growing authority and involvement in legal matters can be explained as a means to extend his power, parallel to what happened in many parts of the world, the particular form this development took as well as the parallel growth of ecclesiastical jurisdiction must be the result of European influence. The

Scandinavian countries thus had the advantage of being exposed to influence from the center at a time when new legal and administrative forms were developing there.

War and the Preparation for War: From *Leding* to Professional Forces

In the mid-twentieth century, four big military camps were excavated in Denmark. They are usually referred to as *trelleborgs*, after the best-known of them, Trelleborg on Zealand. The others are Fyrkat and Aggersborg in northern Jutland and Nonnebakken outside present-day Odense on Funen. Their date was long a subject of controversy, but has now been fixed at around 980 through dendrochronology. Trelleborg has been dated in this way to 981, and although there is not sufficient wood to date the others, the similarities between them indicate that they are almost certainly contemporary. The camps are built in the shape of a circle, varying between 120 and 240 meters in diameter, and filled with houses, placed strictly symmetrically. The date as well as the character of the fortifications indicates that they were built in connection with Harald Bluetooth's conquest, possibly as garrisons to control various parts of the country. They thus give substance to his boast of having conquered the whole of Denmark.

From a military point of view, the trelleborgs differ from the castles that were built some hundred years later in being large and probably low-slung. Although only the foundations have been preserved, they most probably had wooden palisades. They thus would have needed a large number of men to defend them properly. Despite being built to house an occupation force, the number of men needed to garrison them indicates a relatively modest difference between elite soldiers and the common population. The Danish conquest of England shortly afterwards points in the

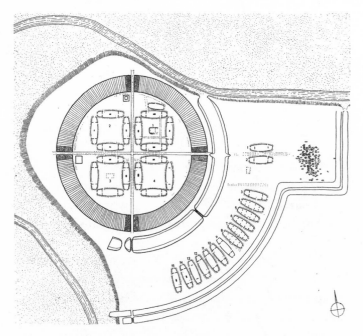

Figure 9. Trelleborg on Zealand. A camp with houses, surrounded by walls and palisades. As the drawing shows, it is built according to a very precise plan, with symmetrical buildings placed exactly in the center. Drawing by Poul Nørlund, from *Nordiske Fortidsminder*, vol. 4, fasc. 1 (Copenhagen, 1948), p. 24. Dept. of Special Collections, University of Bergen Library.

same direction. Although later English sources describe the elite character of Cnut's army, it must have been the result of a large mobilization, for according to one version of the Anglo-Saxon Chronicle it arrived from Denmark on 160 ships.

We do not know how this army was recruited and structured, but we have indications from Danish as well as Norwegian sources of a military organization based on districts, each recruiting the number of men necessary to man a ship, a system normally referred to as *leding* (No. *leidang*, ON *leiðangr*, Da. *leding*, Sw. *ledung*). It is first mentioned in Denmark in a charter dated 1085, but most scholars believe that it is older, possibly going back to the reign of Harald Bluetooth. The organization is described in detail for the first time around 1170 and then in the laws of the thirteenth century. The sagas attribute the foundation of the corresponding organization in Norway to King Håkon the Good (c. 930–960), which has also been accepted by most historians. The term is used in skaldic poetry from the tenth century, but we do not know if it refers there to this particular organization or just to a large fleet. However, there are detailed references to the *leding* in the laws of Gulating and Frostating, usually dated to the late eleventh or early twelfth century. The *leding* is also known from Sweden, but, as usual, the early sources from this country are too meager to give much information about it.

Already in the earliest laws, the *leding* has also become a tax. This transition most likely happened when kings realized that they could appropriate for other purposes the provisions provided for military expeditions. Local communities were obliged not only to muster men for the ship but also provisions for the expedition, which typically lasted two or three months. The king could get hold of these by mobilizing the *leding* for an expedition, but then dismissing the crew and keeping the provisions. This could then easily develop into a permanent tax. The Old Norse sagas dealing with the civil wars, notably the *Sverris Saga*, give numerous examples of the flexible use of the *leding* and of royal demands for tax rather than men; King Sverre in particular often relied on elite forces rather than mass mobilization, but he needed provisions for these forces. Nevertheless, the tax and the elite forces did not replace mass mobilization in Norway but were employed in addition to it. In the Code of the Realm (1274–77), the *leding* had become an annual tax, defined as half the amount due in case of a mobilization. Late-thirteenth-century sources also indicate that the king might demand the full amount every three years, which seems to correspond to a rule that, though never explicitly stated, may be inferred from the fact that the sagas rarely mention full mobilizations more often than every three years. By contrast, such a rule is explicitly mentioned in the Danish laws, with the difference that the period is every four years instead of three.

Denmark also differs from Norway in that the tax eventually replaced military service for the majority of the population, while a minority became fulltime elite warriors, with better training and heavy and expensive arms and armor, but exempt from paying the tax. In consequence, the taxes paid by the common people were many times higher in Denmark than in Norway. This change was already underway in 1170 and was fully implemented during the following period. The military class became *herremænd* (gentlemen), similar to knights in England and other countries, and developed into an aristocratic elite. A similar course of events took place in parts of Sweden.

An important reason for this development was the change from sea to land warfare. The use of heavy cavalry is mentioned for the first time in Denmark in the battle of Fodevig (1134), where King Erik Emune defeated his rival King Niels with a force of German knights. It seems to have come into regular use in the following period, and is frequently mentioned by Saxo. In his account of the conflicts in the mid-twelfth century, he explains King Knud's defeat against his rival Sven by his ill-conceived order that his knights should fight on foot to prevent them from fleeing. They were easily defeated. He gives also a dramatic picture of his hero King Valdemar (1157–1182) fighting on horseback against Saxon knights in the service of his rival King Knud in order to prevent them from crossing a river. Valdemar splits his lance in an encounter with a Saxon knight, has four spears thrown against him at the same time and manages to hold onto his horse despite the fact that it is about to throw him off by bucking backwards.

A similar development took place in Sweden from the late twelfth century onwards. The formal expression of the new order

Figure 10. The king (with a crown on his helmet) as knight on horse-back, on a seal belonging to Eirik Magnusson (1280–299). This is the reverse of the seal; the obverse depicts the king in majesty on his throne. Drawing by Abraham Kall, from *Norske mynter og sigiller* (Christiania, 1815). Dept. of Special Collections, University of Bergen Library.

in this country came in the *Alsnö stadga* (the Statute of Alsnö), probably drafted in 1280, which is usually regarded as a kind of "constitution" for the Swedish aristocracy, confirming the principle of specialized military service on horseback in return for privileges. It would seem logical that land warfare and heavy cavalry would be more suitable to conditions in Sweden, where a larger percentage of settlements were inland, than in Denmark, the whole of which is within easy reach of the coast. The change nevertheless occurred first and to a greater extent in Denmark, and the explanation must be sought in the importance of Northern Germany in twelfth- and thirteenth-century Danish foreign policy. Although the Danes were also engaged in conquests in the Baltic area, which required crossing the sea, most of the fighting there took place ashore, and ships were mainly used for transport. According to Saxo, King Erik II Emune (1134–1137) was the first who transported horses on ships, and whether this is true or not, it is certainly the case that the Danes fought on horseback on their expeditions in the Baltic area.

In contrast to Denmark, sea warfare was still important in Norway, which explains the continued existence of the *leding* there. This applies to the civil wars of the twelfth century as well as to the foreign policy of the thirteenth. During the former, the fleet was used to a great extent, both to fight great battles at sea and for quick raids against enemy strongholds. Indeed most of the decisive battles of this period were fought at sea, including the most famous of them, Sverre's victory over Magnus Erlingsson at Fimreite in Sognefjorden in 1184, when King Magnus and sixteen of the greatest magnates of the country were killed. An exercise of sea power was the best, and in some cases the only way to maintain control over a country where most of the population lived along the coast. This applies particularly to western Norway, where the country's largest town, Bergen, was situated. Traveling on land in this area meant almost constantly crossing mountains, hills, valleys, rivers, and fjords. Avoiding the latter meant traveling through barren country across mountains up to around 1500–2000 meters (5,000 to 6,500 feet) above sea level.

Later, in 1263, Sverre's grandson King Håkon Håkonsson used the fleet to defend Norwegian possessions off the coast of Scotland. The immediate impression one gets of this expedition is that of a fight between a whale and an elephant: the Norwegians on ships along the coast of Scotland, the Scots following on land to prevent the enemy from getting ashore. Only one episode involved active fighting: some Norwegian ships were thrown ashore by a heavy sea at Largs and came under attack from the Scots until the Norwegians managed to launch the ships again and get away. The expedition was a failure and might be regarded as evidence that the Norwegian form of sea warfare had become obsolete. Actually, however, a similar strategy was used with considerable success against Denmark in the 1250s and 1290s, partly as a power demonstration—which clearly had been the intention in Scotland—partly for raiding expeditions ashore, where Denmark had now become vulnerable because of its neglect of sea warfare in the preceding period. Denmark, with its low-lying coast and dense population, was also more exposed to raids from the sea than was Scotland. A treaty with France in 1295 is evidence of the reputation of the Norwegian fleet. According to this treaty, the king of Norway was to assist King Philip IV of France with three hundred ships and fifty thousand men for four months per year in return for a payment of thirty thousand pounds sterling. The size of this force is clearly unrealistic, and the treaty was probably intended as a credible threat against England in the on-going war between France and Scotland on the one hand and England on the other, rather than an actual mobilization. Still, the memory of the expedition of 1263 must have convinced Philip that his money was well spent.

In the fourteenth century, however, Norway was confronted with a similar challenge as the neighboring countries. Warfare along the Swedish and Danish border to the south in the early fourteenth century and then the struggles to regain Sweden for King Magnus and King Håkon in the 1360s and '70s took place ashore and called for land forces. The Norwegian response seems to have been a combination of a peasant levy on foot and elite forces on horseback. Even at this point, however, no full transition took place, probably because the country, at least after the Black Death, was too poor to raise an elite force that could compete with those of the neighboring countries. The peasant levy seems to have managed well enough as a defensive force, however, because when Duke Erik occupied Oslo in 1309 during the conflict between Håkon V and the Swedish dukes, he was attacked by a local Norwegian force and shortly afterwards left the town. Although the *Erikskrönikan* depicts the battle as a Swedish victory, it is obvious that Erik would have continued the siege of the castle of Akershus if he had not been defeated or had not at least found himself in sufficient difficulties to be forced to retreat. By contrast, the Norwegians were defeated in offensive operations. During the fourteenth century, the Norwegian fleet also became obsolete and was defeated by German cogboats, which were higher and bigger and could sink the Norwegian ships or shoot at their crews without fear of retaliation.

A logical consequence of the transition from sea to land and the development of heavy cavalry was the introduction of castles, the first of which were built in the twelfth century. In the 1240s, the king of Denmark had twenty of them, while ten belonged to the duke of Southern Jutland. The greatest expansion took place in the following period, however, as the result of the more intense internal struggles that began in 1286 and of Erik Menved's early-fourteenth-century wars. After a rebellion in Jutland, which was put down in 1313, the king built a number of castles in this region, while up to then most of the castles had been in the border regions and along strategic sea passages. In Sweden, small and simple castles were built in the twelfth century, followed by really large and elaborate constructions dating from the thirteenth century, particularly from its second half, and from the following centuries. These new castles could serve both as residences for the king and his representatives and as fortifications. Similar changes took place in East Central Europe. Western military technology was adopted, partly through imitation, partly as the result of defeats against Western—notably German—armies, and partly as a

Figure 11. A. The medieval stronghold of Glimmingehus (Scania, Denmark), now in southern Sweden, ca. 1500. The castle was built as a residence for Jens Holgersen Ulfstand, commander of Gotland. The foundation stone was laid in 1499 and the Ulfstand family lived there for around fifty years, after which it served as a granary for four hundred years. Photo: Christoph Müller. Wikimedia Commons. B. Åbo Castle in the city of Turku (Swedish Åbo, Finland). The first castle in Åbo dates from the 1280s. In the following period it became a strong fortification as well as a great residence for the many prominent castellans who held it during the later Middle Ages. It was rebuilt by Gustaf Vasa in the 1530s and underwent further changes when his son Johan (later King Johan III) resided there in the 1550s. Photo: Kallerna. Wikimedia Commons.

result of the Mongols' attacks in 1241/42 and later. The result was a strengthening of the top aristocracy who resided in these stone castles and shared the king's governing power.

Castles played a major role in the struggles between King Birger and his brothers in Sweden in the early fourteenth century. The reason for the dukes' success in 1306 was not a military victory, but that they managed to catch their brother by surprise and take him captive. This gave them control of a sufficient number of castles to resist the repeated attempts by Birger's brother-in-law, King Erik Menved of Denmark, to set Birger free to regain his position. Only during the final phase of the conflict, after Birger's treachery, when aristocratic opinion had turned unanimously in favor of the dukes, were Birger's castles conquered. Medieval castles were not impregnable, but they could resist a numerically superior enemy for a long time.

The new military technology not only improved the king's military capabilities; it also led to far-reaching administrative and social changes. Under favorable circumstances, an elite force of heavy cavalry could defeat an ordinary levy on foot that was roughly ten times as large. The change from a popular levy of combined rowers and fighters on foot to heavily armored knights on horseback had obvious social consequences. Whereas the former needed relatively simple and cheap equipment and a moderate amount of training, a knight's armor, equipment, and specially trained horse were very expensive and became increasingly so as armor became heavier and more complicated in the thirteenth and fourteenth centuries. Most importantly, a knight needed special training from an early age; for only then could he hope to perform the kinds of maneuvers the Saxo attributes to Valdemar the Great. Admittedly, the knights did not replace foot soldiers; all medieval armies included both categories of combatants. With the exception of archers, however, whose importance increased from the twelfth century onwards, foot soldiers became less important.

Castles were expensive both to build and maintain, but they enabled the king to exploit the people more efficiently. The castles that became common in this period covered only a fragment of the footprint of earlier fortifications, including the *trelleborgs*, but they were far taller, thus giving their relatively small number of defenders an even greater advantage against attackers than the armor and other equipment of a knight. However, the reduced number of warriors did not lead to any reduction in the costs of warfare, probably rather the contrary. Thus, in reducing the number of armed men the king needed and increasing the cost of keeping them, the castles furthered the transition from the popular levy to a limited number of royal retainers, financed by taxes from the majority of the population. Both for strategic reasons and because of the cost and labor necessary to build and keep up the castles, they were also used as administrative centers. The older royal administration consisted of a combination of stewards of the king's estates, who fulfilled various functions on behalf of their master, and allies among the local magnates. Basically, this system was retained in Denmark and Sweden, but was transformed by the development of castles, their commanders becoming the governors of the surrounding area.

The lack of military specialization and the meager tax revenues collected by the Norwegian king also explain the fact that fewer castles were erected in this country than in Denmark and Sweden. The local administration therefore developed in a different way. A new royal official, called the *sysselmann* (ON *syslumaðr*), analogous to the English sheriff and to continental officials of the same period, was introduced beginning in the second half of the twelfth century. From the first half of the thirteenth century on, the country was divided into fixed districts, around fifty, each headed by a royal official who often had no connection with the district in which he served and who might be replaced or moved from one district to another. Norway thus developed a local administration more directly under the king's control, while at the same time the Norwegian aristocracy became an administrative more than a military class. However, castles were also erected in Norway. The earliest date from the late twelfth century, whereas the largest and most elaborate were erected from the mid-thirteenth century onwards, partly near the main towns of Oslo, Bergen, and Tønsberg, partly on the borders, Bohus on the Swedish and Danish border, and Vardøhus in the north. During the fourteenth century, the first four of these became centers of larger administrative districts, superior to the old ones.

~≈ **CHAPTER THREE** ≈~

State Formation, Social Change, and the Division of Power

IN THE PREVIOUS CHAPTER, we traced a series of changes from the eleventh to the thirteenth century: the development of monarchy as an institution and the end of regicides; the introduction of Christianity and the development of the ecclesiastical bureaucracy; the introduction of public justice and royal legislation; the organization of the military forces under the king's leadership; and the formation of a military elite. To what extent are we dealing here with state formation, and how great were the changes in society from the previous period? Are the changes discussed above evidence of a greater centralization of society under the leadership of the king and his officials, or are we just dealing with a centralization that led to a new form of decentralization? Had the king delegated his power to a small number of prelates and nobles who governed their particular regions with little interference from him? The question can thus be divided into two that concern, respectively, the degree of bureaucratization in general and to what extent it increased the power of the central government.

Social Structure in the High Middle Ages

In the anticlerical pamphlet *A Speech against the Bishops* (c. 1200), the author looks at society through the common contemporary allegory of the human body: the various limbs represent estates and offices that work together for the benefit of the society, or, in the author's terminology, the Church. The treatise gives a detailed description of the various secular and clerical offices, the former being compared mostly to the shoulders, arms, and other limbs, the latter to the organs of digestion. Finally, the common people are compared to the feet, which support and nourish (!) the rest of the body. This picture of society differs in two main respects from the picture presented in the *Rigsthula:* Whereas the commoner in the *Rigsthula* belonged to a kind of middle class, somewhere between an earl and a slave, now all commoners, whether free or slaves, are lumped together at the bottom. One reason for this is that slaves had disappeared (or almost disappeared) by 1200, but the main reason, no doubt, is that a stricter hierarchy was now in place. This is in turn related to a second development, the emergence of the idea of society as an organism with a purpose, that purpose being to ensure justice and God's will on earth. Whereas the slave, the commoner, and the earl in the *Rigsthula* simply express the fact that men are born to different fates, without offering any idea as to the relationship between the classes, the social distinctions in *A Speech* are of benefit to society as a whole. From a modern perspective, it is easy to point out that in fact the main purpose for rigid social stratification was to to defend the privileges of the upper classes—"a defence of those who do not work by those who do not work." Whether we like it or not, however, such ideas of social hierarchy were an important element of contemporary ideology and a way of dealing with a crucial problem: how to maintain an ordered society.

No similarly detailed doctrine of society has been preserved from thirteenth-century Denmark and Sweden, but there are reasons to believe that these ideas were current there as well, at least to some degree. The social hierarchy was probably even more inflexible and the economic and social distance between the lay and clerical aristocracy on the one hand and the peasants on the other was probably greater. *A Speech* attributes a very strong position to the king as the heart of the body, which, in accordance with Aristotle's theory, is the center of the intellect. Its mid-thirteenth-century successor, *The King's Mirror,* follows up by identifying the king as the foundation of the entire social hierarchy, notably by making aristocratic status exclusively dependent on serving the king. A Danish or Swedish aristocrat of the thirteenth century would probably agree that his status depended on his relationship to the king, as there was at this time no formally defined nobility of blood. However, he would probably argue against the idea that aristocratic status depended exclusively on the king's will and particularly against the frequent references to the fact that the king could raise men from the dust, and that such men were often more loyal, because they had only the king to rely on. On this point *The King's Mirror* reflects the situation in Norway immediately after the internal struggles, when many new men had been brought into the aristocracy. More generally, the work also forms evidence of the stronger position of the king in relationship to the aristocracy in Norway than in the neighboring countries.

With these reservations, *The King's Mirror* gives an adequate picture of the transformation of Scandinavian society from the Viking Age to the thirteenth century, a transformation that made the Scandinavian countries, particularly Denmark and parts of Sweden, more similar to their neighbors to the south and west, in social structure, government and administration, and religion and culture. The replacement of the popular levy by landed elite forces reduced the military importance of the peasants and thus their ability to resist pressure from above, and probably also led to an increase in aristocratic landownership. The growth of the ecclesiastical hierarchy worked in the same direction, as the Church eventually became the greatest landowner in all three countries. It is debatable to what extent this increase came from peasant owners and how much was the result of transfers from the king and the aristocracy. A large part of the land no doubt came from the latter. Even so, the Church must have contributed to the increased concentration of landed wealth, partly because it replaced a number of smaller aristocratic landowners, and partly because it was an institution that never died, whereas the wealth of lay landowners might decrease as well as increase, depending on the vicissitudes of hereditary succession. Finally, demographic and economic conditions also contributed to greater social stratification. As in the rest of Europe, the population increased in Scandinavia during the High Middle Ages, and new land was cleared for cultivation, which towards the end of the period seems to have resulted in considerable pressure on land resources. It is debated whether this meant that there were now more people than could be adequately fed by the available land resources, given the technology and social structure of the day, but the land rent had reached quite a high level by the end of the period. Its sharp decline as a consequence of the high mortality caused by the Black Death suggests that this was largely the result of demographic pressure.

Estimates of land distribution in the early fourteenth century give the impression of a very aristocratic society in all three countries. In the case of Norway, the percentages are believed to have been around 7 percent for the king, 40 for the Church, 20 for the aristocracy, and 33 for the peasants, based on the value of the land. These estimates are mostly deduced from later sources (of the sixteenth and particularly the seventeenth century) and are highly uncertain. This applies particularly to the estimates for the aristocracy and the peasants. It is clear that the 33 percent of the land that is ascribed to the peasants did not consist exclusively of small farms owned by individual families. An unknown but hardly insignificant percentage must have belonged to local owners of more than one farm. As the aristocracy at the time was also vaguely defined, there was a flexible boundary between aristocratic and peasant landownership. Most probably, therefore, the percentage suggested for the aristocracy is too low and that for the peasants too high. The corresponding estimates for Denmark in the fourteenth century are 12.5 percent for the king, 37.5 for the Church and the same figure for the aristocracy, and 12.5 percent for the peasants. In Sweden, peasant landownership has been estimated at around 50 percent, but this figure refers to the amount of land itself and not to its value, which means that the figure is not comparable to the estimate for the two other countries, although it is obvious that the percentage of land owned by the peasants would necessarily have been significantly lower if it had been calculated according to value. Sweden is also characterized by great regional differences, with peasant ownership dominating in Dalarna and the north, whereas the aristocracy owned most of the land in the best agricultural areas in the south. Generally, there are reasons to believe that the aristocracy owned more of the land in Denmark and Sweden than in Norway, whereas the Church may have owned less. Peasant landownership was also significantly lower in Denmark than in the two other countries.

This distribution of land and resources must to a considerable degree be explained as the result of the growth of the monarchy and the Church. Another important factor, however, is demographic growth. Calculations for Europe as a whole suggest that the population grew threefold between 1000 and 1350, which amounts to an increase by 0.3 percent per year. Although the evidence is too meager to allow a similar calculation for Scandinavia, there may well have been similar population growth there as well. Studies of place names suggest a substantial increase in the amount of cultivated land and in the number of new farms, the latter mostly small and marginal, which indicates that most of the land that could be worked with medieval technology was already in use. Some evidence of famine in the early fourteenth century may also point in this direction, but this evidence is disputed.

Royal and Ecclesiastical Revenues

In addition to land, both the king and the Church had income derived from their governmental activities: taxes, fines, tolls, and so forth. All quantitative estimates of royal revenues in this period are of course very uncertain. Although the Swedish evidence before the fourteenth century is too scanty to allow any calculation, some attempts have been made concerning Denmark and Norway. Around 1930, the Norwegian historian Asgaut Steinnes estimated the king of Norway's total annual income—from taxes, fines, land rent, etc.—at around 8,000 marks or 1,700 kg. silver. Steinnes's own conclusion from this estimate (and most later historians agree) is that the sum was extremely low and hardly adequate to support a royal government. The sum amounts to between half and one sixth of the payments the Vikings received from England around the year 1000 to abstain from plundering. By contrast, the Danish king's revenues were significantly higher. Thanks to the preservation of a series of documents from around 1230 (the bulk of which are dated to 1231), usually referred to as "King Valdemar II's cadastre," we have much information about Danish royal revenues around this time, although there is considerable scholarly disagreement about their interpretation. The income from the tax (*leding*) is estimated at from 20,000 to 40,000 marks (3,750–7,500 kg. silver), which makes around 40 percent of the total. The other major source was the royal domains with 32 percent, whereas town income made 8 up percent, fines and shipwrecks 8 percent, and the mint 12 percent. With between 50 and 100,000 marks (9,375–18,750 kg.) silver, the Danish royal revenues are thus five to ten times higher than the Norwegian ones in the early fourteenth century. Admittedly, the Danish population was also larger, but hardly more than four times larger, and probably less. On the other hand, the Danish king's income was drastically reduced in the period after 1241, when much land was lost and a large percentage of the tax-paying peasants submitted to aristocratic landowners who were then able to appropriate the taxes previously paid to the king. A revival took place with the strengthening of the monarchy from the mid-fourteenth century on, when parts of the royal lands that had been alienated were recovered and the king succeeded in imposing extraordinary taxes on the population, which became the common practice.

These numbers make the medieval Danish king's relative wealth several times larger than that of his Norwegian counterpart, which demonstrates the former's greater success in imposing burdens on his people. In absolute terms—which are of course the most important when comparing the military strength of two countries—there is even less doubt about Denmark's greater wealth throughout the period. The Norwegian tax was also far lower than it became later, around one fifth of its mid-seventeenth-century level. In total, however, the peasants paid approximately the same to the upper classes in the seventeenth century as in the High Middle Ages; the difference was that the land rent was five times higher in the early fourteenth century. The Norwegian peasants were therefore not so much better off than their counterparts in Denmark and Sweden as the difference in taxes might suggest.

As Scandinavian society at the time was mainly agrarian, calculations of royal revenues have for the most part paid little attention to income from towns and trade. Recently, however, Svein Gullbekk has pointed to minting as a considerable source of income. Although some coins were struck in Norway as early as the late tenth century, regular minting was not introduced until the reign of Harald Hardrada in the mid-eleventh century. Harald, who had brought with him a large amount of silver and other treasures from Byzantium and Russia, began by issuing good quality coins, which then gradually deteriorated over the course of his reign. He seems, however, to have succeeded in having his coins accepted as the regular means of payment and in preventing the use of foreign coinage. After him, there is an unbroken tradition of minting down to the collapse of Norwegian coinage in the later fourteenth century. The fact that a royal monopoly on minting existed in Norway during this period is in itself evidence of some strength in the monarchy: it shows that the people had sufficient trust in the king to accept his coinage as a means of payment at a higher value than its content of silver, and indicates as well his ability to exclude foreign coinage. Moreover, the inflated value of the mint's output gave the king a substantial income, in particular if he managed to have coins with a low percentage of silver accepted at full value. The king of Norway did not succeed completely in this, as there was a distinction between burnt (pure), silver and coins, and between weighed and counted coins, as well as some restrictions regarding the use of coins, but he did derive a substantial profit from minting low quality coins. Gullbekk has estimated that this profit was as high as 300 to 400 percent. Its value in absolute terms of course depends on the volume of coins in circulation, on which there are widely differing opinions, but Gullbekk suggests that it may in some years have reached 7,500 to 10,000 marks burnt (2,500–3,300 kg. silver), or as much or even more than the king's other estimated annual revenues. However,

Figure 12. Swedish *ørtuger*, ca. 1400, a hoard from Masku (Finland).
Scandinavian denominations was based on the *mark*, originally 214,32 g silver
(1 *mark* = 8 *øre* = 24 *ørtuger* = 240 *penninger*). The *penninger* was the only
denomination that was minted—the others were units of calculation.
However, with increasing inflation, the Swedish kings started to issue *ørtuger*
beginning in the late thirteenth century. Collection of the Finnish National
Museum. Photo by Daderot: Nasjonalmuseet i Finland.

this sum seems too large; the Danish king's income from minting
was estimated at only 12 percent of the whole (or 1,100–2,200
kg. silver) around 1230, and money is likely to have been in wider
use in Denmark than in Norway, in addition to the fact that the
Danish population was much larger. The king of Norway's income from trade and taxes in northern Norway and customs
duties from the export of stockfish may also have been considerable; a recent calculation suggests 300 to 550 marks burnt for
the former and 500 for the latter. The king of Denmark's revenues from the markets in Scania are considerably higher; they are

calculated at around 5,000 to 6,000 marks in the fifteenth century, which reflects the greater amount of trade there (see below). Although most of these sums are very uncertain, it would still seem that Steinnes's calculation is too low and that the total must have amounted to at least 10,000 marks burnt, and probably more.

Steinnes's estimate may well be too low, but even recent, higher estimates hardly make the king of Norway particularly wealthy. The regular incomes of medieval monarchs were usually quite small, however, as many examples demonstrate. The crucial question is how much the king was able to mobilize in case of war. There are various hints that extra taxes were levied, but we do not know their size and there is little to suggest that they were very substantial until the early sixteenth century, with the exception of the areas around the main castles, where higher burdens were imposed on the peasants in the form of both extra taxes and labor services. The most important extra resource was of course the *leding*, which put quite a substantial army or fleet at the king's disposal for two months, without costs, and for even longer against extra payments. Nevertheless, the generally cautious and peaceful foreign policy pursued by Norwegian kings in the period from 1240 to 1319 indicates that there were clear limits on how much they could extract from their subjects for such purposes. Neighboring countries, notably Denmark, spent much more, although in some cases—like that of Erik Menved (1286–1319)—with disastrous results.

We do not know exactly what portion of these revenues went directly to the king and what to his officials. In any case, the king of Norway in person received a larger part of the royal revenues than did his counterparts in the neighboring countries. The Danish and Swedish system, like those of most other European countries, probably created greater gross surpluses, in the sense that the number of agricultural laborers rose and each of them paid a larger percentage of the family's earnings to the king or the land-owner. It is questionable to what extent this also created a greater net surplus. Some calculations—admittedly based on very frag-mentary material from the later Middle Ages in Sweden—indicate that most of what was paid in taxes by the peasants went to sup-port the lord of the castle, his household, and his garrison.

Thus, the Norwegian military organization created a smaller surplus than its counterparts in Denmark, Sweden, and East Cen-tral Europe, but gave the king greater control. The military also brought the Norwegian king's rule closer to the classical modern definition of a state as an entity having a monopoly of legitimate violence. Although local officials may well have had greater con-trol over the military than is indicated in the largely official sources, there is no evidence from the period between 1240 and 1319 of local magnates mobilizing the *leding* against the king. The aris-tocracy's potential to emerge as an independent power in opposi-tion to the king was also clearly more limited here than it would have been in a system based on a military elite in which the most important members acted as commanders of the royal castles. In-deed in Norway, it was unusual for members of the aristocracy to have their own castles.

The apparent poverty of the Norwegian king does not there-fore signal a corresponding a military weakness. However, if the kings of more aristocratic countries managed to create a good working relationship with the aristocracy (as in Denmark after 1340, in Sweden under the Sture regime [1470–1520], and in the kingdoms of East Central Europe for long periods during the fourteenth and fifteenth centuries) such an arrangement would strengthen their military and administrative capacities. The rela-tive strength of these different military systems must therefore be estimated on the basis on their actual performance. The greater peace and stability in Norway in the period from 1240 to 1319 enabled the Norwegian king to perform fairly well in the Nordic competition, but in the long run, the military power of the neighboring countries, above all that of Denmark, proved superior.

Modern accounts of state formation from the Middle Ages to the Early Modern Period often focus on the change from a "domain state" to a "tax state," from the king "living on his own" to the head of state exploiting the resources of his country. We find some signs of a move in this direction in the West European monarchies by the later Middle Ages. In Denmark as well as Norway, we find a relatively high percentage of "public" incomes already in the thirteenth century, although there is no clear shift towards an increase in these kinds of income in the following period, with the possible exception of the Danish extraordinary taxes. If the calculation above is correct, however, there is a characteristic difference between the size of the two kinds of public incomes: higher taxes in Denmark, 40 percent against 30 or less in Norway, and higher fines in Norway, between 30 and 50 percent against less than 8 percent in Denmark, corresponding to the greater importance of warfare in Denmark and of justice in Norway.

The income of the Church was to a greater extent confined to two main sources, the tax (tithes) and fines, to which can be added gifts that might be substantial. In contrast to the king, however, the Church could not raise extra taxes to meet real or imagined emergencies. Nevertheless, like the aristocracy, the Church, mainly the bishops, eventually received parts of the royal income. Bishops might hold royal *len* or might become lords of towns. Thus, the bishop of Roskilde was lord of the town of Copenhagen until the king took it back in 1417. Similarly, the bishop of Stavanger in Norway was the lord of the town of Stavanger, admittedly one of the smallest in the country. The archbishop of Lund held a large number of *len* in Scania, a region resembling an ecclesiastical principality. In this way, the bishops were linked to the king in much the same way as the secular aristocracy.

The king and the Church not only increased their incomes during the twelfth and the thirteenth centuries, they received them in a different form. In the early Middle Ages, the king and the bishop most often had to be present in person to receive their incomes, which took the form of provisions supplied during their visits in a particular district. The *leding* and the tithe were to some extent exceptions, but they were not, strictly speaking, income that belonged to these leaders. The *leding* consisted of provisions for ships manned by the local communities themselves, and the tithe mainly went to the local church and its priest. It either was divided into three shares, for the parish church, the priest, and the bishop (in Denmark and Sweden); or into four, the same three plus the poor (in Norway). We do not know how the bishop received his part in the early period, but it would seem likely that he did so during a visitation. According to canon law, a bishop was obliged to visit all parts of his diocese every year. Although this was not put into practice in a literal sense, there is evidence of episcopal visitations throughout the Middle Ages. However, the bishop eventually became entitled to the provisions whether he visited the district or not. In a similar way, the provisions for a king's visits, as well as the *leding*, were converted into a permanent tax that was brought to some central place where it was made available to the king or his representative.

Towns and Trade

In the late ninth century, the Norwegian chieftain Ottar traveled from northern Norway to King Alfred's court in England. His report on the journey was written down in the introduction to the Old English translation of Orosius' world history, which is still preserved. Ottar tells that he lived the farthest north of all the Norwegians, probably near what is now Malangen in Troms, at nearly 70 degrees north. Although he owned only twenty cows, twenty sheep, and twenty pigs, he was a very rich man by local standards because he also owned six hundred reindeer. In addition, he received tribute from the Sami: hides, feathers, the bones of walruses, and the furs of reindeer, bears, otters, and martens. This tribute (*finnferd*) is later mentioned in the sagas as a royal privilege and one of the most lucrative favors that the king granted to his friends. As we have seen (p. 25), the export of such merchandise from northern Scandinavia to Western Europe was already on-going at this time and probably began even earlier. Ottar's case is thus one of many examples of Scandinavian active trade in the period, in addition to the Viking expeditions.

More than five hundred years later, in the winter 1432, a Venetian ship was shipwrecked off Røst, the outermost inhabited island of the Lofoten archipelago. The survivors managed to reach an uninhabited island and were found by the local population and brought to Røst, where they spent several months before they could resume their journey back to Venice in the summer. The captain, Pietro Querini, and some of the other Venetians wrote accounts of their experience that provide a detailed description of the life of the local population. The people of Røst lived, it would seem, in a kind of primitive innocence. They did not lock their doors, men and women bathed naked together without any immorality, they had sufficient food and material goods and were healthy and happy. Moreover, the Venetians discovered to their surprise that these people, living at the ends of the earth, wore clothes woven in London and belonged to a great international trade network. Lofoten had—and still has—one of the richest fisheries of the world. The people of Røst and the other Lofoten islands caught the cod that arrived in great numbers in the shallow waters offshore to breed at the beginning of each year. They cut up and dried the fish without salt in the cold and dry weather that was normal at this time of year and then brought it to Bergen in summer, where they sold it to German merchants. In return, they bought home grain, cloth, and other merchandise. These two examples point to major changes in the character and importance of Scandinavian trade during the half millennium that separates them. In the Viking Age and the early Middle Ages, the Scandinavians mainly exported luxury goods on their own ships. While this trade still continued, its importance was now surpassed by the export of surplus from fisheries and agriculture, which to an increasing extent was bought by German merchants and transported by them. Population growth and the expansion of cultivated land increased agricultural production. Most of Scandinavia was well suited to animal husbandry, and products like butter, hides, and fish were important export articles, especially when population growth in other European countries and the greater wealth of the aristocracy led to greater demand for food. As the landowning aristocracy in Scandinavia appropriated more of the surplus of agriculture, a proportionally greater share of these products was brought to the market in return for products like grain, flour, cloth, wine and beer, and this led to the growth of towns.

German merchants had turned up in Norway already in the twelfth century. In 1186, King Sverre spoke out against them in Bergen, complaining that they imported wine that made people drunk instead of useful commodities like wheat, honey, and cloth, as did the English merchants. From the detailed description of the traveling merchant in *The King's Mirror,* we know that Norwegian merchants must still have traveled abroad in the mid-thirteenth century. They are also listed in the English customs rolls from the early fourteenth century and may have continued their visits well after that, although by then, the Germans had taken over most of the export. There have been various explanations of why this happened. At one time, the prevailing view was that better ships were responsible. Viking ships were excellent for sailing, but they could carry very little cargo compared to the bigger and heavier German cogs. It turns out, however, that the Norwegians actually did use cogs. A better explanation therefore points to organization and the existing trade network. The Germans were ideally placed for transmitting trade goods between the East and West. They had an established system for doing this and also for suppressing competitors and keeping the trade for themselves. From the late thirteenth century on, they settled in Norwegian towns, notably Bergen, where they organized as a separate community with their own laws and jurisdiction.

The description of the merchant in *The King's Mirror* also suggests an explanation of why the Germans succeeded in Scandinavia. Aristocratic merchants like the one in this text, who mostly exported the surplus of their own lands, might occasionally want to travel abroad, bringing their own merchandise to markets in order to see the world and meet other people. However, they had no economic incentive to do so, if the buyers were willing to pick up the goods themselves and bring back what the sellers wanted in return. As long as the main export articles were the surplus from agriculture and the fisheries in the form of land rent, both producers and foreign buyers had a common interest in avoiding the unnecessary mediation of indigenous professional merchants. The land rent was mostly paid in kind—in grain, butter, and fish, the latter notably in the northern and western parts of Norway, so the great landowners received a considerable surplus. The archbishop, for example, was the greatest fish exporter in the country. In addition to his permanent residence in Nidaros, he had a great palace in Bergen, partly because Bergen was the most important royal residence, but also because of the fish trade. For this reason, the archbishop also had a more positive attitude toward the Germans than many of the other lay and clerical magnates. Peasants and fishermen had a similar attitude to German merchants. The fishermen brought their stockfish the long distance from northern Norway to Bergen, but they were unable to transport them further as the voyage to Bergen and back took the entire summer. They too established permanent relationships to individual merchants, which probably meant that they got lower prices, but had the advantage that they could get credit in bad seasons and thus secure the goods they needed even if they could not pay for them at once.

A similar pattern existed in other parts of Scandinavia: Scania in Denmark (now southern Sweden) had extremely rich herring fisheries, and during the thirteenth century the great fair held there became a crossroads for trade between Scandinavia, Germany, and Western Europe. The markets in Scania are mentioned in the sources from around 1170 onwards. In the early thirteenth century, the chronicler Arnold of Lübeck pointed to the wealth that the trade in fish brought to the Danes and mentioned its importance for his own hometown. King Valdemar II (1202–41) issued a law for the port of Skanør, regulating the fishing and trade at this port and the custom due from the exporters. At this time, there were royal castles and some smaller towns in the surrounding area. Foreign merchants had their own plots, where they were allowed to salt their herring and conduct their trade and where they had internal jurisdiction. Merchants from a large number of towns, from the Baltic as well as the North Sea area, came to the market in Scania, which thus became a meetingplace between East and West, where a wide range of goods were sold or exchanged for herring. Scania thus became a market not only for herring but also for wine, beer, furs, hemp, salt, meat and various other commodities. Towards the end of the fourteenth century, the value of Lübeck's trade in Scania was six times that of the city's trade in Bergen. In 1399, 1,218 of 1,760 ships that left Lübeck were bound for Scania, and the value of the trade in this and the following year amounted to one half of the town's total exports and imports.

Sweden's main export article was iron. Iron is one of the most common metals on earth and can be found in a variety of landscapes. However, some of the inner parts of Sweden, Dalarna and the surrounding areas, had the advantage of high-quality iron, readily accessible near the surface of mountains. This resource was increasingly exploited from the late twelfth century onwards, and played a prominent part in the Swedish economy after around 1300. Mining in Sweden was organized and largely controlled by freeholders or members of the lower nobility who jointly owned the mines and worked in teams to extract the ore (Swedish *bergsmän* = mountain men/miners). The smelting took place in privately owned works at the farms of individual miners. Iron mining was very labor-intensive, requiring large numbers of hired laborers; around 20,000 people, men and women, are supposed to have worked in the industry, which may amount to around 3 percent of the total population. In addition, mining created a considerable market for food. Grain was imported from the rich agricultural areas around the Lake Mälaren, and oxen were driven distances of 300 to 400 kilometers from the southern provinces. The existence of a wealthy class of commoners with easy access to arms also had major political consequences: the iron-producing areas formed the core of the popular movement against the union king in the fifteenth century (see Chapter 5).

Iron was transported from the inland mines to the coast and exported to other countries, mostly by German merchants who dominated trade in several Swedish towns, most notably Stockholm and Kalmar, where they may have numbered around one third of the total number of burghers. In contrast to Norway, the Germans in Sweden did not form a separate community, but became burghers with equal rights and the same duties as their Swedish counterparts.

The relationship between the Germans and the Scandinavian kingdoms was somewhat ambivalent. On the one hand, the Germans filled an obvious need for the great landowners, enabling them to sell their products and get others in return, and were also a source of money and credit. On the other hand, their trading conditions and the conditions for their settlement in the Scandinavian cities were a constant source of conflict, and the wealth of the merchants and cities was a temptation, particularly for the Danish king. The events during the last years of Erik Menved's reign and after his death in 1319 showed their financial strength and gave indications of the further expansion that followed. In 1367–1370, they defeated King Valdemar IV in war, and they played a major part during the period of Scandinavian unions. Their main aim was to protect their trading interests, which often led them to interfere in Scandinavian politics, particularly against Denmark, the strongest power in the region.

The growth in trade increased town populations and led to the foundation of new towns. In addition, bishops were normally supposed to reside in towns, and a bishop had a sufficiently large entourage and the wealth needed to support at least a small town with a cathedral, an episcopal palace, and houses for canons and for the meetings of the cathedral chapter. Kings and their courts also increasingly took up residence in towns, normally moving between a number of them, another factor contributing to urbanization. In addition, most towns served as area markets, where peasants and local lords could exchange commodities. But of the around 140 Scandinavian towns founded before the early fourteenth century—fifteen in Norway, twenty-five in Sweden, and the rest in Denmark—only three were significant centers for long-distance trade: Bergen, Stockholm, and Visby, each probably with around 5,000 to 10,000 inhabitants.

The two largest towns in Scandinavia from the late-thirteenth and early-fourteenth century onwards were Bergen in Norway and Stockholm in Sweden, both centers for the export of, respectively, fish and iron, transported by German merchants, who formed a

Figure 13. Sixteenth-century city plan of Visby on Gotland (Sweden). Only half of the area inside the wall has urban settlement; the upper part, which is actually a hill, consists of fields. This may be the result of the decline of the town in the later Middle Ages, although it was quite normal for medieval towns to have agricultural areas inside their walls to provide food for the inhabitants. The many stone houses and the large churches indicate that the city was still wealthy. Today, Visby is one of the best-preserved medieval towns in Scandinavia, although, except for the cathedral (no. 2 from the left), all the churches are in ruins. From Georg Braun and Franz Hogenberg, eds. *Civitates orbis terrarum*, vol. 5., first edition (Cologne 1572, repr. Cologne, 1898).

large part of the towns' populations. Visby was also important from this point of view, although it declined from the thirteenth century onwards because of competition from German towns. By contrast, there was no similar town in Denmark, despite the importance of the Scania market. The reason for this was most probably the short distance between North Germany and the Danish markets. German merchants could easily buy the herring where it was caught and either return to their hometowns or export it to Western Europe during the same summer, whereas they needed to spend the winter in Bergen if they were to do the same with fish from northern Norway. Consequently, despite their greater economic importance, the fisheries in Scania did not give rise to extensive urbanization; the trade was carried on in various marketplaces along the shore. This changed after 1400, when the markets in Scania declined, while the towns, notably Malmö, became more important. Towards the end of the Middle Ages, it was the fourth largest town in Scandinavia, after Bergen, Copenhagen, and Stockholm, with around 4,500 inhabitants. It also played a major part during the Reformation and the Count's War (p. 284–85). The growth of Copenhagen took place after 1417, when the king took it over from the bishop of Roskilde and made it his capital.

There was a considerable expansion of Scandinavian trade during the Middle Ages, which led to closer contact with the rest of Europe, to urbanization, and to the increased use of money; all of which contributed to a substantial economic surplus. Almost all the towns that existed in Scandinavia around 1300 had been founded during the previous 300 years. However, the urbanization trend did not alter the predominantly agrarian character of Scandinavian society. Agriculture was probably more important in the High Middle Ages than in both the previous and the following period. Most of the export consisted of surplus from agriculture and the fisheries, and the greatest exporters were the members of the landed aristocracy. Although the towns were home to a number of indigenous merchants and artisans, export trade was dominated by foreign merchants. Politically, the indigenous merchants were too weak to compete with the landed aristocracy, in contrast to the situation at this period in the most commercialized areas of Europe—Italy, the Netherlands, and parts of France and Germany.

Bureaucracy or Feudalism?

Thus, the division of power in contemporary society—at least at the central level—becomes a question of the relationship between the king, the Church, and the secular aristocracy. In contrast to many other recent scholars, R. I. Moore regards the period from 975 to 1225 as crucial for the development of the European state. An ecclesiastical bureaucracy and an intellectual elite developed an increasingly systematic and intolerant doctrine that was imposed on the population, and a distinctive royal bureaucracy resulted in more effective and oppressive government in Europe than in most other contemporary civilizations. Although there arose a class of professional bureaucrats in the king's service in countries like England and particularly France, which to some extent formed a counterweight to the top aristocracy, Moore exaggerates their importance compared to the prelates and the aristocracy. What characterized the political system of Western Europe in the Middle Ages, compared to that of other civilizations, was not the strength of the bureaucracy under the king's direct control, but on the contrary the king's greater dependence on the leading strata of the population, the prelates, nobles, and burghers. This resulted in corruption, inefficiency, and injustice, but it created a certain amount of stability as well, because the state mattered to its most influential inhabitants. This applies even more to Scandinavia. First, there is little evidence of a central administration recruited from men of lower rank who were completely dependent on the king. In most cases, we do not know the social origin of the men in the king's service, but to the extent that we do, they seem mostly to have been recruited from the aristocracy. Second, the central administration was significantly smaller and less developed.

However, we do note movements in the direction of Moore's bureaucracy in Scandinavia from the late twelfth and particularly the thirteenth century onwards. The central administration in Scandinavia, as well as in the rest of Europe, had its origin in the king's household, as the titles of the various officers indicate: "marshal" or "constable" (head of the stable), "steward" (kitchen manager), etc. These offices continued to exist later in the Middle Ages, but they were sometimes kept vacant. A new officer appears from the late twelfth or early thirteenth century, the "chancellor," who was responsible for the king's correspondence and kept his records and accounts. The development of the chancery in the following period made the chancellor the most important royal official and gave him a role resembling that of Moore's bureaucrats in England and France. Clerical chancellors played an important part during the authoritarian regimes in Denmark under Erik Klipping and Erik Menved, as well as in Norway under Håkon V.

The rise of the chancery was of course a result of the increasing use of script in administration from the thirteenth century onwards. The number of letters extant or known to have existed during the most active period of the royal chancery in Norway, the reign of Håkon V (1299–1319), is twenty per year. The Swedish chancery reached the same figure in the 1330s, while the total number of letters per year in Denmark in the early fourteenth century was eighty. As most of what was written has been lost, these numbers probably represent only a tiny part of what was actually produced. There is also evidence of efforts by the king to attach competent people to his chancery, clerics as well as laymen, for instance the foundation of an organization of royal chapels by King Håkon V of Norway, and the systematic use of canons for the same purposes in Denmark and Sweden. Nevertheless, it is unlikely that the output was anywhere near that of the contemporary English chancery. Henry II (1154–89) already is supposed to have issued 115 letters per year, whereas a dramatic increase took place under his successors, which can be measured in the rise in the amount of wax used per week for sealing: from 3.63 pounds between 1226 and 1230 to 31.90 between 1265 and 1271. It might also be mentioned that the total of all published documents from Norway in the period from about 1000 to 1570, from institutions as well as individual persons, fills twenty-three large volumes, which represents the majority of the extant material; unprinted letters may fill a few volumes more. This amount is roughly equivalent to the material issued by the English royal chancery over a few decades of the thirteenth century. However, medieval England was "a much governed country," and the volume of documents both used and preserved was higher there than in any other country north of the Alps. Although far behind England, the Scandinavian countries show a significant rise in the use of script from the thirteenth century onwards, the late-medieval material from Sweden, and particularly Denmark, being significantly more abundant than that from Norway.

The medieval commonplace about the value of writing was that it served to preserve the memory of things that had happened. This is the theme of numerous introductory statements in the royal charters (*arengas*) and is also mentioned in prefaces to historical works. Most obviously, kings, prelates or great lords needed to keep records of their estates and rights to determine whether they received what they were entitled to from their subordinates. The concentration of property in few hands over widely different parts of the country is difficult to imagine without written records; at the least, such concentrations would likely have been less stable. The importance of the preservation of memory also applies to the legal field, where the reforms carried out in the thirteenth century would hardly have been possible without writing. Whereas in the past it would have been difficult to base legal decisions on a broad knowledge of sentences from earlier courts that had dealt with similar cases, precedence could now acquire greater importance than before. The same principle applied to other administrative decisions. Standardized procedures and routines became possible to a greater extent than in an oral society, and the decisions of lower instances could be backed up by the king's confirmation. The introduction of writing also served to give the elite greater authority as experts on law, religion, and other fields of knowledge, which in turn contributed to further centralization. Most important, even the relatively modest use of script in the thirteenth and fourteenth centuries gave the king and the central government a clear advantage over potential rivals in other parts of the country. The king now could make his will known to his officials all over the country and receive reports from them, which gave him an amount of information that none of his potential rivals in other parts of the country could match.

The consistent application of these principles is more characteristic of Early Modern than of medieval government, but already in the thirteenth century, the use of script made it less necessary for the king to be present in person to have his will respected. Kings, bishops, and other leaders now to a greater extent communicated indirectly, through local officials or through the use of script. The king also normally resided in towns, although he moved between a number of them. In Norway, his usual itinerary in the thirteenth century was by ship along the coast between Oslo and Bergen, spending most winters in Bergen. Winter was also the time for the main festivities of the year, the Christmas celebrations, when most of the leading men in the country gathered around the king. Capitals in the modern sense were a later development. In Denmark, Copenhagen developed into the permanent administrative center in the fifteenth century, but the king continued to travel.

There was also a change in the relationship between the king and his subordinates, at least in theory, a change from "friends" to "officials," that amounted to a degree of what might be termed "bureaucratization." Like ecclesiastical officers and in contrast to previous usage, they now had clearly defined districts and owed obedience to the king, although there was nothing like the total dependence on him propagated by sources like *The King's Mirror*. Here the models for the royal official or retainer are Old

Testament heroes like Joseph, Mardocheus, and Esther, who remained obedient to their masters no matter how unjustly they were treated, and whose absolute subordination to the king is expressed in the passage where the Father explains the advantage in joining the king's service. When all men in the realm are obliged to do whatever the king demands without receiving anything in return, becoming the king's man and receiving a salary from him will be an unquestionable advantage.

Of course, the whole point in joining the king's service was to get something in return. The king would not convince anyone to serve him unless he rewarded them. However, there is some echo of the ideas in *The King's Mirror* in formulas used in the correspondence between the king of Denmark and members of the aristocracy in his service in the later Middle Ages. The latter clearly emphasize the distance between the king and themselves when addressing him. The king is "the most noble lord and mighty prince," and the noble addressing him is his servant who owes him "humble, subservient, dutiful, and faithful service." The king addresses the members of the nobility, like all other subjects, condescendingly as "most dear to Us." While the nobles address the king in the plural, the king normally addresses them in the singular, the exceptions being men who are particularly prominent or close to him, who are addressed in the plural. Such men are also addressed in other formulas that make clear the king's especial favor. On the other hand, when ordering his men, the king normally uses the term "ask," although it is plainly implied that it is their duty to perform his "request." Most probably, this means of address should be read as that of an exalted, gracious lord, so confident in the loyalty of his men that he finds it unnecessary to address them in the language of explicit orders.

This terminology corresponds almost perfectly to the relationship between the king and his men as depicted in *The King's Mirror*. The difference, however, is that these men were not simply

Figure 14. Christoffer II, from his funeral monument in Sorø
Abbey Church (Denmark), second half of the fourteenth
century. Christoffer was one of the most unsuccessful of Danish
kings, but thanks to his more successful son, Valdemar IV, he
got an elaborate and beautiful grave monument in bronze,
which gives an impression of royal majesty. Photo: Mariusz
Pazdziora. Wikimedia Commons.

subjects; they had entered the king's service voluntarily and were
free to leave it as well. Sources of the later Middle Ages give examples of nobles formally renouncing their loyalty to the king.
The formality of the act may indicate that it was considered a
more drastic step than in the earlier Middle Ages. Moreover, all

known examples of such behavior date from periods of crisis or rebellion, when the noble in question could justify his behavior either by the fact that it had proved impossible to serve the king any longer, or because he was taking part in some joint aristocratic resistance to the king. The late-medieval Danish correspondence between the king and the nobles shows a mixture of the new Christian ideology that sees the king as head of state and God's representative on earth, to whom his subjects owe loyal service, and the traditional or feudal ideas of a contract between the king and the individual noble.

Despite these trends in a bureaucratic direction, local administration seems to remain closer to the feudal than the bureaucratic model. This applies particularly in Denmark and parts of Sweden, where landowners exercised considerable legal and political control over their tenants, whereas in Norway the entire population was in principle directly subordinated to the king, and landownership was a purely economic relationship. On the other hand, the term *len* used of the districts governed by royal castellans may suggest inaccurate associations. This term is derived from *Lehen*, the German term for "fief." However, there was a clear distinction between these *len* and the allodial lands owned by the incumbent of the office. The former was an office to which he was appointed for a limited period, whereas the latter was his private property, which his descendants would inherit. The exception to this were *len* granted to members of the dynasty, in practice the king's younger brothers, the most important of which was Southern Jutland, originally granted to Valdemar II's son Abel and held by his descendants until the line became extinct in the late fourteenth century. Another possible exception is the control of the local courts by members of the aristocracy. Admittedly, the lord did not become the judge of the peasants, but as their patron, he had considerable control over them, and he most probably also controlled the local court.

More generally, several aspects of the centralization of society discussed above would seem to have benefited the Church and the aristocracy rather than the king. The existence of castles favored defenders over attackers, which enabled a disloyal castellan to resist the king with some hope of success. Even though castles were an effective means to exploit the population, the profit might not go to the king, but rather to the castellan. The greater gross surplus that resulted from the military transformation was thus not invested only in military efficiency or other services to the king, but also in conspicuous consumption and a higher standard of living for the aristocracy. The king's ability to counterbalance the aristocracy was also limited. In contrast to some other countries—parts of Germany and the Low Countries, for example, and to some extent France and London in England—there was no wealthy town population that might serve the king for this purpose. At least in Norway and Sweden, the king might to some extent use the peasants, but they were too weak to confront a united aristocracy.

Thus, the new military technology might actually weaken the central government and lead to the country's falling apart into smaller principalities, as happened in Germany in the thirteenth century. In the later Middle Ages, Denmark and Sweden and to a lesser extent Norway were mostly ruled by castellans whose districts resembled miniature kingdoms. Above them was the king, the royal court, and the royal chancery and administration, which might issue laws and ordinances for the whole country, serve as an instance of appeal in conflicts between the castellans and possibly their subordinates, and govern the country's relationship to other kingdoms.

In modern Western democracies there is a sharp distinction between bureaucracy and political leadership, such as did not exist in the Middle Ages. Nevertheless, there were some tendencies in this direction. Moore's professional bureaucrats, who were solely dependent on the king, also made important decisions, but they were not alone in this; the king also had to consult with the "people," which increasingly came to mean the prelates and the nobles. In the early period, meetings between the king and the people took place at local assemblies, representing smaller or larger parts of the country. Central assemblies for the whole country became more common in the twelfth and thirteenth centuries. Such gatherings happened at irregular intervals in Norway in the period between 1163 and 1302 and were attended by representatives of the common people as well as the aristocracy, although decisions were in practice mostly taken by the latter. The Danish equivalent to this was the *Danehof* (Danish court), consisting of members of the higher and lower aristocracies. Often, some commoners were also present, but mainly for acclamation. In the 1270s and 80s, this body several times opposed the king and forced him to make various concessions.

At the same time, the king surrounded himself with an informal group of counselors, which eventually developed into the royal council. Until the early fourteenth century, it was mostly an advisory board for the king, and its members were recruited by him. Periods of regencies contributed to this—the regencies for Erik Klipping (1260s) and Erik Menved (1286–1294) in Denmark, for Eirik Magnusson in Norway in the 1280s, for Birger Magnusson in Sweden (1290–1302), and for Magnus Eriksson in Norway and Sweden in the 1320s. In Denmark, the council of the realm gradually grew in importance during the fourteenth century. A formal appointment to the council, accompanied by an oath, is mentioned for the first time in Christoffer II's election charter of 1320. Parallel to this new feature, the character of the council also changed, from a body consisting of the king's trusted friends to one made up of representatives of the aristocracy. The same thing happened in Sweden and, to a lesser extent, in Norway. An important reason for this development is the fact that monarchy became elective in Denmark and Sweden from the early fourteenth century, and a hundred years later in Norway, and that the council in practice became the elective body. The Swedish Code of the Realm of 1350 decrees that the king should have a council consisting of twelve members of the lay aristocracy plus the archbishop, some of the bishops, and other clerics, but this does not seem to have become a permanent feature. A council of the realm is frequently mentioned in the sources of the following period in all three countries, but it is not clearly distinct from wider aristocratic assemblies.

We are thus dealing with an institutionalization of the aristocracy, the beginnings of which we have traced in the previous pages, but which developed further during the later Middle Ages. Whereas the state in the previous period had largely been identical with the king, and institutional conflicts had been between the king and the Church, the following period saw the increasing institutionalization of collective bodies representing the "people" versus the king, notably the council of the realm, dominated by the aristocracy and the bishops. However, the full development of the council of the realm did not take place until the fifteenth century and will be dealt with later (pp. 272–75).

The emergence of central institutions dominated by the aristocracy also led to a formal division of power between the king and these institutions, parallel to what happened in most countries in the rest of Europe. In Denmark, King Erik V Klipping had to issue the first *håndfæstning* (originally: "written obligation") in Scandinavian history, in which he promised to respect the rights of the "people," in practice meaning the aristocracy, on specific points. In the following period, until the king's murder in 1286, the *Danehof* was summoned several times and some of the leading aristocrats served as the king's counselors. The *håndfæstning* (hereafter referred to as the "election charter") eventually became a permanent feature in Denmark and was issued at the king's election as a condition for his being accepted as a ruler. This happened for the first time at the election of Christoffer II in 1320. Formal election charters were not introduced in Sweden until 1371, but a parallel development took place there as well. A similar charter was issued in connection with the deposition of King Birger and the election of Magnus Eriksson in 1319. Both kingdoms thus kept step with the main trends in contemporary Europe and were probably influenced by constitutional ideas derived from the renewed influence of Aristotle's political works in the second half of the thirteenth century. These influences were probably also present in Norway, although the official ideology there was more monarchical, in keeping with the fact that the Norwegian monarchy was hereditary, not elective. The first Norwegian election charter dates from 1449.

The general impression that emerges from these considerations is that of a decentralized society headed by a weak king. The previous sketch of the social and economic conditions would seem to suggest that the real beneficiaries of the development of royal power were the lay and clerical aristocracies and that the local administrations, particularly in Denmark and Sweden but also to some extent in Norway, consisted of smaller principalities under relatively limited central control. Nor is there any doubt that royal power in the Scandinavian kingdoms was weaker than it became in the sixteenth and seventeenth centuries. However, it is also easy to exaggerate its weakness. The gradual solution of the problem of royal succession, the end of regicide, the growth of royal legislation and jurisdiction, and the exalted picture of divine kingship in *The King's Mirror* and other sources may indicate a stronger monarchy than the king's indirect way of ruling and attempts to calculate his resources might suggest. Not least, we have so far discussed the position and role of the king only by looking for equivalents to modern government, the bureaucratic, and the political sphere.

Figure 15. St. Olav, originally from Dale Church, Luster (Norway), thirteenth century, now in the University Museum, Bergen. The statue gives a good impression of aristocratic fashion in hair, beard, and dress at the time, similar to the description in *The King's Mirror*. In his hands Olav must have carried either his attribute, the ax (with which he was killed) or royal insignia. Photo: Svein Skare. Copyright © University Museum of Bergen, with permission.

The Court

However, a third sphere is equally or perhaps even more important, namely the court, which to some extent overlaps with the
two others. There is of course also a social and ceremonial sphere
in modern politics, which is too often overlooked, but whose
importance is nevertheless inferior to its medieval equivalent. In
The King's Mirror, which is our most detailed source for Scandinavian kingship and courtly culture in the thirteenth century, the
Son asks the Father whether the king is allowed to entertain himself by hunting. The Father answers that he may do this to relax
and to get physical exercise, but not at the cost of more serious
duties, which according to the author are sitting in judgment
over his subjects and prayer and meditation. We know very little
about the daily life of Scandinavian kings in the Middle Ages,
whether they were serious, hard-working bureaucrats and politicians or bon-vivants who spent their time hunting, drinking,
feasting, and womanizing. Most probably, there was considerable individual variation. The important point, however, is that it
is difficult to draw a line between proper royal duties and relax-
ation and entertainment. The picture of the drinking, hunting,
and womanizing king who had no serious business to conduct
reflects a modern view of such activities, including the modern
distinction between working hours and leisure hours. Hunting
and festivities—particularly the prolonged celebration of Christmas in mid-winter—were important means whereby the king
could establish a good relationship with the aristocracy, deflate
internal conflicts, and create loyalty to himself. The drinking-
table and the hunting party were as important to the king's relationship with the aristocracy as formal meetings in the council.
Courtly ceremonial seems to have been relatively simple at the
time, far more so than in contemporary oriental cultures or in
the royal courts of the seventeenth and eighteenth centuries. *The*

King's Mirror insists on the obedience retainers owe to the king, but its practical rules of conduct are limited to the need to be polite and well dressed and to respect the normal rules of courtesy. The latter include not standing in the way of those who serve the king food when he is at the table and keeping a sufficient distance from the king when riding with him, so as not to splash mud on him or his horse. Both *The King's Mirror* and other sources indicate that close connections existed between the king and his men and that the court was a meeting-place for the social and political elite. Most importantly, the court was a place of education, comparable to the universities and elite colleges that educate civil servants in our society.

In most of Europe it seems to have been normal practice in the upper circles for nobles to send their sons (and to some extent also their daughters) to their lord's court for fostering, partly for education and to promote their future careers, partly to serve as hostages of a kind. In Scandinavia, fostering seems to have worked in the opposite direction, with those of lower rank fostering the children of their superiors, as in the story of King Harald Finehair sending his son to King Athalstan of England for fostering in order to demonstrate his superiority. Although the story is most probably invented, there is evidence of the custom from other sources. It seems, for instance, that a king's illegitimate children were fostered by his friends or clients. We do not know whether this changed later as a result of European influence. In any case, *The King's Mirror* does not mention fostering at the king's court, but pays great attention to how a young man should dress and behave if he is to be admitted to the king's service. Other sources, from Norway as well as the other countries, refer to the many pages of noble birth who started their careers as the king's servants at court. King Håkon V of Norway asks his officials to look for promising young men of good family who might join the king's body of retainers as pages, called *kjertisveinar* (candlebearers).

There is a chapter devoted to them in the *Hird Law*, which describes their duties and the ceremonies attendant to their appointment. Pages of aristocratic origin are also mentioned in Danish and Swedish sources, performing a variety of duties at court. In 1541, the Danish nobleman Tyge Krabbe described his service as a page at the court of King Hans (1481–1513) from the age of twelve, when he minded the king's dogs ("having with them many a devil's day in moss and scrubs") and carried the king's shield and sword during tournaments.

The extant sources mostly deal with men at court and have little to say about women. Clearly, however, the queen had her own entourage of ladies-in-waiting who were probably recruited from the aristocracy in the same way as their male counterparts. Despite its detailed account of life at court, *The King's Mirror* is surprisingly silent on the subject of women at court, the author confining himself to pointing out that courtesy includes the ability to talk to women of various age and status. There is somewhat more in the *Erikskrönikan*, which elaborates on how Duke Erik charmed his future mother-in-law. Most important, the romantic literature that flourished from the thirteenth century onwards is likely to have had some connection with the presence of women at court and their influence. From a social point of view, noble daughters at court may have had the same function as noble sons, to link their parents more closely to the king. How close such links might be, is open to speculation. In their accounts of the earlier period in Norway, the sagas frequently refer to the king's affairs with women of both high and low status, which served to link their families more closely to him. After legitimate birth became a prerequisite for succession to the throne, the importance of such relationships diminished, but they may well have continued. The sources have little to say about the matter. We know that King Håkon V of Norway had an illegitimate daughter, but not whether her mother belonged to the aristocracy. This daughter, Agnes, was married to a prominent nobleman, whose status increased as a result of the marriage.

The queen herself is less prominent in the sources than her husband, but, formally, her status increased with the introduction of legitimate succession. From the thirteenth century on, she was usually crowned. Whatever the relationship between her and her husband, there can be no doubt at this period of her formal rank, whereas there had earlier been only a vague distinction between her and the other women in the king's life. Most Scandinavian queens who played an important political role were widows, the most prominent of whom was Queen Margrete, the founder of the Kalmar Union. As long as their husbands lived, queens normally acted behind the scenes, for good or for bad. As they were always foreigners, they were often blamed for their husbands' bad acts. For example, King Birger's wife Margareta was accused in the *Erikskrönikan* of urging her husband to murder his brothers and luring them to the fateful banquet in Nyköping by faking her longing for them. As in the rest of Europe, however, approaching the queen was also a means to obtain a favor from the king, as in the story from the *Sturlunga Saga* about how the Icelander Sturla Tordsson became reconciled with King Magnus. Sturla had been summoned to Norway by King Håkon, who accused him of working against his interests in Iceland. Sturla reached Norway in 1263, after king Håkon had left for Scotland, and got a cool reception from King Magnus. He was nevertheless allowed to travel on the king's ship, where he began to tell stories to the king's retainers. Eventually, Queen Ingeborg (recently married to King Magnus [pp. 236–38]) began to listen, received him in a friendly manner, served him wine, and finally reconciled him with her husband.

The recruitment of the king's servants from the aristocracy is a characteristic feature of Western courts in contrast to those of the Middle East, where most of the king's servants were slaves or eunuchs and other people dependent on him. We can thus imagine a normal career for a noble in Scandinavia as starting with a period as page at court and a warrior in the king's entourage, after which he would fill some position in the local administration, its exact nature dependent on his rank and the king's impression of him. Having finished his permanent residence at court, such a man would probably make a regular appearance at royal Christmas parties and meet the king on various occasions during his travels around in the country.

Evidently, such lengthy familiarity with the king did not prevent nobles from opposing him, nor was it without some risk for the king. He could only to a limited extent "hide behind his office," for although his position accorded him respect and deference, his frequent interaction with his subordinates made it difficult for him to hide any personal weaknesses. A heroic or charismatic king could win much support under this system, but one who was clumsy, stupid, or cowardly ran a considerable risk. The kings' sagas give ample evidence of this, celebrating the wit, charm, eloquence, and heroism of great kings, while hinting at myriad flaws in their less successful counterparts. The king had to develop a good relationship with his subordinates, settle conflicts between them, and strike just the right balance between generosity and friendliness on the one hand, and strictness and authority on the other. No small amount of diplomatic skill was called for. In 1256, the Icelanders Tord Kakali, Snorre's nephew, and Gissur Torvaldson, who were bitter enemies, stayed at Håkon's court. Tord urged the king to send Gissur away, declaring that it was likely that conflicts would arise if they both were in the same city. The king answered, "How can you expect me to send away my friend Gissur based on what you have said; would you rather not be in Heaven if Gissur was there?" "I would gladly be there, my Lord!" replied Tord, "but we would have to be far apart."

The personal links established between the king and members of the aristocracy at court may to some extent modify the image we have of aristocratic dominance and opposition to the king. Nevertheless, these ties did not eliminate conflicts, of which there were several in the late thirteenth and early fourteenth centuries.

The Division of Power: Monarchy, Aristocracy, and the Church

Conflicts between the monarchy on the one hand and the Church and aristocracy on the other have played a prominent part in Scandinavian historiography. The most obvious rival of the monarchy was the Church, which in the Middle Ages largely resembled a state, for its hierarchical organization and its involvement in jurisdiction, legislation, and taxation resembled the king's administration.

Whereas at least some scholars have depicted prelates like Eskil and Eystein as charismatic figures promoting high ideals, their successors in the late thirteenth century have met with less approval. By now the Church had become a wealthy and influential institution, and its struggles seem to have had more to do with financial privileges and legal detail than with fundamental issues of *libertas ecclesiae*. An example of this is the jurisdictional conflict that broke out in Norway in the 1270s. A series of negotiations led to an agreement in 1277 in which the king went far in the direction of recognizing ecclesiastical jurisdiction in all cases pertaining to ecclesiastical law, although with some reservations in reference to royal rights. After King Magnus' death three years later, the regency for his son refused to recognize some of his privileges, notably real or alleged tax privileges, and tried to restrict ecclesiastical jurisdiction. The conflict took several dramatic turns. The archbishop excommunicated the regents, whereupon they outlawed the archbishop and the clerics, who refused to obey their decrees. The archbishop and two of the bishops went into exile; the regents took over the archbishop's palace and one of them slept with his wife in the archbishop's bed. When one of the regents died excommunicate, the others broke into the tower of the cathedral in Bergen to sound the bells at his funeral.

The conflict grew into a major confrontation between the two powers, in which the regents used their legal learning to argue for the king's sovereign power. They used the reservation clause in the settlement of 1277 ("with the king's rights reserved in all cases where fines should be paid according to established custom and the law of the country") to claim that the jurisdictional rights granted to the Church were concessions from the sovereign king and remained subject to his interpretation. The background and reason for the conflict are unclear because the lack of sources from the previous period makes it difficult to know how many of the concessions granted by the monarchy in 1277 were actually new. Nevertheless, we can at least see that there were significant differences from previous conflicts between the Church and the monarchy. First, this was strictly a conflict between two organizations; there was no doubt that Magnus and his sons were the lawful rulers of Norway. Second, the expansion of both in the previous period had made the rivalry into something like a zero-sum game: there was little room for one organization to expand without harming the other. This is particularly evident in the case of conflicts over jurisdiction, for both organizations received a large part of their revenues and authority from fines and the settlement of conflicts, so that a gain for one party would immediately translate into a loss for the other. The same principle applies to disputes over taxation, for the Church was now demanding exemption from taxation for all its tenants, not only for the estates run by the ecclesiastical institutions themselves, as had been the case previously.

The conflict ended in 1290 in a relatively vague compromise that largely favored the monarchy. The Church lost several of the privileges it had gained in 1277, and its demand for extended tax exemption was rejected, whereas the question of jurisdiction remained unsolved. Nor were the royal counselors punished for their attacks on the clergy. Competition between royal and ecclesiastical courts of law continued, with the king and the Church unable to reach an agreement about a new Christian law. In their day-to-day dealings, however, the two organizations managed to cooperate reasonably well. There were no serious conflicts in the following period.

Tension between the monarchy and the Church was most prolonged and dramatic in Denmark, where the archbishops Jacob Erlandsen (1252–1274), Jens Grand (1289–1302) and Esger Juul (1310–1325) all came into conflict with the king. Danish historians have held widely different opinions on how to weight the impact of legal and ideological issues versus political interests in these struggles. Jurisdictional and legal arguments played an important role, and the legal positions of both parties can be examined in the detailed petitions that they brought before the papal court. Nor was the question of jurisdiction confined to a dispute over the respective competences of the two powers. The conflict between the king and Archbishop Jacob Erlandsen started as a disagreement between the archbishop and the inhabitants of his diocese, in which the archbishop demanded new legal procedures and more severe punishments for violence, murder, and homicide, whereas the people resisted any change in the law, demanding a return to the old law of the late twelfth century. There was also a conflict over appointments to clerical offices, as in Norway. The most important difference, however, was the feudal aspect of the conflict, which concerned the position of the archbishop as one of the king's main vassals with extensive secular power within his diocese, above all in connection with the *leding*. The king complained that the archbishop did not perform his duties in this regard, while the archbishop demanded greater independence than the king was willing to allow him. To complicate matters, the struggle between the two tended to merge with the other conflicts at the time, whereas in Norway, the secular aristocracy was the main enemy of the Church, as is well illustrated by the aggressive policy of the regency government.

The connection to other conflicts was particularly strong under Jens Grand, who was related to some of the magnates convicted of the murder of Erik Klipping. The conflict between the archbishop and the king was brought before the pope, who, after a long process (the acts of which have been preserved), decided in favor of the king and moved Jens Grand to Riga in 1302. According to the acts, Jens refused to believe that those accused of King Erik's murder were guilty. He is also alleged to have said that it was a pity that Erik was not murdered earlier, as that would have prevented him from having offspring, and further that he would rather have the devil himself than the present Erik on the throne. Admittedly, the archbishop's lawyer denied that Jens had said this, but he did not present any information to the effect that Jens was of a different opinion. It would therefore seem that there was a close connection between this conflict pitting the king against the archbishop and the struggles following on the murder of Erik Klipping. The series of conflicts resulted in a victory for the king, which turned out to be final; after Esger Juul, no archbishop again challenged a king. One reason for this was that the Church was never united behind the archbishop; usually, the majority of the bishops supported the king. Rather than opposing the king as representatives of the universal Church, late-medieval bishops became part of the aristocracy and individually participated in the various alliances and confederations for or against the king.

The Swedish Church had received tax privileges and independent jurisdiction in the early thirteenth century, but there is little indication that these privileges were respected in the following period. The real breakthrough came in 1276, after King Magnus Birgersson (1275–1290) had received aid from the Church to replace his brother on the throne. The Church was now exempted from all taxes on the property that it possessed at the time and had as well the right to receive legal fines from its tenants. However, the regency for Magnus' son Birger, led by the magnate Tyrgils Knutsson, reversed this policy, thus sparking conflict between the two powers. The conflict ended in 1305, when King Birger had reached majority and his relationship to his brothers had deteriorated. King Birger seems, at least initially, to have returned to his father's policy, whereas his brothers continued that of Tyrgils Knutsson, but the lines of division are not consistent, nor was the Church united during the struggles. Whereas the archbishop supported the king, the bishops of Linköping and Skara—the two richest sees in the country—were on the side of the dukes. After 1319, the Church seems to have improved its position, both during the regency and after King Magnus reached majority. Thus, we find the same tendency as in Norway towards rivalry between the Church and the lay aristocracy, while the king might use the Church to counterbalance the latter, which was stronger in Sweden than in Norway. The relative wealth and power of the two churches is more difficult to assess. Ecclesiastical organization was slow to develop in Sweden but had reached an advanced stage around 1300, and the Swedish Church played an important political role during the later Middle Ages.

Thus, open conflicts between the Church and the monarchy most often ended in victory for the latter, although this victory did not greatly reduce the power and wealth of the Church. Throughout the Middle Ages, the Church remained a parallel institution to the monarchy, with large estates, its own bureaucracy, the right to tax the population, and independent jurisdiction in a variety of cases. In so far as we are dealing with a zero-sum game, the Church had a substantial share of the profit. On the other hand, we are also dealing with interests common to both, and there was opportunity for the king to profit from the services of the prelates, employing them in his administration and using ecclesiastical offices to reward his servants. It was also an advantage for the king to deal with two aristocracies rather than one, for if the Church had not existed, he would probably have faced a stronger and wealthier secular aristocracy.

An influential school of thought in Scandinavian historiography sees the conflict between monarchy and aristocracy as the main issue in the political history of the region from the thirteenth to the sixteenth century. The inner struggles in Denmark and Sweden in the late thirteenth and early fourteenth century mark the beginning of this conflict. Unfortunately for the peace of the country, both King Valdemar II (d. 1241) and King Erik Klipping (d. 1286) of Denmark and King Magnus Birgersson of Sweden (d. 1290) left more than one son, which in all three cases led to rivalry and internecine struggles. Valdemar II of Denmark left three sons at his death in 1241, the eldest of whom, Erik IV Plovpenning ("Plow money", named after a tax he imposed on the people), became king, whereas the two younger received *len*. Armed conflicts broke out between them almost immediately and continued after Erik died in 1250, probably murdered by his brother Abel. When Abel was killed on an expedition against the Frisians in 1252, his younger brother Christoffer became king, despite the fact that Abel had a son. This led to a rivalry over the throne that lasted for several generations, with Abel's descendants, in their capacity as dukes of Southern Jutland, sometimes opposing the ruling kings. One of them even became king for a short time (1326–1330) as Valdemar III. However, Christoffer's descendants held on to the throne; his widow Margrete Sambiria managed to secure the succession for her son Erik V Klipping, who was a minor at the time, and after his murder in 1286 the throne passed on to his son Erik VI Menved, also a minor. In addition to other problems, Erik during most of his reign had to fight his younger brother Christoffer, who succeeded him as Christoffer II in 1320.

There is evidence of specifically aristocratic interests arising during these conflicts, notably under Erik Klipping. His mother Margrete Sambiria led an authoritarian royalist government, which continued unchanged after Erik reached majority. In 1282, however, Erik had to issue a charter promising to rule in the interests of the aristocracy on a number of specific points, and in the following years, until the king was murdered in 1286, members of the aristocracy played an important part in the government. The murder resulted in a return once again to a more royalist government. The leading men of the previous regime were accused of the murder and exiled, and the dowager Queen Agnes took control together with some her favorites, for a time including Duke Valdemar of Southern Jutland, Abel's grandson. The government continued strongly royalist during most of Erik VI Menved's reign, but changed after his death. In 1320, his successor Christoffer II had to issue the first real election charter with precise restrictions on royal power, including the provision that the monarchy was to be elective, not hereditary. In the following dynastic rivalries, the aristocracy was undoubtedly the driving force; Valdemar III, the king who replaced Christoffer II in 1326, was only eleven years old. The following changes, Christoffer replacing Valdemar in 1330 and the interregnum after Christoffer's death in 1332, were staged by the king's German mortgagees, who now controlled most of the country.

In Sweden, the struggle between King Birger and his brothers has also been understood as a conflict between monarchy and aristocracy, with Birger allied with the Church and his brothers with the lay aristocracy. In practice, however, it is difficult to find such a consistent pattern; both the Church and the lay aristocracy were divided. Only when Birger murdered his brothers did the aristocracy unite against him; hardly a single member supported him in the spring of 1318; only some foreigners, mostly German mercenaries, remained on his side. In the previous period, the dukes may have had greater aristocratic support than did their brother, because of their personal popularity, possibly combined with greater generosity because of their weaker legal claim, but the universal desertion of Birger must have been determined by moral outrage. The conflict ended in the victory of the dukes' aristocratic adherents who declared Sweden an elective monarchy in 1319 and took over the regency for the infant King Magnus Eriksson until 1331.

Were these essentially conflicts between monarchy and aristocracy, or was the issue the rivalry between the king and his younger brothers? The fact that the aristocracy strengthened its position as the result of the struggles might immediately seem to point in the former direction, but it is actually of little importance. Individually or collectively, the aristocracy may well have profited from the inner struggles without being the cause of them.

The two alternative explanations may to some extent be tested by the example of Norway, which avoided internal conflicts in the period, except for a conflict with the Church in the 1280s. At his death in 1263, King Håkon IV Håkonsson left only one son, who succeeded him, Magnus VI the Lawmender (1263–80). Magnus was succeeded by two sons, both under age, Eirik (born 1268) and Håkon (born 1270). From 1284 to 1299 Håkon ruled one third of the country as duke, but then succeeded Eirik on the throne, which prevented any further division. The relationship between the two brothers seems to have been good, possibly because Eirik suffered ill health from an early age after a fall from his horse and was therefore not in a position to resist his more energetic brother. Håkon's succession led to some replacements in the king's inner circle, including even the execution of one of his brother's main counselors, but it occasioned no internal unrest. The lack of inner conflict in Norway might possibly be explained by the weakness of the Norwegian aristocracy. However, weakness had not prevented the same aristocracy from backing various pretenders in a series of struggles over the course of a hundred years. It would therefore seem more likely that the presence or absence of internal struggles was determined by the number of pretenders to the throne rather than by an opposition between monarchy and aristocracy. As a matter of fact, all the conflicts, with the exception of the one in Denmark in the 1320s, took place in situations of dynastic conflict, as when younger brothers of the king wanted to increase their wealth and power.

Moreover, although there later were struggles over the throne, this is the last period when younger sons posed a problem. Although the impression from the later Middle Ages is that an absence of heirs to the throne was then a greater problem than a surplus of them, several kings in the following period had younger brothers, but no problems resulted from this fact. It would therefore seem that the internal struggles of this period represent the last phase in the consolidation of dynasties, whereas those in the following period represent either aristocratic or national opposition against particular forms of royal government.

Here, however, there is a difference between Norway and Denmark on the one hand and Sweden on the other. The two former seem to have created relatively stable monarchies, Norway by the middle of the thirteenth century and Denmark after the crisis of the 1330s, whereas Sweden experienced a series of rebellions and struggles over the throne in the fourteenth and fifteenth century and was without a king during most of the period from 1470 to 1523. It is tempting to seek the explanation of this in the country's late consolidation. This might in turn have been the result of its geography, which presented greater obstacles to centralization than was the case in the two other countries. It took around three hundred years for Norway and Denmark to develop a relatively stable monarchy. As Sweden did not really begin the process until around 1250, it is perhaps not surprising that it was not finished until the first half of the sixteenth century.

There is of course no doubt that the king had to share his power with the aristocracy in medieval Scandinavia, and that this weakened his position when compared to that of the strong bureaucratic monarchies of the Early Modern Period. The king had no standing army so that his ability to fight a war depended on the support of the aristocracy, and in Norway also on the peasants; and in all three countries, kings mostly depended on members of the aristocracy for civilian government. However, the king did not face a united aristocracy, and the number of castles and their *len* was considerably less than the number of aristocrats competing for them. As a result, although the king's freedom to govern the kingdom directly was limited, he could create some maneuvering room by playing the aristocrats off against one another. The aristocracy was strongest in Sweden. There several kings were deposed during the later Middle Ages and the country was even without a king for a considerable time. The Danish aristocracy was able to appropriate a large part of the royal revenues during the troubled decade from 1241 to 1340, thus weakening that kingdom. In the long run, however, the monarchy and the aristocracy of the country were able to work together. Denmark was also by far the wealthiest of the Scandinavian countries, which explains its dominating position during the following centuries. In contrast to Denmark and Sweden, the king of Norway's reliance on the aristocracy was rather the result of the strength of the monarchy, which made it less necessary for him to recruit men from lower layers of society as a counterweight to the aristocracy. Members of the Norwegian aristocracy who were recruited to the central administration identified their interests with those of the king. Norway had the strongest monarchy of the Scandinavian kingdoms in the sense that the aristocracy depended more on the king than in the two other countries. The thirteenth-century Laws of Succession, defining kingship as hereditary, are clear evidence of this. The strength of the monarchy is also expressed in the lack of aristocratic opposition to the Norwegian king and in the late development of a council of the realm, which continued to be weaker in the later Middle Ages than the councils of the neighboring countries. Nor was there any independent aristocratic judiciary with landowners settling cases between their peasants, as existed in many other European countries. Only the Church competed with the monarchy in this field. Thus, despite its relative poverty, the Norwegian monarchy had the advantage of strength and internal unity.

Despite the fact that the secular and ecclesiastical aristocracy controlled most of the resources of the three countries, the king could exploit the competition between them to achieve greater power than the modest resources under his direct control would indicate. However, we should hardly imagine that the king's position was based solely on the individual aristocrat's fear of losing in the competition with his equals. More fundamentally, the medieval aristocrats' attitude to the king is symptomatic of the general problem of social order. Even a military aristocracy has some need of social stability. Recognition of the legitimacy of the dynasty and of orderly succession, as well as the ban against killing the king, constitute evidence of the aristocracy's acknowledgment that the king was necessary to societal order, an attitude that was probably shared by the general population. The monarch was a neutral or relatively neutral umpire between competing aristocrats and had a sacred status that distinguished him from all other members of society. At the same time, he had a personal relationship with the leading aristocrats, which made it easier for him to gain their loyalty. As we know little about the personalities of most medieval kings, it is difficult to measure the importance of this factor. Scholars therefore tend to regard conflicts between kings and noble as expressions of friction between monarchy and aristocracy, whereas in many cases they may equally well be explained by personal antagonism between the king and one or another individual aristocrat.

It may of course be debated to what extent the notion of loyalty to the king was internalized within the aristocracy and the population in general. Even if we emphasize interests rather than norms, however, there remain arguments for obeying a legitimate authority. The difference between norms and interests is that the former are usually easy to discern, while the latter are not. Once the dynasties had been established, there was rarely doubt about who was the lawful king, but it would often be difficult to know which course of action towards this ruler would be the more profitable. If someone risked losing his property, his position in society, and perhaps even his life should the king continue to rule, rebellion might be the only option, but such persons would normally form a minority. Close adherents and those who were likely to gain from their royal connections, would of course remain obedient, but the vast majority was unlikely to see any obvious advantage in either course of action. They might cheat or disobey when confident that they would not be detected, but would hardly undertake active resistance. Moreover, in addition to the uncertainty regarding the more profitable action for any individual, there is the problem that successful resistance would depend on the support of others, whose intentions might be difficult to ascertain. Consequently, even from a rational-choice point of view, there is much to be said in favor of loyalty towards legitimate authorities.

The end of regicide signals a major social change, the introduction of an authority above the contending parties which embodies the idea of an ordered society. This idea did not protect the king from opposition or even—in special cases—from deposition, but it did give him special status that made it more difficult to oppose him or to remove him than other members of society. The exalted picture of the king in sources like *The King's Mirror* may seem an exaggeration to us and might to some extent have been so even in the thirteenth century, but it nevertheless expresses an essential element in the understanding of kingship at the time. The king was the guarantee of the borders of the country, which were defined as a "king"dom, and he was the guarantor of the rule of law and public justice. Thus, contemporary ideology gave him considerably greater power than his modest resources would indicate, while at the same time making him subject to some amount of control. This was in a way like squaring a circle; there was no definite answer to how to deal with the king's abuse of his authority, but eventually the idea emerged of *lawful* opposition, and, in the worst case, *lawful* deposition. This idea was eventually stated explicitly in the election charters.

The State and the People: Nationalism and Loyalty

As in the rest of Europe, the Church was the main source of explicit ideology in Scandinavia in the Middle Ages, and the evidence of its output is overwhelming. Its precise effect on the people is more difficult to ascertain. Less is known about similar attempts by the monarchy. Recent debates about nationalism have focused on the question of whether this is a specifically modern phenomenon, only to be found in the period after the French Revolution, or whether it goes back to, or at least was anticipated in earlier periods, including the Middle Ages. The answer is largely a matter of definition, but there is at least some evidence of patriotic sentiments in the Middle Ages, in Scandinavia as elsewhere. Despite his strongly religious attitude, even Theodoricus Monachus, writing around 1180, gives voice to some patriotic pride at the exploits of his Viking ancestors who raided all over Europe. Saxo similarly opens his work by pointing to national pride as the main motive for writing history. As all other nations boast of their great deeds and take pleasure in remembering their ancestors, so too the Danish archbishop Absalon, always intent on the glory of his fatherland, could not bear the thought of its being cheated of such fame and remembrance. He therefore commissioned Saxo himself with the task of preserving Denmark's heroic legacy. And Saxo did not confine his accolades to his preface; his entire narrative is filled with heroes; the Danes are a great nation and their enemies (Norwegians, Germans, and others) far inferior in virtue and military skill, only able to defeat Danes by means of treachery and deceit. In Sweden, where the writing of history began late, the early-fourteenth-century *Chronicle of Erik* expresses similar ideas. The prologue, praising God and his creation, soon turns to Sweden:

> There can be found good men
> chivalry and good heroes
> who held their own against Didrik of Bern.

Didrik of Bern is the Gothic king Theodoric (493-526) who in medieval legend was transformed into one of the greatest and bravest knights of all Europe. The Swedes eventually developed a particular relationship with him by identifying themselves with the ancient Goths, allegedly the most ancient people on the earth. The connection is to be found already in a history of Gotland written in the thirteenth century, in which the Goths are said to have emigrated from this island. Later, the myth was further developed in Ericus Olai's (Erik Olofsson's) *Chronica regni Gothorum* of the 1470s or 80s. Swedish representatives at the Council of Basel (1431–1449) used the Gothic origins of the Swedes as an argument for claiming precedence, although unsuccessfully. The *Chronicle of Erik* continues with numerous examples of the Swedes' heroism and great deeds. During an expedition in Karelia against the Russians, they defeat an army ten times the size of their own. When their leader, Matts Kettilmundsson—later the leader of the rebellion against King Birger—challenges the Russians to single combat, no one dares to take up the challenge, even though Matts spends the whole day waiting.

Such examples are not necessarily evidence of a strong attachment to the established kingdom; all of these sources deal as well with internal struggles and often celebrate heroes from both camps. However, we at least see here the king and the central government urging their subjects to defend the country and the common welfare against external enemies. During the war against the Swedish dukes (1308–1309), King Håkon V in a letter expresses his gratitude to the people of Trøndelag for their brave defense of their territory, adding that they will be rewarded for their efforts. Having given instructions for the coming expedition against the enemy, the king ends by expecting that they will defend "the country and their own peace and freedom."

We cannot draw any conclusions from these statements about nationalist sentiments within the ordinary population; only that the king occasionally found it necessary to appeal to such sentiments. We are on a somewhat firmer ground when it comes to the upper classes. Although there are many examples of shifting loyalties within the elites, such as Danish outlaws who fought their own king and raided their home country, there was a sufficient amount of interest within the elites in the continued existence of independent kingdoms.

Nationalism in its nineteenth- and twentieth-century shape is often associated with poets and freedom fighters willing to die for their country, but wealthy businessmen, landowners, and bureaucrats who find their interests best served by an independent state are equally prone to nationalist sentiments, and their influence is probably greater. Nationalism is not only the willingness of idealists to sacrifice everything for an imagined community, but also an expression of the fact that every organized government relies on a number of people who are interested in its continued existence. An example of this is the promise made by his councilors to King Håkon V on his deathbed in May 1319, shortly before Norway entered its first union with Sweden, not to give foreigners military commands or administrative positions in Norway. The king may have believed that native-born men would make better rulers over his subjects than foreigners, but the initiative is more likely to have come from the Norwegian aristocracy, which certainly wanted to reserve such positions for its own members. Both the people and the aristocracy repeatedly articulated these demands in the following period of unions with Sweden and Denmark, thus illustrating the concrete interest they attached to the existence of an independent Norwegian kingdom.

The stakes in independent states were certainly less obvious in the Middle Ages than in the nineteenth and twentieth centuries, but they did exist. Snorri repeatedly points to the difficulties kings experienced in establishing themselves in another country, which clearly derived from their lack of networks. There was a national elite in each country that resented attempts by foreigners to gain influence, whose own position was limited to that particular country, and who could expect prominent and advantageous positions in the royal government. A standard condition in election charters during the union period was that such positions should be reserved for a country's own inhabitants. Moreover, while in the Viking Age raids in foreign countries and even permanent settlement there had contributed to wealth, in the High Middle Ages wealth was increasingly based on landownership. Loss of territory or increased foreign influence might threaten landowners' interests. These considerations apply not only to the lay aristocracy but also to the Church. Although the Church was a universal organization, it was in practice largely local and territorial, having its main income from land, which, at least in Scandinavia, was mostly located within one particular country. The churchmen had the same interests as lay aristocrats in protecting their property and, in addition, needed organized government and peaceful conditions to carry out their work. Their long-term interests therefore largely coincided with those of the king, although there might be periods of conflict between the two. As we have seen, ecclesiastical ideology saw the king, who held his power from God, as a territorial king, whose power was confined to this particular territory and who had to respect the rights of his counterparts in other territories.

CHAPTER FOUR

Royal, Aristocratic, and Ecclesiastical Culture

THE SOCIAL AND INSTITUTIONAL CHANGE discussed in the previous chapters has a parallel in the cultural field, for art, architecture and literature are the products of institutions and social classes: in this case of the Scandinavian monarchy, Church, and aristocracy. The art and literature they created add to our understanding of their values and concerns. These sources also shed light on the question of change vs. continuity over time and help to untangle the threads of culture that derive from local traditions vs. European impulses.

The relationship between Scandinavia and the rest of Europe has been the subject of particularly intense discussion in the cultural field. All three kingdoms had a national-romantic movement in the nineteenth century that attempted to identify what was original to Scandinavian culture in contrast to imports from elsewhere in Europe. The work of N.F.S. Grundtvig (1783–1872) in Denmark and E. G. Geijer (1783–1847) in Sweden are prominent examples of this movement. It was particularly strong in Norway and Iceland, both of which regained or tried to regain their independence in the nineteenth century. These countries also—particularly Iceland—had the richest national tradition in the form of vernacular literature. The founders of Norwegian historical writing, R. Keyser (1803–1864) and P. A. Munch (1810–1863) strongly defended the specifically Norwegian character of Old Norse literature against Danish and Swedish attempts to present it as pan-Scandinavian. Later, the Icelanders in their turn claimed that it was specifically Icelandic, in opposition to Norwegian claims. Nowadays, the issue is less emotional and there is even a strong impulse in the direction of explaining Scandinavian culture as mainly the result of European influences, but the debate still goes on.

Viewed from a wider perspective, this debate appears as part of a broader controversy about unity versus diversity within Western Christendom as a whole in the Middle Ages. On the one hand, the Catholic Church was a centralizing element, boasting a tight, hierarchical organization and a learned elite with its special language, Latin, and promoting a universal ideology, based on a set of canonical texts. On the other hand, the number of local languages and dialects was an obstacle to communication and hence to centralization, as was a manuscript culture that allowed wide distribution to only a limited number of texts. In addition, the enormous legacy of the medieval Church may give an exaggerated picture of its dominance. It was the main patron of architecture and of the visual arts and the main producer of texts, but the latter in particular may have had limited impact in a culture where most people were illiterate. Thus, there are reasons other than nationalistic ideology to examine the relationship between Scandinavian and European traditions. The following discussion will deal mainly with four themes: religious versus secular literature, the social importance of Christianity, the writing of history, and the formation of a courtly culture from the mid-thirteenth century onwards. Historical writing forms one of the most important literary genres and also constitutes an intellectual crossroads where indigenous and external impulses meet, whereas Scandinavian religious and courtly literature are the most prominent examples of European influence. Finally, all four topics raise the question of the connection between cultural development and the social change discussed in the previous chapters. To what extent do we find cultural and literary expressions of the social changes discussed above? And to what extent were such expressions actively used to promote the interests of the monarchy, the Church, and the aristocracy?

Scandinavians and European Learning

The Church was the main institution of learning in Scandinavia as in the rest of Europe, and the main transmitter of European impulses, in the form not only of religious texts but also of classical literature, scientific knowledge, and Roman and canon law. It is not easy to know what and how much of this learning was imported to Scandinavia during the Middle Ages or how widely it was known there. Most of the original texts have been lost or survive only in fragments, whereas some others can be traced indirectly, through library catalogues. Most libraries were small. Bishop Arne of Bergen (1305–1314) had a private library of thirty-six volumes, which was a goodly collection for the day. The largest library in Scandinavia belonged to the Vadstena monastery in the fifteenth century. Around five hundred medieval manuscripts and some incunabula have been preserved from it, but much more must have been lost. Probably because of its size, this library was also, in contrast to most others, arranged like a modern library in which the books have shelfmarks and are placed on the shelves in a particular order. According to extant lists of books, larger cathedral libraries seem to have contained around a hundred volumes. This was fewer than the collections in similar institutions abroad, which, however, were also small by our standards. The cathedral library of Canterbury had 1,300 volumes around 1300, while the private libraries of some bishops and leading intellectuals in the thirteenth century contained around a hundred volumes. Considering the poverty and the small population of the country, Iceland's libraries were remarkably large. The diocesan library in Holar contained 332 volumes in 1525 and even local churches could have more than a hundred volumes. These libraries evidently contained the books necessary for teaching, liturgy, and administration, as well as the Bible, liturgical books, theological treatises, and canon-law texts, but classical authors were represented as well. Bishop Kurt Rogge of Strängnäs (d. 1501) had works by Cicero, by Greek authors such as Demosthenes, Polybius, and Procopius in Latin translation, and by Italian humanists like Boccaccio and Petrarch. A 1519 inventory of books belonging to the cathedral library of Slesvig lists Persius, Juvenal, Martial, and Lucan, plus Latin translations of Herodotus and Plutarch. In contrast to most ecclesiastical libraries, Vadstena had a number of vernacular texts. Bishop Arne of Bergen owned several sagas in Old Norse in addition to Latin texts. Some translations of classical works into Old Norse have also been preserved, such as the *Saga of the Romans,* based on Sallust's and Lucan's works on the Late Republican civil wars, the *Saga of the Trojans,* and works on geography and nature.

A potentially valuable source on literature and reading habits in medieval Scandinavia are the fragments of medieval manuscripts used for binding cadasters and administrative records in the post-Reformation period. A large part of these have been collected and registered, but they are only now being studied for the information they can convey about books and learning. Most come from liturgical manuscripts, but there are also fragments of theological, philosophical, and classical texts. Future research on this material may give us a more complete view of the knowledge available to the clerical elites of the Scandinavian countries. So far, the impression is that although pan-European clerical elite

culture was represented in Scandinavia, the region was nevertheless at a certain distance from the main centers of learning.

The Church introduced writing for literary purposes to Scandinavia; the runic alphabet, which goes back to the beginning
of the Christian era, seems mainly to have been used for shorter
messages and inscriptions. The earliest literature is also religious.
It begins with hagiography. In 1086, the Danish King Knud was
killed in the cathedral of Odense during a popular rebellion
against his attempt to mobilize an army to conquer England. A
short account of the event was composed shortly afterwards, followed by a legend, the *Passio sancti Canuti regis et martiris* (The
Passion of St. Knud, King and Martyr, c. 1095) and the more
ambitious *Gesta Swenomagni regis et filiorum eius et passio glorio-
sissimi Canuti regis et martyris* (The Deeds of King Sven the
Great and his Sons and the Passion of the Glorious Knud, King
and Martyr) by the English monk or cleric Aelnoth. Both conform to common European hagiographic models. Knud is shown
to have possessed the four cardinal virtues—wisdom, justice,
moderation, and courage—even in childhood. After his father's
death, he is passed over in favor of his brother and has to go into
exile, as did Joseph in the Bible as the result of his brothers' in-
trigues. When he returns to Denmark to become king after his
brother's death, he rules as the perfect *rex iustus,* in the mold
of David. Finally, when persecuted and killed by his rebellious
people, he throws away his arms and accepts death meekly, like
Christ himself.

The legend of the Norwegian national saint, Olav Haraldsson
(*Passio Olavi*) was composed in the second half of the twelfth
century and (at least the life), probably by Archbishop Eystein
himself. It presents a similar picture of its protagonist. The story
opens dramatically with a description of the frozen landscape
of the north, where the devil holds sway, and then shows warm
winds coming from the south, represented by Olav, to melt the

ice, a picture of the northern countries that is also found in the hagiography of Knud. Like Knud, Olav is a model of sanctity— his Viking past and acts of violence are discreetly overlooked. Although he is killed in battle, he does not die fighting; rather, he throws away his arms and, like Knud, accepts death meekly, as a martyr. A similar legend about St. Erik in Sweden (d. 1160) is later, probably from the second half of the thirteenth century. A Norwegian collection of sermons, the earliest vernacular text from that country, has been preserved in a manuscript dated around 1200, as has a similar collection from Iceland. In both cases, there are indications that at least some of the sermons, and probably also the collections, are older, of the first half of the twelfth century. The first—and almost the only—flourishing of Latin literature in Norway also took place during Eystein's tenure as archbishop, and most probably under his influence. Eystein is usually credited with the foundation of the cathedral of Nidaros in its present form. The new cathedral was far larger than the old one and is influenced by English Gothic architecture.

Already in the late eleventh century, Pope Gregory in his letter to the king of Norway (above, p. 5) suggested that some young men of good birth be sent to Rome to receive an education that would enable them to teach their compatriots Christian doctrine. We do not know what came of this, but in the twelfth century, we meet Scandinavians in Paris, notably at St. Victor, the Augustinian house known for its learning. Many of the contemporary bishops recruited from the aristocracy had such an education. However, there were considerable differences within Scandinavia when it came to contacts with learned European culture. Denmark, the closest of the three to European centers of learning, was the first to have an indigenous Latin literature. Norway and Iceland followed, beginning in the mid-twelfth century, while Sweden lagged behind. This changed around 1300, and for the rest of the Middle Ages, Denmark and Sweden were better integrated into European intellectual culture than Norway and Iceland. In the early thirteenth century, the Danish Archbishop Anders Sunesen (1201–1221, d. 1228) wrote the Biblical poem *Hexaemeron* (The Six Days), which deals with the creation of the world, the fall, and salvation. Inspired by twelfth-century French theology, the work applies the method of "four levels of meaning" to the Biblical text, uncovering the literal or direct meaning; the allegorical meaning, which reveals the religious significance of the story; the moral or tropological meaning, showing the story's significance for the life and behavior of the faithful; and finally the anagogical or eschatological meaning, which points to the end of the world and the coming reign of Christ.

Whereas Anders is an example of a Scandinavian churchman bringing home learning from Paris and other European centers, there were other Scandinavians who themselves made an impact in these centers. The most prominent of them is Boethius (Bo) of Dacia, one of the preeminent philosophers at the University of Paris towards the end of the thirteenth century. He seems to have spent most of his life in Paris and never to have returned to Denmark. He was a follower of Aristotle, but in a more radical way than the most famous of the thirteenth-century Aristotelians, Thomas Aquinas (1225–1274). Boethius taught at the Faculty of Arts (*artes*), the lower faculty at medieval universities, where all students had to begin before they could move on to one of the three higher faculties of law, medicine, or theology. Ten of his works have been preserved, but much has been lost; his total literary production seems to have amounted to at least three thousand pages. As was usual at the time, most of his works take the form of *quaestiones,* disputations for and against a particular proposition. A few take the form of *sophisms,* a more complex kind of inquiry, necessitating subdivisions into more specific propositions. Finally, Boethius wrote treatises "On the Highest Good," "On the Eternity of the World," and "On Dreams." As a philosopher, Boethius addresses one of the most burning questions at the time, the relationship between faith and knowledge. In his view, nothing in the world is necessary; everything could have been different or might not have existed at all. On the other hand, we can study nature and establish laws that describe it. Theoretically, the consequence of this view is that all knowledge is gained exclusively by human intelligence, which contradicts Christian doctrine. Of course, Boethius did not draw this consequence, but accepted the dogmas of the Church. Nevertheless, he came dangerously close to the idea of a "double truth." He claimed that it was possible to state that there was no first man, meaning that human beings and the world have always existed, as long as this statement was understood as referring to what could be established by biological methods. Theology, on the other hand, taught that there was an actual first man. This and other opinions were condemned by Étienne Tempier, bishop of Paris, in 1277, a condemnation that was most probably explicitly directed at Boethius. Boethius does not seem to have taught in Paris after 1277, and he ended his life as a Dominican.

Another Dane, Martinus de Dacia, taught in Paris in the 1270s and even became a canon at Notre Dame. Several of his works survive, of which the best known is *Modi Significandi* (Modes of Meaning), a theory of language that became very popular during the following centuries. From the point of view of philosophy, Martinus is nevertheless less important than Boethius. On the other hand, he went on to a career in Denmark after his time in Paris. In 1290, King Erik Menved tried to have him appointed bishop of Roskilde—besides the archdiocese, the richest see in Denmark—but this was prevented by Archbishop Jens Grand. Six years later, Martinus got his revenge. He became the king's attorney in the process at the papal curia against the archbishop, which led to the latter's deposition in 1302 (above pp. 159–60). Martinus died in Paris in 1304. Of other Danes in Paris, we might mention Nicholaus de Dacia, who was elected rector of the University of Paris in 1344.

There are no comparable figures from the other countries before the early fourteenth century, but we have evidence of Scandinavians studying in Bologna in the late thirteenth century: altogether nineteen Danes, eleven Swedes, and six Norwegians during the years between 1285 and 1300. Characteristically, some of these were laymen who later made a career in the king's service. Nor is it a coincidence that they went to Bologna, the leading center for the study of law. For those who wanted to make a career in the royal or ecclesiastical administration, studying law was usually the best choice, and Scandinavian sources from the second half of the thirteenth century onwards give plenty of evidence of the knowledge of law, canon as well as Roman. Revisions of the laws during this period created a need for men with a legal education and the laws themselves make it quite clear that such men were available.

A Swedish intellectual of about this same period was Petrus de Dacia (1235–1289), a Dominican (Dacia refers to the Scandinavian province of the order, not to the country of Denmark). Petrus studied in Paris and Cologne and may possibly have had Thomas Aquinas as his teacher. However, he is less known as a theologian than for his close friendship with the German mystic Catharina of Stommeln, whom he visited several times, corresponded with, and whose biography he wrote, including the correspondence between them, in which he also gives information about himself. His aim in this was probably to have her canonized. Catharina was a mystic who had several visions and drastic experiences of God and the devil, including stigmatization, ecstasy, and various kinds of torture attributed to the devil. As she was illiterate, her letters were written by her parish priest or by some literate person in her circle. Master Mathias (d. 1357) was one of the most learned theologians in Scandinavia and wrote a number of works. He was also St. Birgitta's confessor.

Danes and Swedes were far more numerous at the European universities than Norwegians. In the later Middle Ages, 2,146 Danes, 821 Swedes and Finns, and 219 Norwegians are known from the matricula to have studied at German universities. In the fourteenth century, there were three Swedish and two Danish houses for students in Paris. Eventually, towards the end of the Middle Ages, universities were also founded in both countries, in Uppsala in 1477 and in Copenhagen in 1479.

Conforming to this picture, the vernacular literature of Norway and Iceland includes a large number of religious works: saints' lives, sermons, some doctrinal works, and translations of parts of the Bible, but few examples of more advanced theology. The most ambitious theological work is probably a translation of Genesis and the first part of Exodus, commissioned by King Håkon V of Norway (1299–1319), which includes extensive theological commentaries by authors like Petrus Comestor (c. 1100–1187) and Vincent of Beauvais (c. 1200–1264), both of whom taught in Paris. *The King's Mirror,* composed in Norway in the mid-thirteenth century, probably in court circles, includes various kinds of knowledge derived in part from European sources, in part from the author's own experience Its main aim is ethical. The author begins his teaching with the biblical quotation, "the beginning of wisdom is the fear of God," and continues by directing admonitions at people in various ranks of society on how to conduct their lives.

The *Mirror* is clearly based on European learning, but it is plainly an effort to transmit this learning to a Norwegian audience, even largely to a lay audience. This is evident both from the fact that it is written in the vernacular and from its style, which aims to be lively and entertaining rather than terse and precise in the manner of a scholastic treatise. The author rarely mentions his sources specifically, but they seem to have consisted mainly of the best-known writers of the time, such as the great early-medieval authorities Isidore of Seville (560–636) and Bede of Jarrow (672/73–735). Of more recent authors, he can be shown to have used Petrus Comestor.

The author's description of the world and geography largely reproduces what was common knowledge to the learned elite of the day. The earth is a globe, but all the inhabited land is situated on the top, so that the Mediterranean world, with Jerusalem as its center is where we place the North Pole, whereas the northern regions are down the slope, near our equator. The author's geographical descriptions focus on three countries—Ireland, Iceland, and Greenland, probably chosen in part because they were of special interest to his audience, in part to show the contrasts that exist in the natural world. While Ireland is the best country in the world, Iceland and Greenland are the worst, Iceland even furnishing evidence of the existence of hell, the source from which the island's volcanoes and hot springs get their heat. Whereas the descriptions of Ireland seem to be based on literary sources and mostly consist of legends and curious stories, those of Iceland and Greenland are vivid and precise and demonstrate considerable familiarity with the countries and their natural conditions, knowledge most probably derived from the oral testimony of people who had visited them. Although there are few details in the author's description of nature and geography that point to advanced learning obtained from the leading intellectual centers of the day, the author's general attitude indicates that he is more than a compiler. He shows intellectual curiosity and makes energetic attempts to find answers to difficult questions, such as the explanation for the northern lights. Most impressive of all is the comprehensive philosophy he derives from his knowledge of nature, which rests on a parallel between nature and society and advises using God's government of nature as a model for the king's government of society. Man can learn about God's ways by contemplating His creation of the world, which in turn can furnish a model for how society should be governed. The social hierarchy is the expression of God's will, and the author's message to the king as well as to people on various levels of society is that they should behave in accordance with the status God has given them.

In addition to *The King's Mirror,* there are a number of writings in Old Norse about nature and cosmology, mostly translations and adaptations of Latin sources. The *Mirror* is an example of the practical use of European learning in Scandinavia, as a foundation for reforms in legislation and jurisdiction and for both the king's exercise of power and the obedience his subjects owe him.

The moderate influence of advanced theology in Norway and Iceland has as its corollary the fact that pre-Christian culture was to a relatively large degree preserved in these countries. *The Older Edda,* which survives in an Icelandic manuscript of around 1275 but is clearly based on an older original, contains poems about pagan gods and heroes, at least some of which are considered to have been transmitted orally from the pagan period. *The Younger Edda,* composed by the Icelandic chieftain Snorri Sturluson (1179–1241), deals extensively with pagan mythology, referring a number of stories about the ancient gods, allegedly as an aid to skaldic poets or for interpreting this poetry. Thus, there seems to have been considerable interest in the pagan religion, as well as knowledge about it in Iceland and probably also in Norway as late as the thirteenth century. We of course do not know how reliable these thirteenth-century accounts are. Although the extant texts are Icelandic or preserved in Icelandic manuscripts, the Norwegian king and court were an important audience for the poetry as well as the storytelling. This survival of ancient mythology should not be understood as a revival of pagan religion or as imperfect Christianization; there is nothing to indicate that

Snorri and his audience believed in the pagan religion. It should rather be compared to the uses made of classical mythology in contemporary Europe, as an aesthetic resource and a mark of learning. Moreover, in the introduction to his *Edda,* Snorri also sees in ancient mythology marks of "natural religion" that reflect man's faltering knowledge of God before the Christian revelation.

The preservation of mythology, then, does not indicate a reaction against Christian learning, but derives instead from pride in national culture and traditions and a will to preserve them. This is also expressed in the widespread use of the vernacular as a literary language in Iceland and Norway in contrast to Denmark and Sweden, where most writing was in Latin until the fourteenth and fifteenth centuries. Admittedly, this is less original than is often believed; there was an increasing use of the vernacular from the twelfth and particularly in the thirteenth century in most countries of Western Europe, probably as the result of increased literacy among the laity.

In Iceland, however, the vernacular was not only used for most literary purposes, but became in itself an object of study. This was highly unusual. There was a considerable interest in language and grammar in learned circles of medieval Europe, but the object of such studies was normally Latin. The reason for this was partly practical, as Latin always had to be learnt as a foreign language, but it was also in part a consequence of the prestige of this language and of a tradition of grammatical studies going back to Antiquity. The Icelanders, however, made a point of studying their own language theoretically. In *The First Grammatical Treatise,* which dates from the twelfth century and deals mainly with phonetics and orthography, the author states that languages are phonetically different and should therefore have their own alphabets, capable of rendering correctly their specific sounds. He adds a number of examples of sounds that are specific to the Icelandic language and thus require letters not available in the Latin alphabet. The author is familiar with the main grammatical works in Latin but adds a number of original observations that have impressed modern scholars. In *The Third Grammatical Treatise*, which also covers stylistics and poetry, the author, Oláfr Hvitas-kald (1216–1259), a nephew of Snorri Sturluson, claims that skaldic poetry is essentially similar to that of Ancient Greece:

> From this book one can learn better that it is the same art, the poetry that the learned Romans learnt from the Greeks in Athens and then translated into Latin and the meter and poetry that Odin and the men of Asia brought northwards to the northern half of the world. And men learnt this art in their own language, as they had made and learnt it in Asia, where there was most of beauty and wealth and wisdom in the world.

The Rules and the Hearts: Scandinavian Christianity

To what extent did Christianity really penetrate Scandinavian society at levels below the clerical elite? The opinion that the Scandinavians did not really become Christian has been fairly widespread, particularly in the older literature. This view is probably kin to the romantic notion of an original, Germanic culture with its heartland in Scandinavia, which to some extent was able to resist the ecstatic, superstitious, and "unhealthy" aspects of European Catholicism: its belief in miracles, its extreme asceticism and rejection of sexuality and the body, and its unquestioning acceptance of ecclesiastical authority. Romanticism was here reinforced by Protestantism, for it was in the nature of Protestantism that it would approve a "healthy" resistance to the more questionable aspects of Catholicism without offering outright defense of paganism.

We have little evidence of how much ordinary people knew about Christian doctrine, to what extent they obeyed the rules

Figure 16. The Virgin Mary, woodcarving from Nystad (Uusikaupunki) Church (Finland), early fifteenth century, now in the National Museum, Finland. As often in this period, the Virgin is depicted as the woman in the Revelation: "And there appeared a great wonder in the heaven; a woman clothed with the sun, and the moon under her feet, and upon her head a crown of twelve stars … and she brought forth a man child, who was to rule all nations …." (Rev. 12:1–5). Photo: Markku Haverinen. Copyright © Nasjonalmuseet i Finland.

of the Church, or how much Christianity influenced their daily lives. There was certainly a distance between the ideal and reality, but on the other hand, a population devoted 100 percent to the Christian religion in keeping with the ideals of *either* Catholicism or Protestantism is unlikely to have existed anywhere. If we acknowledge that delving into the inner soul of medieval man is beyond the historian's craft and look at the external evidence alone, there can hardly be any doubt of the profound influence of the Catholic Church on Scandinavian society. And this holds true if we regard Catholicism in the strictly religious sense of that word as well as in its broadly cultural meaning. During the eleventh and particularly the twelfth century, a network of churches joined the occasional rune stones and crosses from the period of the conversion, thus enabling the entire population to attend Christian services regularly. The ecclesiastical organization was well developed, and, with the exception of Iceland in the Free State period (until 1262), the Scandinavian Church was at least as wealthy relative to the wealth of the countries as the Church in the rest of Europe. As it received its property through donations from the laity, it is difficult to imagine that such wealth would have been achieved without the laity believing in its message. Further, despite the various criticisms that can be directed against the ignorance and laziness of medieval priests, the strong ecclesiastical organization must have been a powerful instrument in establishing Christianity as the dominant cult and doctrine. A large devotional literature in the vernacular has been preserved from Norway and particularly from Iceland, and from the later Middle Ages also from Denmark and Sweden.

From the point of view of the common people, the most important cultural imports were ecclesiastical art and architecture. The ornamental art characteristic of the Viking Age (as represented by the Jelling stone) continued to be used in churches in the following centuries, notably in Norwegian stave churches, but it was eventually replaced by European models. Most church buildings in Scandinavia resemble local churches in Germany, France, or England, as do their decorations. The Norwegian stave churches, around twenty of which have been preserved, are a partial exception to this rule, although similar churches may have existed in other countries but been destroyed. Opinions differ as to their origins and development, with some viewing them as rooted in pre-Christian architecture, others as a translation of the Romanesque basilica into wood. Both Denmark and Sweden still have a large number of medieval churches, whereas there are fewer in Norway, probably because the majority of Norwegian churches were built of wood and thus more likely to perish. The churches were decorated with altarpieces, statues, and wall paintings that transmitted the Christian message to the mostly illiterate parishioners.

Thus, there is hardly reason to doubt the general importance of Christianity in Scandinavian society in the Middle Ages. Its exact character in the various countries and regions, however, is another and more complicated matter. As in the rest of Europe, most of our source material regarding religion originates in the elite classes, so that considerable caution and ingenuity must be exercised to draw from it information about the common people. Sermons, which have been preserved from all the Nordic countries, give some impression of typical preaching. Extant Scandinavian sermons belong to both of the two main phases of medieval preaching, the early one, based on the tradition of the Church Fathers, and the later, introduced by the mendicants in the thirteenth century. The early tradition employed two main types of addresses, the *homilia*, exegesis of a biblical text, and the *sermo*, which was a freer exposition of a particular theme. The two tended to merge in the Middle Ages. Allegorical interpretation was frequently used in both types. The novelties introduced by the mendicants were the more extensive and systematic use of *exempla*, i.e., concrete stories intended to capture the interest of the audience and underline the preacher's religious and moral message; and an infusion of scholasticism, which led preachers to attempt rather elaborate compositions and to try to convince their audience with logical arguments. The Norwegian and Icelandic *books of homilies*, both probably dating from the twelfth century, belong entirely to the early phase, containing sermons that are largely adaptations of writings by late antique and early-medieval authors: Gregory the Great, Caesarius of Arles, Bede, and several Carolingian authors. Most extant Danish and Swedish sermons belong to the second phase, dating from the fourteenth century onwards. A considerable number of them stem from Vadstena. So far it is mostly the Danish examples that have been subject to examination by modern scholars. They make extensive use of exempla, but, with the exception of some sermons clearly intended for a learned audience, show no influence of scholasticism.

The general impression made by Scandinavian sermons is that they are not very different from sermons in the rest of Europe. On the positive side, this conclusion confirms the impression that Scandinavia was well integrated into Western Christendom, and suggests, further, that written sermons give a fair representation of actual preaching. On the negative side, the sermons were hardly the products of great and original minds. Their lack of originality makes it difficult to decide whether references in sermon texts to the particular sins or habits of the audience or an emphasis on particular aspects of doctrine or ethical teaching are the preacher's reaction to specifically Scandinavian realities. Often, what appears to be inspired by conditions particular to Scandinavia turns out to be directly derived from foreign sources. But then again, it is possible that quotations or allusions from foreign sermons were chosen by the preacher because they applied very specifically to his audience. The problem for modern scholars is to distinguish between these two possibilities.

As to their contents, the sermons have in common a practical orientation, urging their audience to seek salvation by believing in the doctrines of the Church, performing good deeds, and avoiding sin. In accordance with the broader pattern in medieval Christianity, a certain change of emphasis can be traced from the collective to the individual. The early sermons are mainly addressed to a collective audience, while the later ones seem mainly concerned with the individual, emphasizing the relationship between God and the individual soul, and positioning the Church as an institution rather than a community of the faithful. This change is expressed particularly clearly when it comes to eschatology. The Norwegian *Book of Homilies* mainly focuses on the Last Judgment and even contains two sermons devoted specifically to this theme. Danish sermons are almost exclusively concerned with the judgment of each soul immediately after death, in accordance with the general trend in the later Middle Ages towards a more individualized theology.

Earlier sermons are in a sober style, appealing to the intellect more than to the senses by presenting the doctrines of the Church and the alternatives facing the audience in this life and after death, though without elaborating on them. By contrast, later sermons are often strongly emotional, appealing to the senses with dramatic tales of sin and virtue, gloomy reflections on the great majority of mankind ending in hell, and a detailed preview of the sufferings of the damned. However, the greater emphasis on the individual does not lead to a corresponding emphasis on the subjective aspect of morality. Sin is normally understood in a very concrete sense as actions, and drastic punishments are meted out in hell for sins against the ritual commandments or the dogmas of the Church, without any reference to intent or circumstances.

Late medieval art gives a similar picture. A large number of wall paintings have been preserved from the fifteenth and early sixteenth century in Denmark and parts of Sweden, mainly in local churches, and in recent years they have been the subjects of extensive iconographic analysis. There are the standard Old and New Testament scenes from the history of salvation, but these paintings excel in horrific depictions of the devil's temptations and the punishments in hell, an emphasis that echoes sermon *exempla*. The popular character of these paintings may indicate that local peasants had some influence on the choice of themes and thus may give some indication of popular religion, although there is no firm evidence to support such a theory.

These changes in religious expression, observed in art as well as in preaching, have often been explained as expressions of a new mentality of fear and hysteria brought on by the Black Death. No doubt, the frequent outbreaks of this terrible disease must have occasioned fear. Nevertheless, the idea of the entire period being dominated by terror seems extreme, the result of modern scholars imagining their own reactions to such disasters. Medieval people had after all far more familiarity with disease and sudden death than do we. Moreover, most religious expressions of the brevity of life and the terrible punishments in hell pre-date the Black Death. A gradual change in the direction of more vivid and emotional representations of these ideas from the late thirteenth century onwards should probably be understood instead as in part a change in rhetorical expression from abstract symbols to the concrete representation of visual reality, and in part as an attempt by the Church to draw the laity into a more active participation with religious life. These two explanations probably overlap in their impact, and both seem largely to be a result of the new piety introduced by the mendicants.

Sources on the religion of the ordinary people are meager. When it comes to the nobility, more information is available, but it has not been explored extensively up to now. The numerous written sources from the later Middle Ages that originate with the nobility give the impression that the influence of the Church and religion was strong and pervasive. God is frequently referred to in correspondence, whatever the subject matter, in phrases like "by God's will," "if God allows," "may God protect you," and so forth. Such expressions are of course not evidence of personal piety, but they do give some indication of the atmosphere—in the same way as their absence in present-day society reflects its secular character. Extant testaments show nobles leaving enormous sums to the Church, a generosity not always appreciated by society. Relatives clearly had interests that ran counter to the interests of the Church, and we know that they often contested what they considered excessive donations, sometimes successfully.

On the other hand, the value that the aristocracy placed on honor, revenge, and secular display must have been difficult to reconcile with Christian ethics (even if any apparent tension would have been somewhat eased by the fact that prelates and secular aristocrats often held the same values and acted in similar ways). Ecclesiastical criticism of aristocratic values was expressed in sermons and religious art attacking an obsession with the pleasures of this world and pointing to the narrow path that leads to salvation. We are badly informed about how this ethical conflict was experienced or possibly resolved by individual nobles or by the class as a whole. However, it is not simply a question of ideals versus practice. When failing to adhere to Christian norms, the medieval aristocrat often acted in accordance with a specifically aristocratic ethics and set of values. Thus, the noble had to maneuver between various ethical codes. Only on his deathbed would he fully embrace Christian values. With this in mind, one might regard great generosity to the Church as payment for persisting in a specifically aristocratic ethics and lifestyle. The issue may have been less troubling for women, who seem generally to have been more pious than men. This may also have been the case in Scandinavia, but our information is limited.

Generosity to the Church should not of course be regarded solely as an expression of piety, for it could also amount to a display of the ostentation that was so essential a part of the lifestyle of the nobility. Funerals and death anniversaries were celebrated with particular pomp and circumstance. The rite of leading the horse of the deceased into the church at his funeral is an especially impressive example. The horse was guided to his master's coffin in the church, thus symbolically following him to his grave, and offered as a sacrifice to the church. The heirs subsequently redeemed the horse for a large sum of money. Despite all the aristocratic ostentation, the displays—of pride, and care for the pleasures and wealth of this world, noble funerals nonetheless served to unite the ideals of the two estates of society, for they created an occasion for showing off piety as well.

Popular response to the message of the Church can mainly be traced indirectly. Miracles, pilgrimages, and the cult of the saints show ordinary people's attachment to the Church and Christianity, although some sources indicate that magic of a more or less pagan character was also practiced. Both Christian and magic rituals provide us with clear evidence of people turning to the supernatural to seek help in disease and various other life difficulties. They tell less about the search for God and salvation in the life to come. However, the imbalance is largely due to the character of the source material. Our major source, the extant miracle collections, are intended to prove the sanctity of particular persons by showing that they had performed "real" miracles, contrary to the normal workings of nature. Mere conversions or spiritual experiences were too ambiguous to be accepted as evidence, and, perhaps for this reason, were not recorded.

In his great book on medieval sainthood, André Vauchez distinguishes between "hot" and "cold" regions, according to their ability to produce saints. Scandinavia as a whole must be considered relatively "cold." Most of the saints venerated in the region during the Middle Ages were the common saints of Western Christendom as they appear in the Roman calendar. However, some local saints emerged from early on, and a few of them were even venerated outside Scandinavia. Most of these Scandinavian saints belong to Vauchez's northern type; i.e., they are people holding high office, who are mainly venerated for their miracles after death. Their official lives are usually impersonal and stereotypical, as well as fairly brief, while the main focus is on their miracles. The royal saints are typical examples of this. Whereas the popularity of the Swedish St. Erik and the Danish St. Knud seems to have been limited, St. Olav in Norway had great popular appeal, inside and outside the country, and a large number of pilgrims sought his shrine, particularly on his holiday on 29 July. By contrast, the southern type is a charismatic figure, whose reputation for sanctity is largely based on a remarkable life—St. Francis is the best-known example. The preeminent Scandinavian exemplar of this brand of sainthood is St. Birgitta of Vadstena in Sweden.

A Scandinavian Saint

Birgitta was born in 1303 as the daughter of the *lagman* Birger Persson, a member of the highest Swedish aristocracy, while her mother, Ingeborg, was related to the royal house. At the age of fourteen, she was married to Ulf Gudmarsson, also a member of the top aristocracy. The marriage was happy; Birgitta bore eight children and lived as a mistress of a great aristocratic household. However, a pilgrimage to Santiago de Compostela in 1341—a tradition in Birgitta's family—became a turning point. The couple decided to live apart and devote themselves to religion. Ulf joined the Cistercian monastery of Alvastra, where he died shortly

Figure 17. St. Birgitta, sculpture in Vadstena Church (Sweden), c. 1390. There are several portraits of Birgitta, but this is considered to be the most authentic. Dept. of Special Collections, University of Bergen Library. Unknown photographer.

afterwards, in 1344, while Birgitta spent her time in prayer and contemplation in a house nearby. Birgitta had grown up in a pious family and been very religious throughout her life. She had her first revelation, of Christ's suffering, at the age of ten. Nevertheless, the separation from her husband and his death marked a radical change, as expressed in an episode told by her biographer, Peter Olovsson. Shortly before his death, Ulf had given her a ring, asking her to think of the salvation of his soul. A few days after his death, Birgitta took it off. When those around her pointed out that this did not indicate much love for her husband, Birgitta answered:

> When I buried my husband, I buried all carnal love, and although I loved him of all my heart, I would not wish to buy him back … against God's will.… And therefore, that my soul shall lift itself to love God alone, I will forget the ring and my husband and leave myself to God alone.

After her decision to devote herself completely to religion, the revelations became frequent and directed her life. In 1345, she was told to found a new order and given detailed instructions for its organization, but the ecclesiastical authorities stopped her. In autumn 1349—the year of the plague in Scandinavia—she left for Rome to celebrate the Holy Year 1350 and never returned. Now, her great project was to make the pope return from Avignon to Rome, but she was also working for the foundation of her order, which was finally accepted by Pope Urban VI in 1370, although the first monastery was not established until after her death, in 1384. Birgitta also intervened in Swedish politics and supported the opposition against Magnus Eriksson that led to his deposition in 1364. In 1372 she went on a pilgrimage to the Holy Land, where she became ill. She died in 1373, shortly after her return to Rome. She was canonized in 1391.

Birgitta had altogether more than seven hundred revelations, which were written down in four large volumes filling fourteen hundred pages, the *Revelationes celestes* (Heavenly Revelations). Birgitta either wrote them down herself and had them translated into Latin or told them to her confessor who wrote them down. In one of the revelations, she was ordered by the Virgin Mary to learn Latin, and, according to several witnesses who testified during her canonization process, she became quite fluent in the language, although she did not feel sufficiently confident to write her revelations in Latin herself. The revelations have a strongly sensual and visual character, with dramatic descriptions of the suffering of Christ and the saints, the pain of sinners in hell, and the ugliness and horrible stench arising from the devil and the sinners, all this very much in accord with the emotional and concrete character of contemporary art and sermons. On one point, Birgitta even directly inspired artistic representation. During her last pilgrimage, to the Holy Land, Birgitta had a vision of Christ's birth. She saw him lying on the earth while his mother worshipped him. This became a common motif in pictures of the Nativity in the following period. The revelations also testify to Birgitta's knowledge of doctrine and even law—expressed in descriptions of God's judgment of humankind—and include detailed and precise rules for her order. Despite her total break with her former life, Birgitta could draw upon her experience as the head of a large aristocratic household.

Claiming that one has received revelations from Christ and the Virgin Mary might easily have aroused suspicion in the fourteenth century, when the inquisition was in full swing and eager to persecute heretics of all kinds. And the danger was likely heightened when the revelations, like Birgitta's, were often critical of ecclesiastical as well as secular authorities, as for instance in the following outburst against the pope:

He is more disgusting than the Jewish usurers, a greater traitor than Judas, crueler than Pilate. He has devoured the lambs and strangled the shepherds. For all his crimes, Jesus has thrown him as a heavy stone into the abyss, and he has sentenced him to be devoured by the same fire that once devoured Sodom.

Birgitta was nevertheless accepted, and we can only suppose that her personality as well as her status must have been important factors. She was used to moving in high circles, and she had an excellent relationship to the higher clergy in Sweden, which may have helped her to acquire a similar network in Rome. Her advisers included the learned Nils Hermansson, bishop of Linköping, one of the wealthiest and most important dioceses in Sweden, and her confessor, Master Matthias, a leading theologian. Her later confessors, after Matthias's death, Peter Olovsson of Alvastra and Peter Olovsson of Skänninge, were also learned theologians. Thus, Birgitta had access to the best theological minds of her age, and her writings show that she made good use of them, keeping firmly within doctrinal orthodoxy. A widespread feeling of crisis in the Church might also have helped her, for she became part of a broad movement to reform the Church and bring the pope back to Rome.

Institutionally, the most lasting result of Birgitta's activities was the Birgittine Order, officially named the *Ordo Sancti Salvatoris* (the Holy Savior's Order), whose detailed rules were expressed in some of her revelations. Each monastery housed both monks and nuns, although strictly separated, under the leadership of an abbess. The original foundation, Vadstena in Sweden, became an important religious and cultural center with, among other treasures, the largest library preserved from medieval Scandinavia.

Thus, Birgitta was clearly what Vauchez would term a "hot" saint, one of the hottest in the fourteenth century. Of course, people of Birgitta's ilk are exceptional in any society, but, as we

Figure 18. Interior of the Vadstena Church (Sweden). The Church, consecrated in 1430, is built in the late Gothic style and, like most contemporary Scandinavian churches, shows German influence. Unknown photographer. Middelaldernett.

have seen, in Scandinavia she was more different from a "normal" saint than she would have been for instance in Italy or the Low Countries. On the other hand, the support she got from her circle in Sweden shows that there was a place for her kind of sainthood, at least in the higher reaches of society. The royal court and the aristocracy lived in a world filled with religion, which frequent masses, pilgrimages, and other kinds of devotion, and in close contact with the higher clergy. Thus, one of Birgitta's main supporters, Bishop Nils of Linköping, had in his youth been a teacher in her home. Although Birgitta's intense devotion was an exception, she grew up in so strongly religious an atmosphere that she could scarcely have avoided familiarity with Christian cult and doctrine, and was fortunate to find, in the country where she spent her formative years, an audience receptive to her revelations.

Nevertheless, Birgitta probably appealed more to the elite than to the common people. A study of sainthood in the later Middle Ages (by A. Fröjmark) indicates that the ecclesiastical elite was very influential in the promotion of the cult of the saints in this period as well. This was not only the result of the introduction of a papal monopoly on canonization, necessitating a long and costly process that had to be initiated and paid by the ecclesiastical elite. Examples from the miracle collections show that the ecclesiastical authorities were also operative in the process, often leading the people in the direction of particular saints whom they personally wanted to promote. The people were essential, too, in order to achieve canonization, because a saint needed a reputation for sanctity as well as a number of well-attested miracles. In the case of Birgitta, there is clear evidence of a popular cult. This extended to some people in her entourage, her daughter Katarina and Bishop Nils Hermanson of Linköping, who reached the lower rank of beatification.

While there can hardly be any doubt that the Church succeeded in introducing its doctrine and rituals in Scandinavia in the Middle Ages, there is less evidence of the newer trends towards a more personal religion, which in the later Middle Ages were expressed for instance in the *devotio moderna*. This may be due to the nature of the sources; after all, the external aspects of religion are more likely to leave traces than the interior workings of the soul, and the new, Lutheran Church was not interested in preserving Catholic devotional literature. We should also be wary of the "Protestant" tendency to assume that external piety signals the absence of interior devotions. Nevertheless, the extant sermons, as far as they have been analyzed, the number and types of saints, as well as the religious art seem to point mainly in the "traditional" direction. So does also the fact that there was little heresy in Scandinavia. Rather than forming evidence of the Scandinavians' faithful adherence to the Catholic Church, this absence seems to indicate that personal religion was weaker, that religious customs and rituals were well integrated into daily life, but that few people were personally moved by the message of the Gospel.

If we turn to the heresy that eventually did find favor in Scandinavia and in a short time abolished the Catholic Church, namely the Protestant Reformation, we may notice a significant difference between Denmark and Sweden on the one hand and Norway and Iceland on the other. The former countries had a real Reformation movement and even, to some extent, a Counter-Reformation, while in Norway, and to a lesser extent Iceland, the Reformation was introduced from above, with little preparation. Consequently, the new stirrings that were disturbing the calm of the pre-Reformation Church are more likely to be detected in the former countries than in the latter. This impression is also confirmed by the fact that the mendicants were stronger in Sweden and particularly Denmark than in Norway. In addition to the Franciscans and the Dominicans, the Carmelites came on the scene in the fifteenth century, founded a number of houses, and engaged in the reform of the Church.

The Writing of History

Historical writing was the most important literary genre in medieval Scandinavia and was common to the ecclesiastical and secular traditions. It had two main aims: (1) to trace the origin of the people and record the deeds of the ancestors; and (2) to deal with the relationship between this national past and the universal history of salvation. Given its political importance, it comes as no surprise that the dynasty plays an important part in historical writings. Saxo Grammaticus (c. 1150–1220) traces the Danish dynasty back to a founder by the name of Dan, a native of the country, who is supposed to have had twenty successors before the birth Christ. As some of these reigns were very long, the date of the foundation of the Danish kingdom corresponds approximately to that of the foundation of Rome (753 BC). According to Saxo, the Danes have no connection to any other people. He thus rejects Dudo of St. Quentin's suggestion that the Danes are descended from the ancient Greeks; i.e., the Danai, and he omits every reference to the Roman Empire until the age of Charlemagne, emphasizing that the Danes had no part in it. Consequently, the contemporary Roman Empire, bordering Denmark to the south, has no claim on suzerainty. Saxo was not the first to write about the ancient history of his country; both the Chronicle of Lejre, probably from around 1170, and the slightly later work of Sven Aggesen contain such information, but Saxo's work is by far the most extensive. His sources were to some extent ancient poetry and oral narrative—he explicitly mentions the Icelanders—but he clearly arranged the materials drawn from them very freely and probably even invented parts of his narrative. His extensive reading of Roman writers may have been a source of inspiration, as may also Geoffrey of Monmouth's slightly earlier account of early English history, a very popular work at the time.

In his history of the kings of Norway (*Heimskringla*), the Icelander Snorri Stuluson traces the origins of the dynasty back to the pagan god Odin, who is depicted as a human being worshipped as a god after his death. Odin is the prince of the city of Åsgård in Inner Asia and a contemporary of the Roman conquerors. Having prophetic power, he understands that the future of his descendants does not lie in the world of the Romans, so he moves to the North to conquer this area. Rather than a descent from the Classical peoples, Snorri here imagines a kind of division of power between the peoples of the North and the Romans. The link between Odin's empire and the Norwegian kingdom is formed by a genealogy of Odin's descendants, ending with Harald Finehair, the ancestor of the contemporary rulers of Norway. The source for this genealogy is an extant poem, *Ynglingatal,* probably composed in the Viking Age and preserved as quotations in Snorri's text. This genealogy was used for the first time in historical writings in the anonymous *Historia Norwegie,* composed in Norway in the second half of the twelfth century. The entire prehistoric genealogy comprises twenty-eight generations. This means that Odin must have lived around the time of the birth of Christ, and thus have been a contemporary of Augustus. Whereas Saxo shows a connection between the rulers and the people from the beginning, Snorri has nothing to say about the origins of the people and only lets the dynasty arrive in the country at a late stage. As we have seen, Saxo as well as Snorri regard the Christianization as a crucial event. Both tried to show that it had its origins in local attempts to find the Highest God, and both point to the importance of indigenous kings in converting their people.

Iceland was a new country when Ari the Wise (d. 1148) wrote its history in the early twelfth century. The first settler had arrived less than two hundred years earlier, in 870. There was thus no question of any relationship to the Romans. However, Ari tries to show a relationship to universal history in another way, by reconstructing an exact chronology for the history of his country, based on the reigns of the Norwegian kings, which in turn is based on some crucial events in universal history, such as the martyrdom of the English King Edmund in 870. Ari's style is terse and dry, with no attempt at vividness and drama, quite unlike Snorri's style and that of his other Icelandic successors, but he takes the same attitude to the conversion of his country as his successors dealing with the conversion of Norway. The conversion means that the Icelanders accept the truth of Christian revelation and reject their ancient religion. However, the way this happened shows their pragmatism. Seeing that the religious division would make life unbearable, the pagan Thorgeir prudently decides in favor of Christianity (above, p. 63). A later source, the *Landnámabók* (the Book of Settlement) forms a kind of genealogy of the whole people, listing the settlers establishing themselves in various parts of the island and their descendants.

One of the earliest histories of Norway, Theodoricus Monachus's *Historia de antiquitate regum Norwagiensium,* composed around 1180 and dedicated to Archbishop Eystein, takes a different attitude to the pre-Christian history from that of Saxo and Snorri, but indirectly confronts the same problem. Theodoricus refuses to deal with the history before Harald Finehair, because he finds no reliable evidence for it, but nevertheless expresses pride at his ancestors' plundering expeditions over large parts of Christendom. The conversion is the crucial event in his history; the reigns of the two Olavs who carried it out fill around one third of its pages. However, instead of linking Norway's past to universal history by tracing it back to the Romans or the birth of Christ, he achieves the same result by a series of digressions, which create typological parallels between Norwegian history and the history of salvation. Thus, there is a parallel between the death of the pagan ruler Earl Håkon in Norway and the Roman emperor Julian the Apostate (d. 363), who were both succeeded by Christian rulers. Similarly, when Earl Håkon's grandson, also called Håkon, is killed in a maelstrom, the maelstrom forms a parallel to the pagan hordes streaming out of Hungary and killing Ursula and the 11,000 virgins at Cologne, which in turns signifies St.

Olav's martyrdom. The author, whose Norwegian name was probably Tore (ON Þórir) has been identified with either of two contemporary bishops, the bishop of Hamar (1188/89–1196) and one of Eystein's successors as archbishop (1205–1214), both of whom were canons of St. Victor in Paris. The Victorine influence on the work is also striking; numerous references to Latin authors correspond very well with works known to have belonged to the library of St. Victor. Theodoricus himself clearly belonged to the contemporary international intellectual elite. Not only does he show considerable learning, but he also tries to adapt to contemporary scholarly standards by focusing on the reigns rather than the biographies of the kings, by trying to confine himself to trustworthy information, and, above all, by integrating the history of Norway into the international history of salvation through his typological parallels.

The Latin historiography of Scandinavia forms part of the common European tradition, whereas its earlier vernacular historiography, the Icelandic and Norwegian sagas, differs from this tradition in several respects. However, the term "saga" which has become conventional even in English is likely to exaggerate this difference. Admittedly, the term in itself does not exclusively refer to historiography. Literally, it means "what is said," and may thus refer to any story, written or oral, long or short. It is used in modern scholarship of the Icelandic family sagas as well as the kings' sagas, but includes also many fantastic stories about events in distant times or places, mostly composed in the later Middle Ages (*fornaldarsögur*). It is not clear whether contemporaries made a distinction between "historical" sagas, such as accounts of the kings, and fictional ones, but this raises essentially the same issues as attempts at distinguishing between "historical" and "literary" narrative in contemporary Europe.

Despite this common aim, the difference between the Latin and the vernacular tradition is not only a question of language, but also of expression, aesthetic ideals, and historical interpretation. Stylistically, the Latin tradition shows considerable variation (which is also to be found in the rest of Europe), ranging from Saxo's highly complex and rhetorical Silver Age Latin, modeled on Valerius Maximus, to the "simple style" found in other Latin works, such as that of Theodoricus. It is more difficult to find parallels to the saga style. The style of the gospels and some of the saints' lives, with their simple syntax and little rhetorical embroidery, may be a possible source of inspiration, but popular narrative is probably equally important or more so. However, we are not dealing with oral narrative directly transmitted to writing, as can be shown by tracing the gradual development of the saga style, notably the retreat of the author, from the earlier to the later sagas.

The main differences between Latin and Old Norse historical writings can be illustrated by a comparison between the ways in which the two greatest Scandinavian historians, Saxo and Snorri, treat the same story about of St. Olav punishing himself for inadvertently cutting slivers from a stick on a Sunday by burning the slivers in his hand. Snorri creates with words a setting for his story. He describes Olav's deep thoughts which make him forget what day it is and then lets a servant remind him with the words, "It is Monday tomorrow, Mylord." The king then asks for a candle and burns the slivers in his hand. Snorri ends with a brief remark about Olav's willingness to do what was right. Saxo sets no scene. There is no servant and no exchange of words, just enough of the story to give its moral point, which is then elaborated in considerably greater detail than in Snorri. Being convinced that punishment awaits sinners, Olav prefers to suffer temporarily on this earth rather than permanently in Hell. He also thought about the importance of setting a good example and refused to excuse his error on grounds of simple negligence. Finally, Saxo tells the story in his complicated rhetorical Latin, alluding both to the Roman hero Mucius Scaevola, who let his hand be burnt to demonstrate Roman virtue, and to the words in the Bible about cutting off a hand if it presents a temptation to sin.

Heimskringla's version represents classical saga narrative. It is objective, in the sense that the author remains neutral and abstains from comment; visual, in its vivid description of persons and events; and dramatic, in allowing the players to confront one another with brief, succinct, intensely meaningful sentences, delivered in a calm tone and often with understatement that heightens the drama. The sagas generally prefer direct address, in contrast to classical Latin prose, which prefers indirect speech. In this way, the actors in the drama are presented on the stage without interference from the author. The Latin tradition does the exact opposite. The author is constantly present, with comments and analysis, praise or blame, and in some cases offering allegorical or typological interpretations and parallels between the events narrated and the history of salvation.

Most important, the retreat of the author and the focus on dramatic narrative do not make the sagas more "popular" or less "learned" than contemporary Latin works. Most of the sagas have, in fact, a more precise chronology than Saxo's. Although Saxo makes comments on his sources in his prologue, Snorri's approach to this question is more sophisticated. In his discussion of skaldic poetry, he introduces the important principles of contemporaneity and the stability of tradition. The skalds performed their poems in the presence of the king and his men and, because of the meter, these poems are likely to have been transmitted unchanged from their original composition to the present. Although the skalds were not objective reporters—their profession was to praise their patrons—it is not likely that they would have attributed to these people deeds they had not performed, as that would have read as blame and not praise. Consequently, their substantive information should be accepted as truth, as opposed to their praise and embellishments. These conclusions are certainly open to debate, and, in practice, Snorri's attitude to his sources certainly differed radically from those of a modern historian. His observations are nevertheless remarkable set against their medieval background.

Nor does their focus on dramatic narrative mean that the sagas are only concerned with individual episodes; a closer reading often shows a very deliberate composition, aimed at creating a consistent plot. This is particularly characteristic of the *Sverris Saga* (c. 1220) and the *Heimskringla* (c. 1230), whereas some others, notably the earlier sagas, are more episodic. The best example of coherent composition is Snorri's saga of St. Olav, originally written as a separate work and later integrated into the *Heimskringla*. Here Snorri organizes his extensive material—the saga fills around 250 pages in modern editions and is derived from oral as well as written sources—in a coherent narrative that adheres to a strict chronology and provides a detailed account of Olav's movements. He then makes a structural distinction between Olav's first ten years, which were successful, and the last five, which were increasingly difficult, leading up to his exile and death in the battle of Stiklestad (1030) at his return. Particularly in this second division, Snorri manages to integrate the various episodes into a coherent plot, showing how Olav, largely through his own intransigence, fell out with one after the other of the Norwegian chieftains, until it became impossible for him to remain in the country. Here he maneuvers between hagiography and political history. Olav was Norway's national saint and thousands of pilgrims sought his shrine in the cathedral of Nidaros. How then could Snorri write about him as if he were just any ruler, with his good and bad sides, his successes and failures? He solves the problem by delivering most of the hagiography, in concentrated form, towards the end of Olav's life, after he has been exiled from Norway. Although Snorri is respectful of Olav throughout the saga, depicting him as a good Christian, this arrangement enables him to give a vivid account of Olav's conflicts, and one that does justice to the point of view of his adversaries as well to that of his devotees.

The composition of the sagas seems to depend on the relative importance of various elements. Particularly dramatic and important events get more space, and there is a tendency to link events together to explain success and failure. More abstract schemata, like the history of salvation or numerical symbolism, are less prominent, although there are some tendencies in this direction. By contrast, such schemata largely determine the composition of Saxo's work. It consists of sixteen books, seven dealing with the pagan period and seven with the Christian, while two cover the transition from paganism to Christianity. Thus, the history of salvation is strongly present. Further, Saxo's sixteen books can be divided into groups of four, which in various ways show parallels between the history of Denmark and that of Rome. Books I–IV cover the period from the beginning to just before the birth of Christ. In Book I, Dan rather than his brother Angul gives the country its name, in the same way as Rome was named after Romulus and not his brother Remus. Book V is entirely devoted to the reign of Frotho, the great king, conqueror, and legislator, whose long reign ends in a period of peace lasting thirty years. Frotho is thus both a contemporary and a parallel to Augustus. During this period, Christ was born. The next three books cover the period up to the reign of Charlemagne, when Christianity reached the border of Denmark, and here Saxo directly mentions the Roman Empire for the first time. In Book VIII, the Danish and the Carolingian empires are about to confront each other. Charlemagne prepares to engage in battle with the Danish King Gøtricus but is summoned to Rome at the last moment. The next four books cover the period of the establishment of the Church in Denmark, and the last four deal with the period after the foundation of the Church province in 1104. In the second half of the *Gesta Danorum,* Denmark's relations to the Roman Empire become an important theme. At the first stage, Christianization leads to subordination under a "Roman," i.e., "German" archdiocese (Hamburg-Bremen), while at the same time Denmark's imperial power is greatly extended with the conquest of England. The liberation from "Roman" dominance with the foundation of the Church province is dealt with at the end of Book XII. However, there is still a Roman threat in the following books, when Frederick Barbarossa claims feudal suzerainty over King Valdemar I, although Saxo tries to downplay this as much as possible. He ends his work with the crusades in the Baltic region under the joint leadership of the king and his own patron, Archbishop Absalon. In this way, Saxo creates a link between the history of Denmark and the history of salvation, while at the same time presenting Denmark as a northern parallel to the Roman Empire.

The emphasis on dynastic continuity and national independence in the historical writings corresponds to the importance of these phenomena in the actual history of the Scandinavian countries. Saxo and Snorri, as well as most other historians, insist on the ancient origins of their respective dynasties and, at least to some extent, on the antiquity of their nations. On this point, Saxo is more explicit than Snorri, as the link between dynasty and nation is ever-present in his work, whereas Snorri only brings the dynasty into Norway at a comparatively late stage. Whereas Saxo was closely connected to the contemporary rulers of Denmark, Snorri's relationship to their Norwegian counterparts is more difficult to determine. As an Icelandic chieftain during the period of independence, he seems to have had a somewhat ambivalent attitude to the Norwegian king. During a visit to Norway (1218–1220), he was commissioned by his friend, Earl Skule Bårdsson, then acting ruler of the country during King Håkon's minority, to convince the Icelanders to accept the king of Norway as their ruler. Apparently, he used his connection to Skule more to further his own interests in Iceland than those of his patron for he ended by being killed by King Håkon's Icelandic ally (1241).

Some scholars have therefore regarded Snorri as a kind of Icelandic freedom fighter and interpreted his work as anti-royal propaganda, whereas others have detected in him a more positive attitude towards the Norwegian monarchy. Based on the *Heimskringla,* which only covers the period until 1177, a year or two before Snorri's birth, it is very difficult to uncover a consistent attitude to the Norwegian monarchy and its relationship to Iceland. It is quite clear, however, that Snorri is not a spokesman for the theocratic ideology expressed in *The King's Mirror* and the official documents issued by the king and his council in the second half of the thirteenth century. Snorri's work reflects the competitive society of the previous period, when unpopular kings could be killed by the people and victory and defeat depended on personal charisma and political skill rather than legal claims and divine vocation. This is largely the case also in Saxo. When Knud is rejected in a royal election, Saxo almost has to excuse him for not taking up arms against his brother. Knud is above all a warrior hero, fighting for his own honor. The reason for the rebellion against him is not his piety but that his lazy and cowardly people were unwilling to risk their lives in an expedition against England. Although Saxo strongly condemns Knud's killers, his reason for this is that Knud deserved better, not that it is a crime to kill a king. Saxo's account of the internal conflicts in the mid-twelfth century resembles Snorri's of the contemporary struggles in Norway; neither of them is much concerned with ideas of lawful succession or with the ideal of the *rex iustus.*

The preeminent example of a royal biography based on the idea of the king holding his office from God and ruling according to the Christian principles of justice is the *Saga of Håkon Håkonsson,* composed in 1264–5, shortly after the king's death in 1263. This saga can to some extent be characterized by Beryl Smalley's term "civil service historiography," given its rather bureaucratic environment and greater focus on civil government. This saga is a goldmine of detailed information for later historians, but it is often considered dull in comparison with the earlier sagas, as it is largely without the dramatic confrontations in which they excel. Moreover, its protagonist, Håkon, comes across as a pale figure. He is depicted as a good Christian and a good ruler, but he is rarely shown in action or in relations with other people. The reason seems to rest in the greater prestige of the royal office in this period and the stronger influence of Christian *rex iustus* ideology. In contrast to his predecessors, Håkon does not compete with other prominent men, nor does he use charm or eloquence to attract adherents; he rules in virtue of belonging to the dynasty and because he is God's elected representative on earth. Håkon's election at the age of thirteen is described in great detail, and the author insists that it took place because he was the rightful heir to the throne. Håkon refuses to take up arms to secure the kingdom, trusting that God will grant to him what is rightfully his. Later in the saga, Håkon defends the royal office against encroachments from the Church, the unity of the kingdom against rebels, and the possessions of the king of Norway against other kings, as when he launches a great expedition against Scotland to defend Norwegian possessions in the west, the Hebrides, and the Isle of Man. The saga ends with Håkon's death, followed by a detailed account of his character and his achievements as a ruler. The latter include a number of civilian accomplishments normally neglected in the saga literature: building projects, revisions of the laws, and a Christianizing mission among the Sami.

The later Middle Ages saw a decline in historical writing in Denmark, Norway, and Iceland, but its apex in Sweden. Here a revival of historiography took the form of the rhymed chronicle. Whereas prose had earlier been the usual medium for historical and other narrative writing—even French verse romances were translated into Old Norse prose—most late-medieval Swedish chronicles were composed in verse, probably under the influence of German models. The first and, according to most scholars, from a literary point of view the best work in this genre is the *Erikskrönikan* (the chronicle of Erik), composed between 1322 and 1332, but a series of other such chronicles were composed from the 1430s onwards, eventually forming a continuous history of Sweden from around 1250 to the 1520s.

Having traced the history of Sweden back to Didrik of Bern (above, p. 170), the author moves to the mid-thirteenth century, narrating the history of Sweden until 1319/20. Around three quarters of the work deals with the reign of King Birger Magnusson (1290–1319), with the main emphasis on the conflict that began in 1304 between Birger and his two younger brothers, the dukes Erik and Valdemar. Erik, "gentle Duke Erik," is the main hero. He is the perfect knight—brave, courteous and generous, but also clever. Two dramatic events mark the climax of the narrative. The first is the "Håtuna game" in 1306, which saw the dukes taking their brother captive and forcing him to divide his kingdom with them. King Birger was celebrating Michaelmas at his manor Håtuna without his brothers. "The king did not invite them / although they would have liked to see him." The dukes prepare carefully, ordering their men to travel by different routes, so as not to arouse suspicion, before gathering together near Håtuna, while they themselves make the journey by sea. They catch Birger unawares and take him and the queen captive; only his son, aged six, escapes. King Birger is brought to Nyköping, where he is kept in captivity but given all he needs, both food and beer—this in contrast to what later happens to the dukes.

The second episode takes place in 1317. Immediately before, the chronicler has described one of the dukes' greatest successes, Erik's marriage to King Håkon of Norway's daughter Ingebjørg, and Valdemar's to his niece of the same name. The account makes much of the pomp and lavishness of the occasion. Then the scene shifts to Duke Valdemar's visit to King Birger, an event that in the chronicle appears to have happened immediately after the weddings, but actually took place five years later. The dukes are ignorant of what is going to happen, but the author foreshadows disaster, comparing Birger to Judas, with whom he sits in the deepest hole of hell. Then he builds up to a new climax: Birger's friendly reception of his brother, the queen's complaint that she never sees her brothers-in-law, and the formal invitation to celebrate Christmas with them in Nyköping. Valdemar returns with the invitation, Erik is skeptical but agrees to go. The dukes are warned on their way to Nyköping, but they press on. Birger receives them with great friendliness and hospitality; they eat and drink and celebrate the whole evening long until at last, late at night, the dukes go to bed. Birger is ready now to carry out his plan, but first, another scene is inserted: some of his men refuse to aid him and are thrown into prison. Birger thus has no excuse: he cannot claim that he has not been warned against committing such an outrageous act. Finally, Birger enters the dukes' bedroom with an armed entourage, wakes them and speaks the ominous words: *Minnes ider nakot aff Hatuna lek?* ("Do you remember anything of the Håtuna game?"), throws them into prison and has them starved to death. Having also taken the dukes' men captive, King Birger laughs and boasts, "Now I have Sweden in my hand." One of his knights replies, "It is my belief that you will lose everything." The man turns out to be right; the chronicler describes Birger's downfall and replacement by Duke Erik's son Magnus, aged three: *Wil Gud innan himmerike / han ma wel werda faders like* ("May God in heaven grant that he will resemble his father").

The aristocracy of the *Erikskrönikan* differs markedly from that of the sagas. While in the latter, the ruling class consists of popular leaders, its counterpart in the former has become an elite, whose ideology and values find expression in the chronicle: the focus now is on pomp, magnificence, and chivalry. This conforms to actual developments in contemporary Sweden. On the other hand, the chronicle has even less in common with the bureaucratic elements of the later sagas and thus represents a return to the classical saga. War and dramatic events are depicted directly and vividly, without much in the way of explanation or analysis. However, the author is more present than in the sagas, often commenting on good or bad acts, particularly towards the end of the work where he deplores the dukes' tragic fate and condemns Birger to hell. Moreover, the dukes are not only chivalrous heroes but also astute politicians; the author delights in their cleverness in hiding their movements so as to take Birger by complete surprise at Håtuna.

Although the rise and decline of historical literature is to some extent independent of historical reality, there seems to be some pattern in its timing in Scandinavia in the Middle Ages. The establishment of kingdoms was, it would seem, a stimulus to historical writing. There was clearly a need to trace the origins of one's own people after the conversion to Christianity, and to give an appropriate explanation of the latter. This motive is prominent both in Saxo and Snorri, as well as in other early works. It is also significant that Scandinavian historiography is for the most part heavily dynastic, this in accord with the importance of the dynasties in the development of the kingdoms. The longer works are normally organized according to the reigns of the kings. Such dynastic historiography was very important during the early consolidation of the dynasty, but became less so as a dynasty was more firmly established. Moreover, the particular style of the sagas (and to some extent also the style of Saxo), focusing on individual interests and competition in which the best man won, was more suited to the competitive society of the period before the mid-thirteenth century than to the ordered hierarchy of the following period. Finally, periods of conflict are more likely to stimulate historical writing than periods of peace. This may serve to explain the decline of historiography after the consolidation of the kingdoms, although there must have been enough conflict in Denmark in the period between 1241 and 1340 to stimulate more historical writing than the few, brief chronicles that have been preserved from this period.

Against this background, Sweden seems to be an exception. However, as the consolidation of the Swedish monarchy was late, the *Erikskrönikan* shows some similarity with early works in the other countries. The chronicle mainly deals with the dynasty descended from Earl Birger, who became the real ruler of Sweden around 1250 and whose descendants became kings after his death in 1266. In addition, of course, the dramatic events of the early fourteenth century were a great stimulus to historical writing. The chronicle is also the expression of the ideology of the rising aristocracy. This ideological aspect is equally prominent in the later Swedish chronicles, which are products of the troubled fifteenth century, when Sweden opposed the Kalmar Union, entered into in 1397 by the three Scandinavian kingdoms and dominated by Denmark. This is the clearest example in Scandinavia of historiography as propaganda.

Political Thought

The writing of history is a prime example of intellectual culture in the service of the monarchy in Scandinavia. In addition, the king, as we have seen above, made extensive use of educated people in his administration, who formulated the doctrine of the king as God's representative on earth, responsible for the welfare of the people, and embedded that doctrine in charters and other documents as well as in oral propaganda. From the late thirteenth century on, we also find explicit discussions of the relationship between the king and the "people," by which is meant in practice mainly the aristocracy. In the rest of Europe, there was an increasing volume of formal treatises discussing such questions, notably from the second half of the thirteenth century onwards, and traces of their influence are to be found in Scandinavia. We can distinguish three phases of this literature. The first includes the pamphlets from the Investiture Contest in the late eleventh and early twelfth century, discussing the relationship between the monarchy and the Church but also formulating some principles of royal government. The second phase begins with the revival of the genre of the "mirrors of princes," around the middle of the twelfth century, which detail the virtues proper to a king and give advice on good government. The genre persisted until the end of the Middle Ages, but it changed character under the influence of Aristotle, after his *Politics* was translated in the 1260s, a milestone that marks the beginning of the third phase. Royal government was now seen against the background of a theory of society, and the division of power between the king and the people became the subject of explicit debate: Should the king rule with independent power (*regimen regale*), or should he share power with the people (*regimen politicum*)? In practice, the difference between these doctrines was often expressed in the attitude taken to dynastic succession; that is, to the question of whether the king should inherit his throne or be elected by the people. The first work of this kind was Thomas Aquinas' *De regno*, written probably around 1270.

All three phases can be found in Scandinavia, but the volume of explicit theoretical literature is rather limited. The main example of the first phase is the Norwegian anti-clerical pamphlet *A Speech against the Bishops*. Written around 1200, during King Sverre's conflict with the Church, it uses the Church's own law,

Gratian's *Decretum,* to argue for the king's control of the Church as well as of society in general. The author shows familiarity with his source and considerable rhetorical skill, appealing directly to his audience to prove the obvious truth of his conclusions, with expressions such as, "Everyone to whom God has given a minimum of intelligence must understand ...". The main representative of the second phase is *The King's Mirror,* also Norwegian, which has been referred to several times already. Its third part resembles earlier and contemporary mirrors of princes in dealing with the king's virtues, notably with how he should exercise his power of judgment, which in the author's opinion is a king's main duty. This discussion is closely related to reforms in jurisdiction and legislation that took place at the time. However, the author also deals extensively with the king's power, in a way that foreshadows the later doctrine of *regimen regale.* He regards the monarchy as hereditary, strongly emphasizes the obedience that his subjects owe to the king, and insists that he can only be judged by God, not by men. Here, however, he gives no hint of any influence from Aristotle. His doctrine is derived instead from theology, notably from the Old Testament: the king's power is grounded in his relationship with God, not on a theory of society. Aristotelian influence is strongly present, however, in the anonymous Swedish tract, *On the Government of Kings and Princes.* This work contains quotations from Aristotle as well as a number of other authorities. Large parts of it are also based on Aegidius Romanus' *De regimine principum* of around 1280, a work deeply influenced by Aristotle, which develops his theory in a strongly monarchist vein. Aegidius argues in favor of hereditary monarchy, a doctrine that is taken over in the Swedish adaptation, despite the fact that Sweden had been officially declared an elective monarchy in 1319. *On the Government of Kings and Princes* probably has its origin in courtly circles and may have been intended for the education of the young Magnus Eriksson (1320s) or of his sons, Erik and Håkon (1340s). There are no formal treatises of a similar kind later, but royal government has an important place in Birgitta's revelations, which contain admonitions to King Magnus, and later, after he failed to heed her advice, support for Magnus's aristocratic opponents as well.

Judging from these theoretical works, one might think that *regimen regale* had strong support in Scandinavia in the thirteenth and early fourteenth century. This was the case in Norway, but hardly in the two other countries, where various attempts at limiting the king's power were made in this and the following period, notably in the election charters. Given the extensive contacts between Scandinavia and European centers of learning there is every reason to suspect that these documents were influenced by the contemporary reception of Aristotle's political thought, but as they mostly confine themselves to making detailed and specific demands of the king, this is difficult to prove. However, a 1281 Norwegian propaganda letter issued by the regency government for King Eirik and Duke Håkon during the conflict with the Church and addressed to all *sysselmann* gives a hint in this direction. The two rulers begin by thanking all good men who have been obedient and loyal to the monarchy during their own reign as well as those of their predecessors and express their confidence that this will continue. However, they have heard a rumor that they find difficult to believe. It seems that some clerics and even laymen want to deny them their due obedience and loyalty by failing to pay fines and contribute to the defense of the country. If this proves true, there will once more be petty kings in the country. The text then goes on:

> ... and we and the good men who act as our counselors find that if we will uphold the king's name and the honor of the crown, we will only let those people remain and live in the country who will act as our loyal subjects and obey our commands. And those who will

shrink from this, let them go where they need to belong to nobody but themselves, nor have any power, whatever kind of people they are.

The two rulers conclude by declaring that they will grant both clerics and laymen the same freedom as in the reigns of their predecessors, despite the unprecedented threats that now face them.

The letter is composed with considerable rhetorical skill. Thanking the subjects for their loyalty and obedience serves as an appeal for continued support as well as a contrast to the description of the clergy that follows, while the rulers' pretended disbelief underlines the enormity of the clerics' behavior and prepares for the final climax in which the clerics exclude themselves from human society. Furthermore, the regents allude to several important arguments that support the power and independence of the monarchy. The term "honor of the crown" had long played an important part in the defense of the monarchy and shows a clear awareness of its character as an institution. The greatest novelty, however, is the final line of the quote, about the disobedient clerics excluding themselves from society. This is an echo of the Aristotelian doctrine of man as a social animal, according to which human beings can only live a good life in a larger community. This doctrine was in in contemporary political thought used as a defense of organized society under the leadership of the king. Thus, the two rulers imply that the clerics, by their disobedience, act against nature, and that they therefore cannot live in society but have to go where there is no community, no ruler and no ruled, in other words, to the wilderness and anarchy.

The Courtly Culture

Although not prominent in historical writings, courtly and aristocratic culture is represented in the Scandinavian countries by translations of European chivalrous literature and in songs and poetry. The translations began in the 1220s at the Norwegian court, when one Brother Robert, probably an English monk, translated Chretien de Troyes's *Tristan et Iseu* into Old Norse. A series of other romances and heroic tales, including Marie de France's twelfth-century *Lais*, named *Strengleikar* in Old Norse, were translated in the following period, both at King Håkon Håkonsson's court in Norway and in Iceland. A later collection of chants from the early fourteenth century is associated with Håkon V's German Queen Eufemia (d. 1312). A series of ballads, performed by local singers in the countryside and written down in the nineteenth century, is usually considered to have originated in the Middle Ages. It seems paradoxical that this courtly culture is best known from Norway and seems to have developed first in this country, the least aristocratic of the three kingdoms. There are in the narrative sources occasional references to singers performing ballads on contemporary events, such as a German singer dealing with the murder of King Erik Klipping. There are also a large number of Danish ballads transcribed in the sixteenth century, which are usually believed to have a medieval origin. Thus, there do exist a variety of literary expressions of Scandinavia's aristocratic culture, although considerably less than for its religious counterpart.

Corresponding to the composition and import of romantic and chivalrous literature and the more elite character of the court and the aristocracy, there is evidence as well of new norms and patterns of behavior in courtly circles. The clearest example of this is *The King's Mirror*. In it, for example, we find the Father urging the Son to address the king and great men in the plural and himself in the singular, a custom that was introduced at this time. The use of different pronouns for addressing different categories of people—or at least the attempt to establish such a custom—clearly signals a heightened awareness of hierarchy. An

Figure 19. Wall painting of a hunting scene, Höjby Church (Zealand, Denmark), c. 1380–1400. National Museum, Denmark. The religious motive is sudden death, which may strike the young and healthy as well as the old and sick. Death, depicted as a naked man sitting on an ox, aims his bow at the elegantly dressed aristocratic hunter, riding a strong and beautiful horse and carrying a falcon on his arm. Photo: Nationalmuseet, Danmark.

even greater change was the rule that a man should take off his cloak when appearing before the king. The Son finds this ridiculous, pointing out that if anyone did this among ordinary people, he would be considered a fool. He demands an explanation, and the Father gives three. One is purely practical and thus less interesting from our point of view: a cloak can conceal a weapon intended to be used against the king. Of the two remaining examples, the first has to do with hierarchy: taking off one's cloak means that one is willing to serve. The second—which in fact comes first in the author's presentation—is simply that this is done by good and noble people, and that one must follow their example if one wishes to be included in fashionable society, an answer that is also to be found in more recent discussions on such matters. It tells us that dress, custom, manners, etc., serve as symbols that distinguish the elite from ordinary people. The more pronounced this distinction, the greater the class difference.

The King's Mirror also discusses fashions in dress, hair, and beard styles. The Father refers to German customs and clearly implies that fashions change and that it is important to keep abreast of them—although he finds it difficult to imagine that there will ever be a fashion more suitable than that of the present day. The importance of fashion is further demonstrated by a later source. In his great statute of 1308, issued in a moment of crisis and intended to secure the king full control over his men, King Håkon V strictly forbids anyone to introduce new fashions into the kingdom, threatening his own men with the loss of their aristocratic rank and his own friendship if they should do so. It is an important royal prerogative to be the trendsetter in such matters, and the king's men show their loyalty by following him. In a similar way, fashion serves to distinguish the king and his men from the rest of the population.

The use of fashion to set them apart evidently aims at creating a stronger sense of solidarity between the king's men and is in keeping with the king's aim of putting an end to internal conflicts. Some further rules more directly serve this purpose. The organization of the king's retainers (the *hird*) consists of different ranks, and it is important for each man to know his own place in the system. When these men are in the king's company, they should arrange themselves so that there is an equal number on each side of him. They have their fixed seats at the table, two together, and these two should also wash their hands together before the meal. They should walk to the table in the same order as their seats. At the table they should engage in quiet conversation, keeping their attention always directed towards the king, in case he should require some service from them. And they should show moderation in drinking, taking care not to get drunk. This latter admonition is particularly significant. Although warnings against excessive drinking can be found long before the examples in *The King's Mirror*, drinking parties were an essential part of the culture of traditional kingship. They served to put the king and his men on equal ground of a sort, although at the same time they were competitive. These were the occasions when a man had to show how much he was able to drink while keeping his wits about him so that he could still tell a good story or respond to a verbal challenge, and it was here that the deeds of the participants and other men were discussed and evaluated.

Compared to the manners and etiquette at the great courts of the seventeenth century, the rules in the *Mirror* were quite simple, but they had essentially the same aim, to make obedient royal servants out of unruly and quarrelsome warriors. Thus, through a number of more or less complicated rules of etiquette and behavior, the contemporary Norwegian monarchy sought to unite the aristocracy under its leadership, teaching them respect for the king and urging them to mutual solidarity. This aim was achieved in part by the rules, but also through the emphasis placed on the difference between the king's retainers and the population in general.

The King's Mirror gives a glimpse of how exactly these rules were formulated and transmitted to the members of the court. The chivalrous literature that was introduced during the same period, and which gives evidence of a new literary taste, also provides examples of behavior that accords with the same rules and attitudes. This can be illustrated by a story from *Strengleikar*, the song of Gujamar. Gujamar is a noble and courteous young man, strikingly handsome and such a brave and skillful knight that he defeats all others. However, he lacks one quality; he is unable to love a woman. One day he goes hunting and shoots a white hind.

The animal is wounded, but the arrow flies back and hits Gujamar in the thigh. Before she dies, the hind tells him that she has
avenged her death by giving him a deadly wound that can only
be healed by a woman. Severely injured, Gujamar walks away and
at length sees a beautiful ship with a lavishly decorated bed on
board. Tired from walking, he lies down on the bed and is suddenly transported to a strange country and brought before its
king, who is old but has an incredibly beautiful wife whom he
jealously guards against all other men. "For old men who have no
appetite for women and want what they cannot do and nature
denies them, they hate and envy those who are young." Gujamar
and the young woman fall in love and start a relationship. The jeal-
ous husband learns about it, Gujamar has to flee, and only after a
much danger and suffering do the two lovers become united.

This is a kind of fairytale, similar in many ways to the folktales
collected by the brothers Grimm and others in the nineteenth
century, but it also contains reflections on the nature of love. The
two lovers belong to each other as they are the best man and the
best woman. Their fates are similar, but also different: the man
rejects love because he finds no one who is worthy, while the
woman rejects love because she has been given to an unworthy husband. Gujamar's wound is apparently his punishment for killing
the hind—it is no coincidence that she is a female animal—but
in reality love's revenge. The hind is also described in a way that
makes it a symbol of love. Its white color as well as the fact that
it has only one horn points to a similarity with the unicorn, the
symbol of pure and innocent love. Thus, Gujamar is punished on
account of his contempt for love, a punishment that is both physical and spiritual, but which also makes him a better and nobler
human being. His perfection in the beginning of the story turns
out to be an illusion, for he lacks love. Only the experience of love
can make him perfect and at the same time give meaning to his
warrior skills; he must defeat an enemy and conquer his castle to

be united with his beloved. Finally, the mysterious ship that leads to the meeting between the two lovers shows that the whole order of the world serves love, which is the strongest force in the world.

It would be difficult to imagine two forms of literature more different than this fairytale and the classical saga with its terse, matter-of-fact representations of wars and conflicts between men ruled by a combination of honor and interest. Courtly culture was indeed a radically new phenomenon, and it had a close connection with the new monarchy. To some extent it may be regarded as a kind of "cultural rearmament" directed by the king. This is explicitly mentioned in some of the prefaces, e.g., that of the *Strengleikar*. There the translator points to the importance of reading the stories of the past so as to learn virtues and the fear of God from them, adding that his translation was made on King Håkon's initiative. Considering the actual contents of the collection, one is not quite convinced of this noble purpose, for the stories celebrate illicit love and sensual pleasure. It is matter for debate to what extent this literature was introduced because its contents were considered suitable and to what extent it was attractive simply by dint of its foreignness. This latter possibility accords with Gellner's theory that elites were created by increasing the separation of their members from the ordinary population, while increasing their similarity to elites in other countries. The widespread use of the vernacular in the Nordic countries might seem an argument against this. But writing in any language was exclusive to the elite, and the contents of this imported literature was more different from popular taste than the sagas, although it would be an exaggeration to regard the latter as a genuinely popular literature. There is thus a clear connection between political, social, and cultural development. As the court was an important instrument in linking the aristocracy to the king's service, courtly culture may be regarded as a further means to this end. One might then assess to what extent this connection was a result of the king's deliberate policy and to what extent it can be understood instead as the result of the changing tastes of thirteenth-century Norwegian aristocrats, who were becoming more closely attached to the king and more exposed to foreign influence.

Some modern scholars, notably the famous Norwegian writer Hans E. Kinck (1857–1924) had only contempt for the romantic literature and regarded its introduction as a tragedy because it destroyed the authentic Old Norse culture represented by the sagas. Implicit in this criticism is the romantic notion of a *Volksgeist*, the spiritual essence of a people. Whereas the Norwegian elite had previously been part of a larger national community, it had now become isolated from the people under the influence of a foreign elite culture. It may be objected to this that the sagas and the skaldic poetry were also mainly for the elite and that there are traces of romance in some of the sagas. We do not know how contemporaries reacted to the two cultures, but there is no direct evidence of cultural conflict in thirteenth-century Norway. Maybe people at the time were able to enjoy widely differing literary genres, in much the same way as we can enjoy Shakespeare, Ibsen, Beckett, and popular detective stories. Nevertheless, the introduction of courtly literature does point to some changes in the direction of a more exclusive aristocratic elite, similar to the introduction of new rules of behavior in *The King's Mirror.*

Whereas *The King's Mirror,* despite its concern for the king's honor and proper manners at court, gives little impression of great luxury, and chivalrous literature mostly describes a world far removed from the Scandinavian kingdoms, the *Chronicle of Erik* represents a courtly culture nearer to home. When Duke Erik visits his future father-in-law, King Håkon, in Oslo for the first time, the townspeople are full of wonder, remarking that "God has made him well." He completely charms the queen as well, who "addressed sweet words to him from her rosy mouth." His failure to delight his fiancée in a similar way was caused by the fact that she was only one year old. When he leaves, the queen calls him her "friend and Christmas brother," and he addresses her as "my dear sweet mother," and promises to serve her wherever he finds himself. As he goes his way out of town, all the ladies lean out of their windows to watch him.

The Chronicler also dwells in some detail on the dukes' wedding in Oslo in 1312. Before leaving for Norway, the dukes give their men two or three new outfits. The brides are the most beautiful women ever seen; no man, however full of sorrow, can watch them without joy in his heart. The guests receive beautiful clothing as well, and good horses; they leave richer than they have arrived. There are tournaments, dances and games, pleasant words and great joy. Even more magnificent are the festivities Duke Erik gives the following year. He builds a large hall for the purpose and fills it with velvet and beautiful textiles. In a cellar under the earth, he stores wine, mead, and all kinds of food. The king and the court arrive from Norway. The celebration lasts for four days with feasting, drinking, tournaments, and rich gifts for the guests. The first dish is served by knights, followed by gifts of horses and clothes. Many men are knighted, including two Germans who receive the accolade from Duke Erik.

Tournaments are mentioned already in the sagas. Snorri lets King Sigurd boast of having participated in one on his expedition to the Holy Land, and Sverre challenges his rival Magnus to fight from horseback. *The King's Mirror* also includes a description of such contests. However, none of these sources can be regarded as evidence that actual tournaments took place in Norway in the twelfth and thirteenth centuries. The *Chronicle of Erik* furnishes the earliest near-contemporary evidence, although we cannot exclude the possibility of earlier occurrences. King Magnus of Sweden and King Erik Klipping of Denmark fought a tournament during their meeting in 1275. There are several other examples, all suggesting that Scandinavian tournaments were largely confined to royal and princely circles. Evidence from the *Chronicle of Erik* leads us to conclude that other aspects of the courtliness described in the romantic literature also were put into practice by the aristocracy. Gifts and parties are of course traditional means of gaining followers and keeping them, but the chronicle suggests greater refinement and luxury in these gifts than ever before and gives some substance to the idea of new manners in the wake of the introduction of chivalrous romance. As a whole, however, the chronicle pays more attention to war than to romantic love and courtly behavior towards women.

This examination of Scandinavia's elite culture has confirmed the impression of increasing European influence after Christianization, but has shown also that there was a specifically Scandinavian reception of this culture. This is particularly prominent in vernacular literature from Norway and Iceland, notably the sagas and the skaldic poetry, but also in Saxo's Danish patriotism and his elaboration of traditional myths and tradition. Moreover, Saxo was not only a recipient of the common Latin culture, but also made an original contribution to it. The examination of Scandinavian culture also shows a connection between trends in the cultural sphere and the political and social trends discussed previously; namely, the formation of royal and ecclesiastical institutions and increased social stratification.

CHAPTER FIVE

The Later Middle Ages: Agrarian Crisis, Constitutional Conflicts, and Scandinavian Unions

THE MID-FOURTEENTH CENTURY marks a new epoch all over Europe. A new and terrible disease, the Black Death, arrived from Eastern Asia late in 1346 and spread from Italy to the rest of Europe over the course of the following years. Calculations of mortality vary from one third to half of the population. Moreover, the disease returned at irregular intervals until the mid-seventeenth century (and in some places well into the eighteenth century), although its spread and mortality seem gradually to have decreased. Thus, the relationship between land and people changed drastically; there was now plenty of land but few people to cultivate it. From the point of view of ordinary people who survived the disease, this was in many ways an ideal situation. There are also many indications that their standard of living improved; it has even been maintained that in many places it was better than at any time before the second half of the nineteenth century. By contrast, the landowning classes suffered drastic reversals after their expansion in the previous period.

In the 1960s and '70s, a large research project looked at the consequences of the Black Death in Scandinavia. Although its sources are meager, posing a number of problems, the project has given some indication of the rates of farm desertions and declines in land rent. The calculations show great differences between the countries, with Norway the most seriously affected according to both criteria. In fifteen of the nineteen Norwegian areas that have been examined, more than 40 percent of the farms were deserted. An equally high percentage is found in only one of the areas studied in Denmark. Similarly, the land rent was reduced to somewhere between 20 and 25 percent of its previous level in Norway, while the reduction was considerably less in Denmark and Sweden, where the peasants continued to pay well over 50 percent of the previous rents. To some extent, this difference can be attributed to the way the research was conducted and the available source material. The Norwegian researchers went further in the attempt to reconstruct old farms on the basis of much later sources than did their Danish and Swedish colleagues. It was also easier to trace desertions of farms in Norway than in Denmark and the main agricultural areas of Sweden, because individual farmsteads were the rule in Norway in contrast to village settlement patterns favored in the other countries. Nevertheless, there is hardly any doubt that the numbers also indicate real differences. This is evident particularly from the decline in the land rent, which was clearly greater and lasted longer in Norway.

There is no reason to believe that mortality in Norway was higher than in the other countries; on the contrary, it seems more likely that it would have been lower, since the population was more widely dispersed. However, two other explanations are possible. The first is the nature of the terrain. In Norway most of the cultivated area consisted of small and scattered farms, many of which were deserted. It would have been more difficult for the landowner to use these farms himself for pasture or other purposes than in Denmark or England, where owners turned to animal husbandry, to sheep in England and oxen in Denmark.

Second, and for the same reason, it was easier for the owners to force the peasants to pay more rent than they would have if the rent had been determined solely by market conditions, the more so as the aristocracy in these countries was stronger than in Norway.

In general, landowners suffered more as a consequence of the agrarian crisis than did public authorities. Tithes and taxes were reduced approximately in proportion with the decline in the number of taxpayers, while land rents declined considerably more. Moreover, the king could compensate for reduced revenues by imposing extra taxes, which is known to have happened with considerable frequency. Consequently, the Church and particularly the king were better off than the lay aristocracy, and within the Church, the bishops fared better than the monasteries, which often suffered heavy losses during the later Middle Ages, and not only because of the agrarian crisis. They were also negatively impacted by competition from other forms of devotion and other institutions of learning. The lay aristocracy as a class suffered the heaviest losses, but the losses were not the same for all its individual members. As the number of dioceses, bishops, and canons was probably more or less the same before and after the crisis, each individual's income would have been reduced by about the same amount, even if the death rate among the higher clergy were the same as in the population at large. By contrast, the loss for individual aristocrats might be lessened by a reduction in the number of aristocrats, because survivors would inherit the land of their deceased relatives. The wealthiest and most fortunate of the class might actually have profited from the crisis. They could buy large stretches of land previously owned by the deceased or by their less fortunate colleagues and use it for pasture. The result was a reduction in the number of aristocrats as well as greater inequality within the class as a whole. The members of the lower aristocracy were largely reduced to serving as retainers or servants of the leading magnates.

Turning to the political consequences of the crisis, we might expect to find a reversal of some of the trends discussed earlier. We might expect to see a strengthening of the monarchy and to some extent of the Church, and above all a reduction in the power for the upper classes relative to the peasantry. What we actually find is just the opposite. The later Middle Ages is the age of aristocracy. The movement we have seen towards the greater exclusivity of the ruling elite becomes more pronounced; there is increasing rivalry between the monarchy and aristocracy; the council of the realm is at the height of its power and the constitutional ideology that was detected in the previous period is developed further.

Common to all three countries was the institutionalization of the aristocracy. We saw the beginnings of this process in the previous pages, but it progressed during the later Middle Ages. Whereas the state in the previous period had been largely identical with the king and institutional conflicts restricted to disagreements between the king and the Church, the following period saw the increasing institutionalization of collective bodies representing the "people" against the king, notably the council of the realm, dominated by the aristocracy and the bishops. Admittedly, this is not the whole picture; there were also trends that reflected the economic development. The peasants did strengthen their position at the local level in all three countries, but only in Sweden did they have significant influence at the national level. Those who did, however, were not the tenants in the central areas who had their land rent reduced, but the freeholders and miners in the outskirts, particularly in the north, who had held a strong position even in the previous period. Moreover, we find no evidence of an increase in the number of freeholders. As for the relationship between the king and the aristocracy, increasing competition for *len* among the members of the latter and the attempts of the class as a whole to reserve them for itself may be connected to some degree with the crisis, but it was also a continuation of trends from the previous period. The reduction in the number of *len*, particularly in Norway, is also connected to the crisis; larger districts were needed to give castellans sufficient incomes, while a reduced population would also make it easier to govern larger areas.

In Scandinavia, the later Middle Ages are known not only as the period of the Black Death but also as the period of the Scandinavian unions. Some scholars have pointed to a connection between the two phenomena: the union was a means both to reduce the cost of government and to protect a weakened Scandinavia against aggression from abroad, particularly from Germany. The clearest connection between the Black Death and union is to be found in Norway, whose elite seems to have regarded a union with one or both the neighboring countries as inevitable and which eventually succumbed to Denmark. Otherwise, it is difficult to find a clear connection. In any case, the origins of the union must be sought on the dynastic and political level rather than in the economic and social consequences of the Black Death. As we will discover, these origins go far back in history.

Towards Renewed Scandinavian Integration, 1261–1397

In summer 1260, a Norwegian delegation, led by a friar, Nikolas, turned up at the residence of the Duke of Saxony and asked him to consent to the marriage of his granddaughter, the Danish princess Ingeborg, to King Håkon of Norway's son Magnus. The duke answered that he had no say over Ingeborg's marriage and referred the Norwegian envoys to the queen of Denmark. He then showed the envoys his two daughters, both beautifully dressed, and told them, "I decide over these two, if anyone will ask for them." The envoys were apparently unimpressed and left Saxony.

Nikolas continued his journey to Denmark and according to the saga returned with the message that the queen had accepted the proposal and promised to outfit the princess in the most honorable way. However, when a new and higher-ranking delegation, led by Bishop Håkon of Oslo and traveling with an armed force on seven ships, arrived the next year at the convent in Horsens where the princess was living, they found that no preparations had been made and that the queen had no plans in this direction. The bishop then approached the princess directly, urging her to trust in God and the king of Norway. The princess was finally persuaded, and Bishop Håkon betrothed her on behalf of Magnus. Shortly afterwards, the Norwegian delegation returned and quickly brought the princess back to Norway, taking care to avoid the Swedes, whom they suspected of wanting her for themselves. The delegation arrived safely in Norway, to the great satisfaction of King Håkon, who was very impressed by his daughter-in-law and arranged what according to the saga was the most magnificent wedding ever to have been celebrated in Norway.

The saga describes the proposal in unusual detail and gives a curious impression of the proceedings. Why the embassy to Saxony, rather than a direct approach to the Danish court? And why did the Danish queen do nothing to fulfill her alleged agreement with Friar Nikolas? The most likely answer is that the saga was trying to obscure the fact that Ingeborg was married without the consent of her relatives. The relatives, first King Christoffer (1252–1259) and then his widow, the formidable Margrete Sambiria, who headed the government on behalf of her minor son Erik, had good reasons to prevent the marriage. Ingeborg and her three sisters were daughters of the late King Erik IV Plovpenning (1241–1250). Christoffer, and later Margrete, wanted to confine them to nunneries in order to prevent claims for dowries that would threaten their financial resources (which were in bad shape) and to avoid the risk of new heirs who might endanger the position of their descendants. The same reasons made the princesses extremely attractive to neighboring kings—another of them was married to the king of Sweden. King Håkon may well have been impressed by Ingeborg's beauty and charm—this story as well as some others indicate that she must have been a resourceful woman—but the main reason for his satisfaction was no doubt the potential political consequences of the marriage.

The wedding in 1261 introduced a period of increasing interaction between the three Scandinavian kingdoms, which eventually led to the Kalmar Union of 1397. Historians, particularly Norwegian historians, have often pointed to the shift from the North Sea area to Denmark in Norwegian foreign policy from the mid-thirteenth century onwards. Rather than a shift, however, we seem to be dealing with a new field of interest in addition to the old ones—the 1290s represent a climax in Norwegian foreign policy, towards England and Scotland as well as towards Denmark. At the same time, Sweden launched a crusade in Finland while also strengthening its links with Denmark. The greatest difference compared to earlier times was that Norway and Sweden now interfered in Danish matters. This in turn resulted from the fact that Denmark had been weakened by inner conflicts, which broke out between the sons of King Valdemar II at his death in 1241 and continued intermittently over the course of the next hundred years. At the same time, central power in Norway and Sweden had been consolidated. As Denmark was the richest of the three countries, expansion towards Denmark was more attractive to the Norwegians and Swedes than expansion towards these countries had been to the Danes.

The main form this intervention took was marriage, which was more likely now than before to lead to dynastic unions. The greater importance of descent in the direct line increased the chance that a woman or a member of the dynasty in the female line might inherit the throne, as did also the rule requiring legitimate birth as a precondition for succession. This latter rule, however, also increased the risk of the king dying without a direct heir. These factors, together with the customary practice of kings and princes marrying foreign princesses, increased the likelihood that the same person would be the nearest heir to the throne in more than one country. We therefore find an increase in dynastic unions all over Europe in the later Middle Ages. In East Central Europe, the indigenous dynasties died out in the male line in Hungary (1301), Bohemia (1306), and Poland (1370). In the two latter countries, a woman became the heir to the throne; Jadwiga in Poland was even formally proclaimed "king" of the country (1384). In both Bohemia and Poland, however, the female heirs later married foreign princes, who took over the throne, John of Luxembourg in Bohemia (1310) and the Lithuanian Duke Jogaila in Poland, who converted to Christianity and became king under the name of Ladislaus (1386). In both cases, political considerations were decisive. John of Luxembourg was the son of the Emperor Henry VII, and the union between Poland and Lithuania created a powerful alliance that inflicted a crushing defeat on Poland's main enemy, the Teutonic Order, in 1410. In Hungary, Andrew III, the last king of the Arpad dynasty, was succeeded by Charles I of Anjou, who traced his claim from his grandmother Mary, who was the daughter of King Stephen V and married to King Charles II of Sicily. Although he was the nearest heir, the election of Charles was by no means automatic, and he had to fight rival pretenders and rebellious nobles for a long time after his election. The rules of succession were thus combined with political considerations, as the political elites sought pretenders who could strengthen the international status of their countries, and the kings themselves used marriage as a means to strengthen the position of their dynasties. The two main Central European dynasties, the Luxembourgs and the Habsburgs, worked systematically to extend their power through marriage alliances, as expressed in the motto of the latter, the most successful of all medieval and early modern dynasties: *Bella gerunt alii, tu felix Austria, nube* (Others wage war, but you, Happy Austria, marry!).

Inter-Nordic marriages had occurred, probably as far back as in the tenth century, but they were not particularly frequent. Nor would they necessarily have major consequences, as long as the rules of succession were vague and illegitimate sons had access to the throne. Moreover, royal daughters and other female relatives often served as means to link prominent magnates to the king's factions during civil wars, leaving fewer daughters to be exported. This changed during the following period, with more settled conditions and a greater distance separating the king from the aristocracy. Kings and princes now married women of foreign royal houses exclusively—which had been their usual custom even earlier—and women of the royal house did the same. Royal marriages were used to gain important allies and also, to some extent, in the hopes of extending the power and influence of the dynasty by inheriting the throne in another country. The Norwegian kings, who had limited military resources, made steady and systematic attempts in this direction. Before Magnus's marriage to Ingeborg, Håkon had let his elder son marry a Swedish princess, but the marriage was dissolved by his death in 1257. By contrast, Håkon married his daughter off to a Castilian prince, possibly in order to avoid claims for her hand from the neighboring countries. Later, the marriage of Håkon's grandson Eirik to a Scottish princess almost brought a Norwegian queen to the throne of Scotland. After the death of King Alexander III in 1286, his granddaughter Margaret, King Eirik's daughter, was his nearest heir, but young Margaret died before she could reach Scotland.

Of the two marriages to Danish princesses mentioned above, the Swedish one was without negative consequences from a Danish point of view, because the husband of the Danish princess, King Valdemar, was deposed by his younger brother Magnus with

Danish aid. By contrast, the Norwegian marriage led to claims for a dowry in the form of Danish lands, which after 1280, when Ingeborg, the former Danish princess, held a prominent position as dowager queen, occasionally led to war between the two countries. The conflict was intensified by the murder of King Erik in 1286, because the nobles convicted of the murder found refuge in Norway and in the following years joined the king of Norway in attacks on Denmark. Thanks to this alliance, the Norwegians gained a foothold in Denmark, notably in the border region of Halland, where one of the outlaws, Count Jacob, had his lands. In the following years, they launched a series of attacks on Denmark, which resulted in a temporary peace in 1295 on fairly favorable conditions from a Norwegian point of view.

However, a Danish revival occurred when Erik Klipping's son Erik Menved came of age in 1294. Erik strengthened the alliance with Sweden through a double marriage; the two kings married each other's sisters (1296 and 1298). He emerged successful from a conflict with the archbishop (1302) and at about the same time embarked upon an ambitious policy in Northern Germany (above, p. 42). All of this placed the new king of Norway, Håkon V (1299–1319), in a tenuous position. His solution was to seek an alliance with King Birger of Sweden's younger brother, Duke Erik. Whether this was an attempt to reach an understanding with Birger himself or Håkon was already sensing the bad relationship between Birger and his brothers, remains unknown, but the result was an alliance between the ruling kings in Denmark and Sweden against the king of Norway and against their opponents in both countries. During the following conflicts, the Danish outlaws gradually lost their importance and were replaced by the Swedish dukes, Erik and his brother Valdemar, who had the upper hand in Sweden after their coup at Håtuna in 1306, when they took their brother captive and eventually forced him to divide the country with them in three equal parts. Håkon's great asset in this situation was his only daughter Ingebjørg, born in 1301 and likely to succeed him. Håkon hesitated for some time over the choice between two potential sons-in-law, Duke Erik and Birger's son Magnus, but decided in favor of the former in 1312, after the formal division of Sweden two years previously. The advantage of Erik's marriage to Ingebjørg from Håkon's point of view was that he would be succeeded, in reality if not formally, by Erik, who was a very competent politician and who would join the western third of Sweden plus the Danish province of Halland to the possessions of the dynasty. King Birger's murder of his two brothers resulted in Håkon gaining even more. In 1319, Birger was replaced by Duke Erik's son Magnus, aged three, who also succeeded Håkon as king of Norway.

The union between Norway and Sweden in effect lasted until Magnus's death in 1374, although a decision was taken to dissolve it in 1343–44, when Magnus's younger son Håkon, born in 1340, was elected king of Norway. Håkon took over the government when he reached majority in 1355. However, Magnus still ruled a part of the country. Moreover, after the death of Magnus's elder son Erik in 1359, it became possible to envision a renewal of the union after Magnus's death. In 1363 Håkon married Margrete, daughter of King Valdemar IV of Denmark, while Valdemar's only son Christoffer died in the same year. Consequently, Margrete and Håkon's son Olav, born in 1370, became the nearest heir in all three countries, opening the possibility of a Scandinavian union.

The union became a reality towards the end of the century, and the main reason must be sought in the revival of Denmark after the crisis in the 1320s and '30s. A lament over the sad fate of the country was composed during this period in Latin by an anonymous author, who longed for a return to the glorious days of Erik Menved and condemned the cowardice and decadence of his contemporaries. A famous event, celebrated by contemporaries as well as later ages, would seem to have been the answer to the poet's complaints. On April 1, 1340, a squire from Jutland, Niels Ebbesen, accompanied by forty-seven of his men, entered the castle of Count Gerhard of Holstein, one of the main mortgagees during the interregnum, and killed him. The turning point had arrived. The Danish people rose against their German oppressors and killed them or chased them out of the country. The reality behind the story is more prosaic. We know nothing of Niels Ebbesen's motives, but he was hardly the champion of a national movement. Nor was the main issue a conflict between Danes and Germans. The German mortgagees did not aim at ruling Denmark; their main interest was to get back their money. Gerhard himself was about to exchange his mortgage in Jutland with Duke Valdemar of Slesvig. Nor did the mortgagees control Denmark in such a way that the monarchy could be restored only by removing them. The problem was that the previous period had resulted in so many encroachments on royal estates and rights that it would take a long time and much hard work to restore the royal government.

This process had begun two years before, when Christoffer II's youngest son Valdemar (born in 1321) started negotiations with the mortgagees about taking over the Danish throne. In May 1340 he married Helvig, a sister of Duke Valdemar of Slesvig, and received parts of Jutland as her dowry. In this way, he ended the conflict between the two lines of Valdemar II's descendants. He was acclaimed king of Denmark shortly after, on St. John's Day (June 24). He spent the next twenty years transforming his nominal rule over the country into a real kingship. His assets in this effort included good contacts in Germany—he had spent his youth at the court of the Emperor Louis of Bavaria—but most important of all were his political and military abilities. He was clever, ruthless, and energetic, according to a contemporary chronicle a man who would not even allow water to run out into

244 • CHAPTER FIVE

the sea without its having done any useful work (to this end he built watermills all over the country). He recovered castles and *len* with a combination of threats, violence, and promises. His particular skill was the ability to turn up unexpectedly and catch his opponents by surprise. He was clever in hiding his movements.

In 1360, Valdemar had got control of most of Denmark and at a great meeting in Kalundborg in Zealand, he issued an ordinance about royal government and peace in the country that strongly resembled an election charter. Now, he was ready for his next strike. As a consequence of the Danish dissolution after Erik Menved's death in 1319, Sweden had gained hold of the Danish lands east of Øresund: Scania and Blekinge (1332). The people there had approached the king of Sweden about getting rid of the Germans who held the area in mortgage from the king of Denmark, and the Swedes had paid that mortgage, 34,000 marks of silver. The sum was enormous and contributed to the financial difficulties that beset Sweden for the rest of Magnus's reign. After the revival of the Danish monarchy with Valdemar IV after 1340, the Swedish king and aristocracy had lived in constant fear of a Danish reconquest and had taken various steps to avoid it. Internal struggles in Sweden from 1356 gave the Danes the opportunity they were looking for, and in 1360–61 King Valdemar reconquered the area and in addition got hold of Gotland, an important trading center under the nominal superiority of the Swedish king. This was apparently no incentive for the rapprochement between the two dynasties that resulted in the marriage between Håkon and Margrete, but King Magnus was faced with an even greater danger than these losses, namely an aristocratic opposition that threatened to depose him in favor of his cousin Albrecht, son of the duke of Mecklenburg. The deposition actually took place in February 1364.

From now on, Nordic politics would be a struggle between two dynastic alliances, the old Nordic dynasties, represented by Magnus, Håkon and Margrete, and their descendants, and the

Mecklenburgers, who traced their claim through the 1321 marriage between Magnus's sister and the duke of Mecklenburg. Territorially, this meant an alliance between Denmark, Norway, and some of the western landscapes of Sweden against the rest of Sweden and Mecklenburg, with both sides seeking various allies outside the Nordic countries and both in fact trying to gain control of all three kingdoms. After Valdemar's death in 1375, Håkon and Margrete's son Olav (Danish, Oluf) was elected in Denmark, with Margrete as regent, in competition with Albrecht of Mecklenburg. When Olav died at the age of seventeen in 1387, Margrete replaced him with her sister's son Erik, son of the duke of Pomerania, who is usually referred to as Erik of Pomerania in Scandinavian historiography.

Whereas Denmark overcame its internal conflicts during the fourteenth century, there was frequent discord between the monarchy and the aristocracy in Sweden. The first Scandinavian union, between Norway and Sweden, was the result of a united aristocratic opposition against King Birger, who had murdered his brothers, and led to government by an aristocratic council of the realm in both countries during Magnus's minority (1319–1331). Having taken over the government of the two kingdoms himself, Magnus eventually met with aristocratic opposition in both of them, first in Norway, and then, and more seriously, in Sweden. It is open to discussion to what extent we are dealing here with a radical opposition between monarchy and aristocracy or with reactions to a temporary financial crisis, as in Sweden in the 1350s, or dissatisfaction on the part of particular groups or individuals, as in Norway in the 1330s and '40s. In any case, it is clear that the Swedish aristocracy in the second half of the fourteenth century had strong and well-defined interests and was able to defend them against the king.

The dynastic conflict in 1357–1359, when King Magnus' eldest son Erik rebelled against his father, may possibly be interpreted as a result of aristocratic discontent with the king, for which the young Erik—aged eighteen—was only an instrument. This discontent persisted after Erik's sudden death in 1359 and King Magnus's replacement by Albrecht of Mecklenburg in 1364. Albrecht gave Swedish *len* to nobles from Mecklenburg, which provoked the Swedish aristocracy. In 1371, however, the aristocracy exploited an attempt by Magnus' son Håkon to bring back the old dynasty and forced Albrecht to leave control of the *len* to the council of the realm. Albrecht now became king in name only, but in 1386, he saw an opportunity to regain power. The occasion for this was the death of the most powerful man in Sweden, Bo Jonsson Grip, who held the largest number of *len* in the country. Albrecht attempted to take control of them and distribute them to his adherents. Although Bo had made an elaborate testament calculated to keep the *len* for his relatives and other Swedish aristocrats, Albrecht found an ally in Bo's widow, who was from Mecklenburg, while at the same time concluding an alliance with a number of German princes. This made the Swedish aristocracy turn to Margrete and conclude an alliance with her in Dalaborg early in 1388. Here they not only elected her their ruler, but also accepted royal control of the *len*, although on the condition that they be given to Swedes. To some extent, they thus agreed in what they had rebelled against Albrecht to prevent. They found themselves in a difficult situation and chose the lesser evil.

A Danish army invaded Sweden, defeated Albrecht, and took him captive in the battle of Åsle in 1389. The war continued with the Mecklenburgers still in control of Stockholm and their allies plundering the coasts of the Scandinavian countries, until a temporary peace was concluded in 1395, which became permanent three years later, resulting in Margrete gaining control of Stockholm and Albrecht in effect giving up his claim on the Swedish throne. A union of the three Scandinavian countries was established in Kalmar in 1397.

Figure 20. Queen Margrete, from her alabaster funeral monument in Roskilde Cathedral (Denmark), 1423. National Museum, Danmark. Margrete is portrayed as a young woman, despite the fact that she was fifty-nine years old at her death. There is less of royal majesty here than in the portrait of Christoffer II; the monument rather expresses the dead queen's piety and humility. Margrete was originally buried in Sorø, like her son, father and grandfather, but King Erik moved her to Roskilde and built the magnificent sarcophagus, which was finished in 1423. Photo: Nationalmuseet, Danmark.

The Kalmar Union

The Kalmar Union has been the subject of much discussion among Scandinavian historians. The national revival in the nineteenth century led to a negative view of the union in Sweden and Norway: it was a Danish project aimed at conquering the neighboring countries. This view received scholarly sanction from the Danish historian Kristian Erslev, who did not seek a specifically Danish interpretation of the union, but on the basis of his examination of the sources concluded that this was the most likely interpretation. Erslev was challenged by the Swedish historian Erik Lönnroth in 1934. According to Lönnroth, the lines of division during the conflicts over the Kalmar Union were not between nations but between monarchy and aristocracy, represented by political ideologies—the monarchical *regimen regale* (royal government) versus the aristocratic *regimen politicum* (government by the people). This was expressed already in the founding documents of the union and remained the main issue throughout the union period.

Two documents have been preserved from the meeting in Kalmar, usually referred to as the Coronation Charter and the Union letter. In the former, a number of prelates and noblemen, listed according to rank, regardless of country, acclaim Erik as king of all three countries, without adding any specific provisions about the form that the government should take or the relationship between the countries. This charter is issued on parchment and with pendant seals, in the manner of formal charters. The second document gives detailed provisions for a permanent union between the three countries. It is written on paper and issued by seventeen men, only ten of whom impressed their seals on it, but it refers to more formal charters to be issued in the future. The relationship between the two documents and the interpretation of the Union letter have been the subject of considerable controversy. Some scholars regard the latter as only a draft, while others claim that it was regarded as valid in at least some circles and point to some later evidence in support of this position. According to the national interpretation, the Union letter was an attempt by Margrete to link the three kingdoms more strongly together. Lönnroth disagreed, regarding the Coronation Charter as the expression of *regimen regale* and the Union letter as the expression of *regimen politicum*. Margrete did not want to include in the Charter any hard and fast rules about the government, which Lönnroth interprets as an expression of *regimen regale,* giving the ruler maximum freedom, whereas the aristocracy wanted a union that would grant greater influence to the council of the realm and limit royal power. As Margrete did not want the latter, she managed to prevent the Union letter from being formally issued. Lönnroth dismissed the importance of national considerations, regarding the relationship between monarchy and aristocracy as the only issue.

Although Lönnroth may be right in perceiving different attitudes toward the monarchy in the two documents, he most probably exaggerates this difference. The opposition between *regimen regale* and *regimen politicum* was hardly as pronounced as Lönnroth assumes and, more to the point, it is difficult to find a consistent and well-developed theory of the former in the terse and vague wording of the Coronation Charter. Moreover, whatever the importance of constitutional matters, the documents show a clear contrast between a loose union, consisting only in the election of a common king, and a tight union, intended to last forever and with specific conditions, including the obligation that each country aid the others in war. It may well have been a divisive issue, either alone or together with the opposition between monarchy and aristocracy. It may also be objected that most of the men who issued the Union letter are known to have been Margrete's adherents. There is today growing sentiment against Lönnroth's interpretation for rejecting the national issue, not only in his interpretation of the Kalmar documents but also in his account of the following period.

The fundamental factors explaining the Kalmar Union are the dynastic development and the revival of the Danish monarchy. When the marriage between Håkon and Margrete resulted in a son who was heir to all the Scandinavian kingdoms, it became obvious policy for the Danish monarchy to seek his election in all of them, and, after his death, to secure a replacement for him. There was a good chance that this policy would succeed, for Margrete and her father Valdemar IV had revived the Danish monarchy and reconquered or otherwise regained lost provinces, rights, and estates, including a substantial part of the royal lands appropriated by members of the aristocracy in the previous period. Moreover, although such a policy may not have been entirely in the interests of the Danish aristocracy, neither was the previous interregnum or the mortgage of the country to the king's German creditors. In addition, both Valdemar and Margrete, particularly the latter, were skillful and efficient rulers, who contrived to gain support through the right mixture of promises, threats, concessions, and privileges. When Denmark, the strongest of the three Scandinavian countries, had overcome its internal weakness and, for the first time since the Viking Age, defined the other Scandinavian countries as its main field of interest, a Scandinavian union seemed a likely result. There was at the time much to be said in favor of such a union, for the Mecklenburgers were in alliance with German pirates who plundered the coasts of all three countries.

The Struggle over the Kalmar Union, 1434–1523

The poor people who lived in Dalarna suffered much from their bailiff. He tormented them greatly and forced them to

pay most of what they had in taxes. He let peasants be hanged
up in smoke—so much did he hurt them. Their women did
he treat very badly. They were harnessed to hay-loads, to drag
them, and thus fell into such misery that they gave birth to
dead children.

With these words, the verse chronicle of Engelbrekt Engelbrekts-
son explains the origins of the rebellion that broke out in Sweden
in 1434. The people of Dalarna, the iron-producing highland region in northern Sweden, complained about their bailiff, the Danish nobleman Jøsse Eriksen, and Engelbrekt, a man of the lower
nobility, brought their complaints before the king and the council of the realm. When this proved in vain, he became the leader
of a rebellion and in a short time gained control over most of
Sweden. After some hesitation, the aristocracy joined the rebels,
and together they deposed King Erik, first in Denmark and Sweden (1439) and finally in Norway (1442).

The chronicle gives a vivid picture of the dramatic course of
events, presenting Engelbrekt as a great hero and celebrating his
and his followers' triumph over the tyrannical bailiffs and his
success in forcing the reluctant Swedish aristocracy to join the
rebellion. We see Engelbrekt entering Vadstena, where a number
of councilors and leading men are assembled, proclaiming, "All
of you should now join the kingdom if you want to live longer. I
now intend to win the freedom of the realm." When they refuse,
Engelbrekt grasps one of the bishops around the throat and threat-
ens to throw him and his colleagues to the rebel army outside,
after which he dictates a letter of deposition to the king, which he
forces the assembled lords to seal. Jøsse Eriksson's fate is described
with considerable glee in the somewhat later *Karl's Chronicle*:

> In the hall of the convent Jøsse was taken
> And dragged down the stairs after his feet
> He was hauled like a beast for slaughter

And his neck beat against the steps.
He was tied to the sledge like a pig
...
They placed him on the nearest stock
And cut his head from his body.

In traditional Swedish historiography, as expressed in Erik Gustaf Gejer's early-nineteenth-century interpretation, Engelbrekt was the great hero who saved his country from Danish tyranny and took the first steps towards the dissolution of the Kalmar Union. This interpretation also receives considerable support from the many and vivid verse chronicles of the fifteenth and early sixteenth centuries, which depict Margrete and her successors as tyrants and their Swedish opponents as heroes fighting for the freedom of their country. As already mentioned, Erik Lönnroth rejected this interpretation in an influential book, published in 1934, five hundred years after Engelbrekt's rebellion. He dismissed the stories of Jøsse Eriksson as propaganda and identified the real reason for the Swedish rebellion as King Erik's war against Lübeck, which created problems for the export of iron from Dalarna. Thus, for Lönnroth, far from being a national hero, Engelbrekt becomes an instrument for German mercantile interests in Sweden—a role not likely to endear him to the liberal circles in 1930s Sweden to which Lönnroth belonged! Above all, Lönnroth attached greater importance to the role of the aristocracy in reacting against King Erik's authoritarian regime, thereby pointing to class interests rather than national sentiment. He found support for his constitutionalist interpretation of the conflict in the fact that Erik was deposed by the Danish as well as the Swedish aristocracy and that the union was reestablished afterwards, through the election of Christoffer of Bavaria, Erik's sister's son, as king in Denmark in 1440, in Sweden in 1441, and in Norway in 1442.

No doubt, there were conflicts of interest between the king and the aristocracy over the government of the countries, and the many complexities of the Kalmar Union prevent a simple return to the national interpretations of the nineteenth century. Nevertheless, Lönnroth's dismissal of the national—as well as the social—issue is facile. Lönnroth rejects not only the stories referred to above (or at least their importance), but also the account of the popular rebellion referred to in the *Engelbrekt Chronicle*, on the ground that it is a late invention. This chronicle survives only as a part of the *Karl Chronicle*, which was probably composed in the 1460s. In Lönnroth's opinion the *Engelbrekt Chronicle* was totally rewritten at about this time, roughly thirty years after the 1430s conflict that it depicts but now interprets as a popular rebellion rather than what it actually was—a conflict between a part of the aristocracy and the king. However, later research has largely succeeded in reconstructing the original *Engelbrekt Chronicle* and given strong arguments that its account of the popular rebellion, including the story of Jøsse, is almost contemporary. Although this is not necessarily proof of its historical accuracy, it at least makes it likely that Jøsse's behavior was one of the motives for the rebellion. Above all, it makes it difficult to dismiss the importance of Engelbrekt and the popular movement under his leadership. More generally, the national propaganda in the chronicles—also recognized by Lönnroth—becomes difficult to understand unless there really were national sentiments at the time. Foreign influence might easily be resented. Swedish and Norwegian peasants enjoyed a freer status than their Danish counterparts and tolerated less from their superiors, an attitude that is consistent with rebelliousness and demands that they be governed by their countrymen—although there are also examples of reactions against the latter. The lay and ecclesiastical aristocracy wanted to keep offices in their country for themselves and reacted against foreigners. A conflict over the archbishopric of

Uppsala at about the same time as Engelbrekt's rebellion may have contributed to the aristocracy's willingness to join it at the second stage. Finally, later research has found little evidence to support Lönnroth's thesis that the main interest of the rebels was to secure trade with Lübeck. After the temporary peace of 1432, the Hanseatic blockade had been relaxed, and besides, it is difficult to explain why problems with the export of iron from Dalarna would lead to a rebellion that involved the whole of Sweden.

Apart from people like Jøsse Eriksson, what did the rebels react against in the 1430s, and why did the Swedish rebellion eventually lead to the deposition of King Erik? Erik's foreign policy was not doubt an important factor, not (at least not mainly) because his conflict with the Hanseatic League created problems for the export of iron, but because of the extra taxes needed to finance the prolonged war he waged against the count of Holstein in order to conquer Schleswig. Another important factor is the character of Margrete and Erik's regime, which is commonly depicted as a *regimen regale*. The three countries were governed from a union chancery in Denmark, after 1417 increasingly located in Copenhagen, and the traditional offices in the central administration held by members of the high nobility were vacant. The council of the realm was rarely summoned to meetings, with some exceptions for Denmark; instead, the ruler sought advice from individual councilors. The principles underlying this form of government are aptly expressed in Queen Margrete's instructions to King Erik on his first visit to Norway in 1405. He should be pleasant to everybody he meets, but never give any exact promises. In particular, he should avoid promising anything in writing. If forced to do so, he should not issue charters in the most solemn and binding form, on parchment and with the great seal pendant from the document, but preferably on paper with a signet stamped on the back. He should speak to the councilors individually but not summon any meeting of the council as a whole. Apart from the frequent admonition not to take any decision himself without consulting his "mother," "because we know more about this than he does," this advice corresponds perfectly to Margrete's own political practice, which made her one of the most successful rulers at the time and one of the great politicians of the later Middle Ages. Unfortunately, however, Erik did not follow her advice. He had the same aims as his "mother" but pursued them stubbornly and undiplomatically, which eventually led to his fall.

Margrete's advice is thus not only evidence of her political skill but also of the restrictions facing an ambitious ruler at the time. *Regimen regale* might work, but only if it was carefully disguised. The king had limited resources. He had no standing army and tax revenues were insufficient for any major enterprise and had to be supplemented with extra contributions, which needed the consent of either the council of the realm or of popular assemblies. Nor was there any class that could counterbalance the aristocracy. It was thus not possible to challenge this class a whole, though a monarch might gain considerable independence by playing its members off against one another. Margrete succeeded in this, whereas Erik did not. So far, Erik's fall can be explained by a too direct and provocative *regimen regale*. However, this policy was not equally provocative in all three countries, which means that we also have to consider the national issue.

Erik's regime was most constitutional in Denmark. Here he often consulted with the council of the realm and normally appointed Danish nobles as castellans; this in some contrast to Margrete who had made more use of low-ranking Germans and had more rarely summoned the council. In Norway, both Margrete and Erik ruled through a few select nobles, mostly Norwegian, in addition to a few Danish ones, in particular the bishop of Oslo. The council of the realm was rarely summoned. In Sweden, it is no coincidence that the rebellion was sparked by complaints against a Danish official. While few foreigners held royal office in Denmark, a number of Danes held office in Sweden, which provoked not only the peasants but also the Swedish nobles. Although the rebellion started as a peasant rebellion and the nobles were in the beginning reluctant to join in, eventually the nobles took over and finally broke with Erik. Engelbrekt was dead already in May 1436. Although his killing was the result of a private feud, there had already been tension between him and some of the nobles, notably Karl Knutsson who now took over as the leader of the movement.

Admittedly, however, Erik was deposed by the Danish aristocracy, even before he was deposed in Sweden, a fact that would seem to support Lönnroth's interpretation. At a meeting in Kalmar in 1436, the Danish council mediated between King Erik and the Swedes and made him accept their demand to rule in cooperation with the council of the realm and according to Swedish law and to respect the privileges of the aristocracy. The councilors also used the opportunity to gain similar rights for themselves as those of their Swedish counterparts. However, the king left for Gotland and did nothing to fulfill his promises, apparently believing that his absence would result in chaos and that he would be invited to return on his own conditions. Rather than trying to placate the councils, he pressured both the Danes and the Swedes to accept his cousin, Duke Boleslaw of Pomerania, as his successor. The principles of *regimen regale* and *regimen politicum* were thus clearly articulated from both sides, and both the Danes and the Swedes wanted to preserve the union. However, the members of the Danish council did not act solely out of solidarity with their Swedish counterparts. They were provoked by Erik's plan for the succession and by his refusal to return to Denmark and deal with the problems there, including a peasant rebellion that broke out in summer 1438. In these circumstances, they found it better to cut their losses, get rid of Erik, and replace him with someone who could deal with the problems. They invited Christoffer to Denmark late in 1438, elected him protector of the realm in the following year and king in 1440. The fact that the Swedes also elected Christoffer shows that the union had its adherents in both countries, but is not evidence that the aristocracies thought exclusively in constitutional rather than in national terms.

Although the Engelbrekt rebellion was not necessarily directed against the union, which was actually restored after Erik's deposition, Christoffer's death marked the end of the period when all three kingdoms were united for any significant period of time. When Christoffer died childless in 1448, the nobleman Karl Knutsson managed to be elected king in Sweden, whereas the Danes after some searching and negotiation chose Count Christian of Oldenburg, whose successors in the direct line would rule the country until the mid-nineteenth century. The 1448 Swedish election was not necessarily intended as a break with the Kalmar Union, although it was contrary to earlier agreements about a joint election by representatives from all three countries. However, the Danes had broken this agreement previously by electing Christoffer. Although the circumstances are not quite clear, Karl may have hoped that his election in Sweden would lead to his acceptance in the other countries as well, or he may have convinced the Swedish assembly that this would happen. There was no obvious heir, and Karl or his electors may have believed that the fact that he had estates and connections in Denmark might make him acceptable to the Danish aristocracy. Both kings later tried to gain Norway, but Christian won, and a treaty establishing a permanent union between Norway and Denmark was concluded in 1450.

Christian also managed to gain Sweden in 1457, but he lost it again to Karl in 1464. The rebellion against Christian in 1464 marked the start of a chaotic period, during which Karl was reelected, deposed, and reelected again, without ever managing to take control of the kingdom. His death in 1470 would seem to have presented an opportunity for Christian to get hold of Sweden once more, but he was defeated by Karl's successor Sten Sture in the battle of Brunkeberg outside Stockholm in 1471. Sten Sture turned out to be a more clever politician than Karl and managed to keep the country under his control and outside the union until his death in 1503, with the exception of the period between 1497 and 1501. He was succeeded by Svante Nilsson Sture (1504–1512) and Sten Svantesson Sture (1512–1520). None of these rulers claimed the kingship but used instead the title "protector of the realm." They based their power on an alliance between a considerable part of the aristocracy and the free peasants and miners in other parts of Sweden, notably Dalarna in the north. The faction held together thanks to skillful propaganda in the form of letters, speeches, and a number of verse chronicles clearly intended for oral performance, which celebrated the Swedish nation, blackened the Danes, and stamped the opponents of the faction as traitors. One piece of their propaganda is still to been seen: the magnificent statue of St. George and the Dragon in the Great Church in Stockholm, which was erected as an allegory of Sten's victory over the Danes at Brunkeberg.

During most of this period, the protectors of the realm managed to hold on to power by skillful maneuvering, but there were tensions within the aristocracy that could be exploited by the Danish kings. In 1497, open conflict broke out between Sten and some other magnates, including his later successor Svante Nilsson, which gave King Hans the opportunity to invade Sweden. After some defeats, Sten decided to come to terms while he still had something to offer in the negotiations. The result was a loose union that left the Swedish council and aristocracy a considerable amount of control and Sten an impressive assembly of *len*.

When in the following period Hans broke his promises and sought to increase his control of Sweden, his former enemies joined in a new rebellion (1501), which led to a prolonged conflict between the two countries, interrupted by periods of armistice. Finally, Hans's son and successor Christian II invaded Sweden with a large army in January 1520 and defeated Sten Sture the Younger in a battle where the protector himself was killed. Once more, the Swedes decided to come to terms. Sten had made many enemies—including the archbishop, Gustaf Trolle—some of whom wanted an agreement with the Danes. Like his father, Christian also promised to respect the council of the realm and the privileges of the Church and the aristocracy. He was crowned in Stockholm in November to great festivities, which, however, were suddenly broken off on the third day. A number of prominent men were accused of heresy because of their support for Sten Sture in his previous conflict with the archbishop, whom he had imprisoned and whose castle he had pulled down. Altogether nearly a hundred men—bishops, noblemen, burghers, and others—were executed in the great square in Stockholm, either beheaded or hanged, depending upon their status. Their blood flooded the streets in the rain and the event came to be known as the "Bloodbath of Stockholm." Similar massacres took place in other parts of the country.

Christian apparently believed that he had secured his hold of Sweden and prevented a setback such as his father had experienced, but the opposite happened. A new rebellion soon broke out under the leadership of Gustaf Eriksson Vasa, who belonged to one of the wealthiest and most prominent families in the country. Gustaf concluded an alliance with Lübeck and soon conquered most of Sweden. He was elected king on June 6, 1523. Meanwhile, the Danish aristocracy rebelled against Christian and elected his uncle, Duke Frederik of Schleswig-Holstein, to replace him.

Why Was the Union Dissolved?

The brief summary above represents a considerable simplification. It leaves out a bewildering number of people and events—the formation and breaking of alliances, war and peace. Lönnroth managed to create order from this chaos, but at the cost of too great a simplification. His account needs to be supplemented with a least two main observations. The first is that there was a distinction between collective and individual aristocratic interests. The aristocracy was not always united, either nationally or across borders. Nor would it be possible to conduct a monarchic policy without aristocratic support; no other class was strong enough to compete with the aristocracy. Individual interests among the aristocrats are therefore as important as shared class interests. The aristocrats competed for royal favor; and those who succeeded in gaining it had no desire to join their equals in attempts to limit the king's power. Thus, it might be suggested that *regimen politicum* was for hungry aristocrats, while *regimen regale* was suited to well-fed ones. Attitudes also depended on circumstances. It was usually easy to present a common aristocratic front in support of the best possible conditions for the aristocracy during negotiations over election charters, but far more difficult to maintain this front in the daily running of government, when the king was able to secure allies through favors and privileges and play individual aristocrats off against one another.

The second observation, as already pointed out, concerns the national issue, or, perhaps more adequately, the connection between this issue and the constitutional one. We are not dealing with a union king versus a union aristocracy but with a union king versus national aristocracies. Whereas it is relatively easy to imagine a royal power common to the three kingdoms, it is very difficult to imagine the three aristocracies embracing a similar commonality. The aristocracy's main instrument was the council of the realm, consisting of the bishops and some other clerics and the most prominent members of the lay aristocracy. It was difficult enough for each country to arrange regular meetings of this assembly. It was almost impossible to bring all three together. Although such joint meetings did occasionally take place, most often in connection with royal elections, it would have been impossible to conduct the on-going government of the countries in this way. Consequently, the only way for the aristocracy to retain its influence was to insist on the prerogatives of the national council of the realm. In this way, aristocratic and national interests tended to coincide. Characteristically, Christoffer of Bavaria had to promise in his Swedish election charter of 1441 that the country during the king's absence would be governed by indigenous court officials together with the council of the realm.

This also means that the many examples scholars have found of aristocrats pursuing their own private interests rather than national ones are of only limited interest. The great Swedish leader in the late fifteenth century, Sten Sture the Elder, may well have been a cynical power politician who cared for his own interests rather than those of the Swedish nation. The point, however, is that most of the time he found his interests better served by Swedish independence than by submission to the Danish king, as did the majority of the Swedish aristocrats most of the time.

From the king's point of view, the need to accommodate national demands meant that he had either to travel regularly between the countries—which was a usual requirement specified in the election charters—or to delegate most matters to the national council of the realm. Neither alternative was very attractive. The same applies to an experiment attempted in Erik of Pomerania's reign, when a union council was set up that consisted of a few members of the council of each country. It was not continued in the following period. It is doubtful whether such a council would prove sufficiently representative to replace the national ones. Although the king traditionally had traveled quite a lot within his own country, the required distances increased enormously as a consequence of the union, which covered the largest territory of any political unit in Europe at the time. On the other hand, leaving most decisions to the council meant being a king in name only. Nor was the council of the realm suited to form a permanent government, the more so as government now became increasingly bureaucratic. Delegation to the council would in practice equate to establishing a permanent chancery with wide powers of decision in each country, which would reduce the king's power even more. The greater distances also meant less personal contact between the king and the aristocracy than before. Only the Danish aristocracy continued to have a regular relationship to the king, although young aristocrats from Norway and Sweden might spend some time at court. The *Sture Chronicle* even hints that Sten Sture the Elder had been a page at Christian I's court.

Regimen politicum thus in practice meant national government, whereas *regimen regale* meant a strong union. This is also evident in its actual history. The first union, between Norway and Sweden when the king was a minor, illustrates well the aristocratic ideal. The countries were governed by the councils, partly under the leadership of a regent, and links between them were kept to a minimum. A similar practice was introduced during the short reign of Christoffer of Bavaria (1439/42–1448). By contrast, Margrete and Erik built up a union administration in Denmark, after the acquisition of Copenhagen in 1417 increasingly centered in that city, and governed the other countries from there. They managed to increase their control of local administrations by appointing men they could trust to most of the larger and more important *len*, notably those with a castle. They also imposed stricter conditions on the *lenholders*, requiring that they render account for their administrative expenses and leave the surplus to the king instead of keeping the whole in return for services.

Christian I and his successors practiced the same kind of central administration as Margrete and Erik, but, except for Christian II (1513–1523), were somewhat more cautious regarding the local administration.

To the king, loyal men meant men dependent on him, either lowborn or foreigners or both. In Sweden and Norway, noble foreigners, Danes or Germans, might serve the purpose equally as well as lowborn men, which had the additional advantage of satisfying the aristocracy nearest at hand. In Denmark, lowborn men and Germans might be used as a counterweight against the Danish aristocracy, but, on the other hand, it was easier to rule in cooperation with the council of the realm in the country that was the king's main residence. Moreover, the career opportunities the union offered Danish aristocrats were incentives for cooperation with the king and would make some amount of *regimen regale* palatable to them. Despite the common front that the Danish and Swedish aristocracies eventually formed against Erik of Pomerania, the Danish council of the realm normally sided with the king during union conflicts, and its members showed no solidarity with their Norwegian counterparts when the Norwegian council was abolished in 1536.

Another issue of national relevance was foreign policy. As we have seen, the three countries had widely different interests in this field, but the union monarchs normally pursued the traditional Danish aim of expansion in Northern Germany. This was a particularly prominent concern under Erik of Pomerania, whose main aim was to get hold of the Duchy of Schleswig, the southern part of the country that had been given as a fief to a sideline of the dynasty in the thirteenth century and whose duke was now the count of the neighboring area of Holstein, a fief under the emperor. Erik carried out a prolonged and costly war in these areas, which was financed by increased taxation in all three countries, and which contributed to the resentment against him in Sweden. Christian I in 1460 managed to get control not only of Schleswig but also of Holstein, against the payment of 30,000 marks silver, almost as much as the sum Magnus Eriksson had paid for Scania (above p. 244). To finance this, he imposed a tax in Sweden that led to his deposition four years later.

Increased taxation was normally resented by the common people, but it might be supported by the elites if they found that it served their interests. However, the Swedish and Norwegian elites would hardly be interested in Danish conquest in Northern Germany. In the case of Sweden, there was the additional problem that the Danish kings' policy in Germany often brought them into conflict with the Hanseatic League, on which the Swedes depended for their export of iron. Such conflicts might also create problems for the Norwegians, although there were more varied attitudes to the Hansa in that country. Otherwise, the Norwegians were as uninterested in Danish expansion in Germany as the Swedes, whereas the Danish king for his part showed little interest in the traditional Norwegian possessions in the Atlantic Islands. Thus, when Christian I married his daughter to the King of Scotland in 1468, he mortgaged the Orkneys and Shetland in order to pay her dowry, which resulted in the islands being permanently ceded to Scotland. This was probably also Christian's intention; he preferred a good relationship with Scotland to some distant islands that probably produced little profit. The Norwegian council of the realm was offended, however, and Christian's successors had to promise in their election charters that they would redeem the islands, a promise that they never kept.

The incompatible aims of Danish and Swedish foreign policy were revealed in a drastic way around 1500. To put pressure on the Swedes before the 1497 invasion, King Hans had concluded an alliance against Sweden with the Russian Grand Prince Ivan III (1493), who shortly before (1471) had taken control of Novgorod.

The Russians launched a massive attack against Finland and almost managed to storm Viborg, but were defeated and had to conclude a six-year peace agreement in 1497. When Russian envoys arrived in Sweden in 1501 to complain that the Swedes were not fulfilling the agreement, they revealed the previous arrangement with the Danes, which contributed to the new rebellion in Sweden in the same year.

The main argument in favor of the union for the Norwegian and Swedish aristocracies was peace. The union would eliminate rivalry between the countries, whereas the Swedes' cession from it provoked Danish attempts to force them back. It also worked in the interests of aristocrats with lands in more than one country, notably as the result of Scandinavian intermarriage, which became more frequent during the union period. Thus, the union king could often rely on the support of the aristocracy in the border region between Denmark and Sweden. In most cases, however, such aristocrats had one country as their main residence and often exchanged lands so as to concentrate most of their possession in one country. Men who established themselves in a country other than their fatherland would most often identify their interests with those of their new country. Provisions about reserving offices for the aristocracy of one country normally included such men. The majority of at least Norwegian and Swedish aristocrats were therefore more likely to prefer having *len* and offices in their home country reserved for themselves over opening up the whole of Scandinavia for competition between aristocrats from all three countries.

At least from a Swedish point of view, the arguments against the union would seem to outweigh those in its favor. In Norway, the weakest of the three countries, the peace argument seems to have been strongest. The Norwegian aristocracy remained loyal to Erik of Pomerania longer than its Danish and Swedish counterparts did, and there were no serious attempts to elect a separate

Norwegian king. The Norwegian alternative to the union with Denmark was therefore a union with Sweden. Karl Knutsson had considerable support in Norway in 1448–1450 but finally had to give up. The most serious rebellion in Norway, which started in 1501, was closely connected with that in Sweden and, if successful, would probably have led to some kind of union with Sweden.

Against this background, it comes as no surprise that the union of the three countries eventually collapsed. Sweden became a fully independent kingdom under its own king and Norway became a Danish dependency. It is a more open question when the point of no return was reached. The fact that the Swedes did not elect their own king in the period between Karl's death in 1470 and Gustaf Vasa's election in 1523 may indicate that they regarded the union as a possibility throughout the period. However, a more plausible explanation is that they intended to keep the Danish king at bay by means of endless negotiations, while ostensibly keeping the door open for a revival of the union. In addition, the protectors may have been afraid of offending their fellow aristocrats by claiming a higher rank; Karl Knutsson's failures would likely have served as a warning.

Although the union was renewed as late as in 1520, it seems gradually to have become a less realistic alternative. In 1457, the Swedes on their own initiative chased Karl Knutsson out of the country and invited Christian I to be their king. In 1497, there was a rebellion against Sten Sture, but it would hardly have succeeded had not King Hans arrived with an army. In the years between 1517 and 1520, Christian II repeatedly mobilized great and costly armies against the Swedes and was repeatedly defeated. His last and greatest mobilization only succeeded because Sten Sture was killed. Even then Christian was aided by a Swedish opposition movement, which was, however, more anti-Sture than pro-Danish. Thus, Swedish support for a union was gradually diminishing between 1457 and 1520. Whether or not a different course of action by Christian might have saved it in the 1520s, remains an open question, but the most likely answer is no. In any case, the best he could hope to achieve would be to become a figurehead in the aristocratic republic of Sweden. By contrast, Gustaf and his successors developed a strong monarchy in Sweden, partly based on the foundations laid by the Stures, which made Sweden into a great European power in the next century.

Recently, however, Harald Gustafsson has argued that the union was a realistic alternative throughout the period and that even Gustaf Vasa's election in 1523 did not put a definitive end to it. Gustaf did not confine his ambitions to Sweden but tried to get hold of as much as he could from the other countries as well. He occupied the Bohuslän region of Norway and parts of Halland and Blekinge in Denmark, and he tried to hold on to them as long as possible. Gustaf was an ambitious man who may well have wanted to extend the borders of Sweden. However, when he proclaimed himself king on June 6, 1523, he knew not only that the Danes had rebelled against Christian, but also that their candidate to the throne was Christian's uncle Frederik. Although Gustaf would not have declined the union throne for patriotic reasons, it seems extremely unlikely that he believed it would be offered to him. In addition to satisfying personal ambition, Gustaf's election must have aimed at blocking any attempt to renew the union under a new and more acceptable Danish ruler.

As we have seen, dynastic unions were a common phenomenon in the later Middle Ages. The likelihood of any such union becoming permanent seems to have been greatest when one of the partners was significantly stronger than the other, and when they were situated close to one another. Castile and Aragon (from 1479) and England and Scotland (from 1603) are examples of this. However, both of these unions met with considerable problems later in their history and within both there has recently been a revival of separatist movements. A successful example that does not fit this pattern is Poland-Lithuania, in union from 1386. The populations in the two countries were about equal, but the territory of Lithuania was about three times as large as that of Poland. This was a loose union, however, and the two countries themselves were not very centralized, which meant that there was no strong incentive to oppose the union. The Habsburg Empire would also seem to be an exception. It consisted of a large number of countries without any core area strong enough to dominate the others. Considerable diplomacy was therefore needed to hold it together, but the emperor also had some extra advantages: the imperial title, which gave some prestige and symbolic power, and the Counter Reformation, which enabled him to defeat the Protestants in Bohemia and achieve stricter control of the country. Finally, the threat from the Turks enabled him to come forward as a liberator of Christians from Turkish rule.

Within Scandinavia, Denmark was clearly the strongest country in the later Middle Ages, but it was not strong enough to force the other two to remain in the union. Geography was a further obstacle. Although there was a common border between Denmark and Sweden and even a point where the borders of all three countries met, the territory covered by the union was far larger than that of England-Scotland or Castile-Aragon, and the leading country was situated at its southern end. Thus, the odds for an enduring union were not great. If successful, a long-term Scandinavian union would more likely have conformed to the Poland-Lithuania model than to the two Western examples. It would have been a loose union under a common king, with considerable independence granted to its individual partners.

State Formation in the Later Middle Ages

The Kalmar Union raises the issue of medieval versus early modern state formation, which has been so frequently discussed among historians and political scientists—the latter particularly after the publication of Charles Tilly's 1975 anthology on the subject and his account of European state formation from 990 to 1990, published in 1990. Was the union a step backwards compared to the formation of the three kingdoms in the previous period, or even evidence that this formation rested on a weaker foundation than assumed in the previous pages? Were the previously independent kingdoms merged into a union in such a way that their borders became blurred? And were the borders endangered by castle administration?

The building of castles from the thirteenth century onwards initially increased the king's control over his territory and facilitated the extraction of resources from the peasants. With a castle and a garrison of armed knights, they could easily be forced to pay taxes and serve the king in other ways. On the other hand, the king became more dependent on the castellan, who often appropriated most of the revenues for himself. Consequently, as this system was gradually introduced all over Scandinavia during the fourteenth and fifteenth centuries and the same king ruled over the whole area, there might seem little reason to uphold the traditional national borders. There are examples also of territories on both sides of the border being joined under the same lord. It has even been claimed that the borders between the countries were still unsettled in the early sixteenth century and that it was pure coincidence that they were reestablished as they had been in the previous period (Harald Gustafsson).

However, the very fact that the borders were so quickly and relatively easily restored and remained intact despite conflicts and unions argues against Gustafsson's thesis. Admittedly, the division of Sweden might have continued if King Birger had not murdered his brothers, although we might also predict that a new series of struggles would sooner or later have resulted in the kingdom once more being united. The inter-Nordic principality in the border region between the three countries had disappeared by the settlement of 1319. The division of Norway between Magnus Eriksson and his son Håkon was abolished with Magnus's death in 1374. Scania was acquired by Magnus in 1332 but not incorporated into Sweden, and it was easily reconquered during the Danish revival and Magnus's troubles in the 1360s. Concerning the territories temporarily occupied by Gustaf Vasa and returned to king Fredrik of Denmark and Norway, Gustafsson may be right that the attitude of the population in the area would not have posed a serious obstacle to permanent possession. However, the fact that this had been Danish and Norwegian land for centuries probably would have. No doubt, medieval and early modern kings fought for land, but they fought even more for rights. Gustaf Vasa must have known that it would be very costly in the long run to keep these territories and that the more prudent course of action would be to respect King Frederik's rights. He soon returned the occupied territories and concluded a formal treaty with Frederik's successor Christian III in 1541.

Concerning the relationship between the union and the individual countries, it is significant that the union as such had no particular name—the term "Kalmar Union" is modern. It was referred to as "these three kingdoms," evidence that the individual kingdoms were regarded as the real units. This may seem paradoxical against the background of our previous discussion about the importance of the dynasty, which in the beginning served as the only criterion for distinguishing between the countries. However, the distinction between the king's person and the monarchy as an institution was developed further as a consequence both of the union and the strengthening of the aristocracy. The council of the realm became the highest authority within each country and was understood as sharing in the king's power. When the first union, the one between Norway and Sweden, was entered into in 1319, the two councils of the realm met for the first time without a king—he was three years old at the time—and concluded a treaty on the government of the two realms during his minority. In the early fourteenth century, both Sweden and Denmark were defined as elective monarchies and Norway followed suit in the fifteenth century. The union between Denmark and Norway in 1450 was concluded by the two councils of the realm, despite the fact that the king was not a minor as he had been in 1319, and (also in contrast to 1319) it was explicitly stated that the union should last forever. Thus, the union strengthened the institutionalization of government and confirmed that individual realms were its fundamental units. Neither the borders between the countries nor their political institutions were merged as a result of the union. The term "these three kingdoms" was thus no empty formula but a precise description of the character of the union. Both the local and the central administrations may have been weak by later standards, but there was an idea that the individual *len* were part of a legally defined territory, from which they could not be separated, at least not under normal circumstances.

From this point of view, we may also consider the discussion about national versus constitutional interests. Rather than rejecting the importance of national interests in favor of constitutional ones, we should regard the former as an important factor in the development of the latter. Admittedly, the growth of constitutional ideas can be traced back to the gradual formation of an "aristocracy of the realm" from the thirteenth century onwards, which would in any case have led to some kind of division of power between the king and the aristocracy, parallel to what happened in countries like England and France at about the same time. The council of the realm increased its importance during the fourteenth century, although even during the Swedish rebellion against Erik of Pomerania in the 1430s, the members of the council are not clearly identifiable. The definitive institutionalization seems to have occurred shortly afterwards. From the mid-fifteenth century, the councils in all three countries consisted of members of the top aristocracy and the bishops, and they took over the decision-making functions of the larger assemblies. A country's council now became the aristocracy's main tool for limiting the king's power. It also elected the king and regarded itself as the main representative of the people. As the bishops were *ex officio* members of the council, it also represented the interests of the Church. Although the Church was still a powerful organization, it now to a greater extent acted politically through the council of the realm and by securing its rights in the election charters. This was in line with developments all over Europe, the later Middle Ages being the great period of aristocratic constitutionalism and attempts to limit the power of monarchs, kings as well as popes.

It is no coincidence that the formalization of the council of the realm and aristocratic government took place after the deposition of Erik of Pomerania in 1439–1442. Ideologically, this marked the transition from the realm being defined by the king to its being defined by the people. The realm was a collective entity, with laws and institutions specific to it, and it was governed by a council of the realm. This was stated with especial clarity in Sweden, which actually managed without a king for around fifty years. Although opposition between the king and the council was less marked in Denmark and Norway, similar ideas were formulated there also, notably during interregnums. In such a situation, the council insisted on taking control of all the castles in the country until the new king had been elected. There was both a practical and a theoretical reason for this. Practically, it was important to prevent the candidate for the throne from presenting the council with a fait accompli. Theoretically, it expressed an idea of sovereignty as delegated by the people as represented by the council of the realm. Admittedly, this was a highly theoretical "people"; the council was an exclusively aristocratic assembly and not in any practical sense representative of the people as a whole, but we are nevertheless dealing with an important constitutional principle. These constitutional principles were further developed in King Hans' 1483 election charter, in which the king had to accept his subjects' right to rebellion. Its wording stipulates that if the king acts unjustly, the good men of the realm should "teach" him to mend his ways, and, if this fails, they are allowed to use force against him. The paragraph was probably introduced in hopes of convincing the Swedes to accept King Hans, but it was used again in the election charters for Denmark and Norway issued by Christian II (1514) and Frederik I (1524).

What were the consequences of the union for internal development in the three kingdoms? During the last two centuries of the Middle Ages, are we dealing with the continuation of an ongoing process of state formation or with a reversal of the trends of the previous period? As we have seen, no Scandinavian ruling king was killed by his subjects in the over five hundred years between 1286 and 1792. Apart from that, however, the succession to the throne seems to have been at least as problematic as in the previous period, and there were depositions of kings as well. However, in contrast to the previous period, the political elite at the time repeatedly had to deal with the problem of dynastic discontinuity. The Danish dynasty became extinct in the direct male line in 1375, and two grandsons of the previous king—both minors—were candidates to the throne. Thanks largely to Margrete's political skill, her son was elected, but the important point was that there were institutions, notably the council of the realm, that could carry out an election and guarantee that it was respected. A disputed election did not lead to a prolonged civil war as happened several times in the previous period. The next crisis, Olav's death and the succession of Erik, was solved in a similar way. After the deposition of Erik, the urgent need for a king resulted in the unanimous election of Erik's sister's son, Christoffer of Bavaria, an election that was accepted in all the three countries.

Christoffer's death without issue might have created a new crisis, but the Danish council of the realm solved the problem by quickly electing Christian of Oldenburg. There were alternative candidates, including a Danish nobleman, but once more, the elected candidate was universally accepted. Christian's election solved Denmark's problem with dynastic discontinuity for the next four hundred years. The problem of younger brothers was also solved, despite the fact that Christian as well as many of his successors had more than one son.

Once elected, a Danish king could normally expect to rule until his death. However, as many as two of the six kings who ruled between 1375 and 1523 were deposed. Erik of Pomerania can to some extent be said to have deposed himself by remaining in Gotland instead of returning to Denmark to deal with the problems there. His deposition was a clear expression of the constitutionalist ideology of the council of the realm, but was also an expression of lawful procedure. A king who does not carry out his duties is a king no more. Again the council was able to carry out a unanimous election; the new king was universally accepted, and no attempt was made to reinstate Erik. The second deposition, of Christian II, was more problematic. It started as a rebellion by the aristocracy in Jutland—traditionally of rebellious temper—but quickly spread to the rest of the country. Lacking money to recruit an army, Christian fled Denmark without serious resistance. However, this was only a temporary retreat; he was the brother-in-law of the Emperor Charles V, received aid in Germany, and formed a continuous threat in the following period, even after he had been captured and imprisoned during a failed attempt to conquer Norway (1532). The disputed succession after Frederik I's death in 1533 resulted in a new attempt to restore him, the so-called Count's War (1534–1536), named after the leader of the rebellion army, Count Christoffer. At first glance it would appear that we are back to the internal struggles of the twelfth and thirteenth centuries, but in fact, the situation was extraordinary. The Reformation was under way, accompanied by peasant rebellion, tension between the burghers and the aristocracy, and an intervention from Lübeck, where a radical Protestant and populist government had replaced the old merchant aristocracy.

Rather than reverting to the internal strife that characterized the previous period, however, the political system in Denmark seems in most cases to have been able to solve the problems that resulted from the lack of a direct heir to the throne. This in turn points to the common interests of the monarchy and the aristocracy and the advantages for the monarchy as such, if not directly for the individual king, of the elective system that had developed in Denmark. There was now an institution with sufficient authority to elect the king, to see to it that his election was respected, and even to depose a king without exposing the country to a civil war. At the same time, the council of the realm did not try to exploit its authority to manage without a king. Despite the increasing importance of constitutionalist ideas, the aristocracy needed the king. The king was essential for order and stability and for solving, or at least minimizing conflicts between individual aristocrats. Characteristically, the Danes also rejected the idea of electing a member of the aristocracy king, this in contrast to the Swedes. They preferred foreigners with some links to the old dynasty. We might in this context think of the ancient idea that royal blood confers special power, but the most important consideration must have been the relative independence of factional loyalties. In contrast to what happened in East Central Europe when the national dynasties became extinct, the Danish council did not elect their kings from prominent foreign dynasties, but instead chose German princes of moderate rank. Apparently, the principal motivation was not to gain powerful allies, but to have a king whose main interest would be his new country.

The situation in Norway was basically similar to the one in Denmark, which is not surprising, partly because succession crises there seem to have been overcome already in the mid-thirteenth century, and partly because of Norwegian dependence on Denmark. The exception is the situation after the death of Christoffer, when the Norwegians were divided between the Swedish and the Danish candidates, and the choice was determined by the greater strength of Denmark.

This situation also illustrates the fact that what worked well for Denmark and Norway, did not work for the union as a whole, and particularly not for Sweden. Whereas the two former countries had institutions able to deal with a shortage of heirs and disputed successions, there was nothing similar for the union as a whole. Despite promises, a common royal election never took place, except the one in Kalmar in 1397; and as has already been pointed out, a common union council is difficult to imagine as a permanent institution. Although this might not prevent the occasional common meeting of the three councils, such a meeting seems in practice to have been difficult to arrange. In 1439, the Danish council acted alone and was followed by the Swedish one. In 1448, the Swedish council acted alone—in retaliation?—but the Danish council did not accept the Swedish candidate. An attempt at a united election was made after Christian I's death in 1481, with a common election charter, but the Swedes failed to attend.

The failure of the attempt to introduce royal elections by the whole union seems in particular to have been due to the Swedes, who also had great difficulties in agreeing about royal elections. Factional struggles were almost endemic from the second half of the fourteenth century, after which the union monarchy created some kind of stability. Erik's rule was respected for a long time, whereas the rebellion against him created a united front, which continued, despite considerable tension, throughout the reign of

Christoffer. The election of Karl Knutsson illustrates the problem of choosing an indigenous aristocrat as king. Karl was an ambitious and aggressive man who made enemies easily, and his reign was one of the most chaotic in Swedish history. He also had the problem that his resources did not measure up to his ambitions; he was far behind the leading families, the Vasa and the Oxenstierna, in wealth. His successors, the Stures, learned from his example and did not try to become kings. They also behaved more diplomatically toward the people and their fellow aristocrats.

These observations show that state formation continued in the later Middle Ages but to a different degree in the different countries. In addition to its greater wealth and population, Denmark had the advantage of a relatively harmonious relationship between monarchy and aristocracy. Admittedly, Valdemar IV and Margrete had used both violence and manipulation to recover lost crown lands and extend their power, but they had succeeded, and despite some tension and hard negotiations over election charters, their successors mostly managed to rule without arousing the aristocracy to open rebellion. The Danish kings could exploit the fact that individual aristocrats were dependent on their favor, and their union policy gave career opportunities outside Denmark to members of the aristocracy.

In addition, they had a good relationship with the Church. The support of the bishops was crucial to Valdemar's revival of Danish power and was an important asset for his successors as well. The Danish kings also maintained friendly relations with the pope—they had during most of the period their own representative at the curia—and were to a considerable extent able to elect bishops of their own choosing, an important prerogative as bishops were often important as royal counselors and administrators. Although Denmark was an aristocratic country and most bishops were recruited from the aristocracy, there were also a number of humble background who had made a career in the king's service, such as Archbishop Birger Gunnersen in the early sixteenth century.

The Danish monarchy also increased its power during the fifteenth century. In 1429, Erik of Pomerania introduced the Øresund toll, which had to be paid by every ship passing through the sound. After some initial conflicts, he and his successors eventually managed to make it effective. This meant an enormous profit, amounting to around a quarter of the annual royal revenues in the early sixteenth century. Until the Kiel Canal was built in the late nineteenth century, Øresund was the only sea connection between the Baltic and the North Sea, the main trading route in Northern Europe. In addition, the toll had two other advantages. It went directly into the king's treasury and could be used by him, without interference from the council of the realm. Secondly, it was paid in cash and thus provided ready money that the king could put to immediate use wherever he wished, unlike most other taxes, which were paid in kind. The Danish kings also developed a more professional central administration in their new capital Copenhagen, particularly under King Hans (1481–1513), who also built a modern navy that was used with some success during his and his successors' attempts to gain Sweden. The increased cash income also enabled the Danish kings to hire mercenaries, who played a decisive part in their attempts to gain Sweden. Thus, Denmark had much the greatest military power of the three countries, but Sweden was nevertheless sufficiently strong defensively to resist Danish attempts at conquest.

The Swedish aristocracy was more difficult for the king to control than their Danish counterparts. The fact that the king was Danish may be part of the explanation, but it should be remembered that two Swedish kings had been deposed already in the fourteenth century, before the union with Denmark. It also says something about the character of the Swedish aristocracy that the country was without a king almost continuously for fifty years. As might be expected, the Swedish Church had strong links to the aristocracy. Most bishops were aristocrats, although there were some exceptions. The Danish king occasionally managed to impose a lowborn favorite on a Swedish see during the union, but there are also some examples of broader recruitment towards the end of the Middle Ages—Archbishop Jakob Ulvsson from the lower aristocracy, for example, and Kurt Rogge of Strängnäs and Hans Brask of Linköping, both from burgher families. Like Danish aristocrats, the Swedish nobles also competed for *len*, which often led to internal unrest. Here the lack of a strong king may have been a disadvantage; there was no arbiter above the competing nobles who could referee their disputes and secure some balance.

By contrast, the Danish kings constantly mediated between the two leading (and competing) families, the Rosenkrantzes and the Gyldenstjernes (Shakespeare's Rosenkrantz and Guildenstern!) and saw to it that both of them received some *len* and offices. A king doing the same might possibly have worked in Sweden, but the union king was of course often absent, and in addition he had a habit of giving Swedish *len* to foreigners. The Sture had difficulties in acting as neutral arbiters between the nobles; they were sometimes more readily viewed as competitors. Admittedly, Sten Sture the Elder managed to gain the same protection from the Church as if he had been a crowned monarch (1474). Apart from that, he and his successors based their power on a number of important *len*, while the rest were distributed among the Sture's allies. Here, however, they had to balance carefully to prevent rivalry and discontent. Nevertheless, the Sture were considerably more successful than Karl and did manage both to hold the Danes at bay and to limit internal conflicts. Important factors contributing to their success were, in addition to their personal skills, their mobilization of the peasants and their effective propaganda. Nevertheless, as we have seen, even towards the end of the period, the Danes were able to find allies within the Swedish aristocracy. A comparison between King Christian I of Denmark and Sten Sture the Elder shows the advantages of a stable monarchy. Sten Sture was a brilliant politician and propagandist but had to deal with a series of crises throughout his reign, was never safe from opposition, and towards the end of his career had to submit to the Danish king. Christian I was a mediocrity who admittedly failed to hold onto Sweden but was unchallenged in Denmark and Norway.

Despite the Sture's almost royal position, the council of the realm was officially the highest authority in the country. However, as the Sture had many competitors among the bishops and the nobles, they made considerable use of larger assemblies, where the lower nobility, the townspeople, and the peasants were represented. Although these assemblies were mostly local, they form the background for the development from the sixteenth century onwards of the Swedish *Riksdag* or diet, consisting of four estates. This was in clear contrast to the conditions in the two other countries, where such assemblies regularly took the form of extended meetings of the council of the realm. The paradox is that this "noble republic of Sweden" in the following period developed into one of strongest and most centralized states in Europe, surpassing Denmark politically and militarily to become a great European power in the seventeenth and early eighteenth centuries. The immediate explanation may be sought in the new king who came to the throne in 1523. Gustaf Vasa was the Swedish parallel to Valdemar IV in Denmark. He belonged to one of the wealthiest noble families, he had led a war of liberation against the Danes, he could profit from the heritage of the Sture and their prolonged struggle with the Danes, and he was a ruthless and clever politician. It has also been suggested that Christian II had done part of the job for him by executing a number of potentially rebellious nobles. The strength of the Swedish state over the long run depended upon an alliance between the king and a relatively poor aristocracy that enabled Sweden to profit from a war of conquest in Northern Europe.

Norway shows the greatest continuity from the previous period. Although the importance of castles increased in this country as well, there were fewer of them, and the aristocracy was weaker and more dependent on the king. The consequences of the Black Death were more serious for the aristocracy in this country than in the other ones (pp. 233–34), and despite the fact that the king was mostly absent, there was less aristocratic opposition against him than in Sweden. As in Sweden, the king to some extent appointed foreigners as castellans, particularly from the beginning of the sixteenth century. By contrast, the king had less influence on the Church than in Denmark. After a whole series of twelfth- and early-thirteenth-century archbishops from high-ranking aristocratic families with strong links to either of the two dynasties, first that of Magnus, then that of Sverre, later archbishops had a somewhat more distant relationship to the king. The later pattern seems to have been to recruit bishops from the lower aristocracy, often from families some of whose members were canons. The cathedral chapters, which elected the bishops, were apparently able to recruit family members; although sons could not succeed fathers, nephews could and often did succeed or join uncles.

The later Middle Ages in Scandinavia give an impression of almost continuous struggles and rivalries, war, plundering, and violence. Medieval warfare was certainly cruel and its effects on the common population should not be underestimated. Still, war was conducted with small forces and was less destructive than in later ages. The vast social inequality of the time took the form of greater cruelty towards peasants and commoners than towards members of the aristocracy. Peasants might have their farms burned during wars and they were punished more severely than aristocrats if they rebelled; the leaders were usually executed, while the others had to pay heavy fines. Moreover, in contrast to aristocrats, who were executed by beheading, commoners were hanged (which was considered shameful), or, even worse, they might be broken on the wheel or burned alive. Conflicts between aristocrats were usually conducted in a chivalrous manner, and although they were not as well protected as kings, they were relatively rarely executed. Periods of war were usually brief and were preceded and followed by elaborate negotiations. Wars, moreover, were fought not to destroy an adversary, but to force him to concessions in the following negotiations. Admittedly, what is probably the best-known event in late-medieval Scandinavian history gives an entirely different impression. The Bloodbath of Stockholm was a display of a shockingly new kind of behavior, and a radical departure from fifteenth- and early-sixteenth-century political culture. There was, however, some precedent in the previous acts of Christian II. Christian's Swedish opponents had received all kinds of guarantees of life and property, which almost all of them trusted—Gustaf Vasa being an exception. Moreover, the aftermath of the story shows that Christian's action was not only immoral but ineffective; it had the exact opposite of the intended result, leading to the final loss of Sweden for the Danish king.

Historians have usually expressed limited sympathy for the late-medieval aristocracies and their attempts to limit the power of the king. In practice, their constitutional principles were often the expression of narrow class interests and might even endanger the survival of the country in question, as it is claimed happened in Hungary. There the Turkish conquest of most of the country during the first half of the sixteenth century has been blamed on the aristocratic reaction after Mathias Corvinus's death in 1490, which weakened the country militarily. The aristocratic policies in late-medieval Scandinavia had less disastrous consequences, possibly because the area was less exposed to foreign enemies, but in part also because aristocratic policy was more moderate and responsible there than in Hungary. The level of violence was relatively low by medieval standards, and there was a willingness to negotiate and compromise. Moreover, despite the many selfish demands they embodied in the elections charters, the aristocrats had a clear awareness of the need for a king as a guardian of the social order and the rule of law.

Late-medieval constitutional thought was far from democratic, and in most countries the aristocratic constitutions were overthrown by a strong monarchy in the following period. Nevertheless, there is a connection between the principles articulated in the later Middle Ages and the new wave of democratic constitutionalism that coincided with the American and the French revolutions of the late eighteenth century. Intellectually, the ideas of the medieval theorist survived and were developed further by thinkers like Locke and Montesquieu, and in some countries, notably England, even the medieval constitution survived. Within Scandinavia, Sweden forms a parallel to England. Although the Sture regime was replaced by a strong monarchy, the Swedish king never became formally absolute, and the late-medieval diet survived until 1866, when it was replaced by a modern parliament with two chambers.

The Reformation and Its Consequences, 1523–1537

The Swedish rebellion under Gustaf Vasa was followed by the deposition of Christian II in Denmark and Norway in 1523. The next year the new king, Frederik I, issued separate election charters for Denmark and Norway, in which he gave the usual promises about ruling justly and respecting the privileges of the Church and the aristocracy. Danish attempts to rule the whole of Scandinavia were a thing of the past, and the traditional government of

a king ruling in cooperation with the aristocracy had replaced
Christian II's attempts at royal absolutism. Actually, however,
Frederik's accession to the throne introduced one of the most
dramatic periods in Scandinavian history, which ended in the fall
of both the Catholic Church and the independent kingdom of
Norway.

After Luther's break with the pope in 1520, the Reformation
movement had spread quickly over Germany and soon reached
Schleswig-Holstein and Denmark, and, a little later, Sweden. The
movement was particularly strong in the towns, but segments
of the nobility were influenced. King Frederik was friendly to the
movement and protected the Protestant preachers. Already in
1523, he broke the Danish Church's connection with the pope,
but he did not interfere with Catholic doctrine and religious
practice and left the bishops in possession of their estates. After
Frederik's death in 1533, the bishops were reluctant to elect his
eldest son Christian to succeed him, because he was, even more
than his father, a convinced Protestant. This resulted in a post-
ponement of the election to the next year, but before it could
take place, a civil war broke out, usually referred to as the "Count's
War," after the commander of the rebel forces, Count Christoffer
of Oldenburg, a distant relative of the royal house. The rebels
did not represent a Catholic reaction, but on the contrary were
staunchly Protestant, with Copenhagen and Malmö as their main
strongholds and Lübeck, led by a radical weaver who had replaced the merchant aristocracy as the town's ruler, as their main
ally. Their aim was to reinstate the captive Christian II—who
had also converted to Protestantism—as king. The rebellion thus
had elements of a social revolution. In the beginning, however,
the rebels, thanks to their mercenary army, managed to gain control of Scania and the islands, where they also, at least for a time,
received the support of the nobility. In this situation, the bishops
reluctantly rallied behind Christian and elected him king in the

summer of 1534. Christian gained the upper hand already late in 1534 and won the final victory when Copenhagen surrendered on July 29, 1536. A few days later, on August 12, he arrested the bishops, and on October 30 the Reformation was officially declared. Lutheran superintendents replaced the Catholic bishops, the bishops' estates were taken over by the king, and the monasteries were dissolved. In 1537, a new ecclesiastical constitution was issued after close consultation with Luther and the theologians around him.

By that time, the Reformation had already been introduced in Sweden. This happened at the diet of Västerås in 1527. Sweden also had a Reformation movement, although it was weaker than the movement in Denmark. The king's attitude was also very different. Whereas Christian III was a convinced Lutheran, Gustaf Vasa seems to have had little interest in theology and to have embraced the Reformation for political and financial reasons. The result of the diet was to give the king control of the Church, but very little was said about cult and doctrine. The Swedish Church continued to have bishops and even an archbishop, and the Catholic bishops continued in their offices, but were normally succeeded by men with Protestant sympathies. The Swedish Reformation was therefore gradual; there were even attempts to reintroduce Catholicism as late as in the second half of the sixteenth century. Gustaf Vasa's son Johan III (1568–1592) married a Polish princess and their son, Sigismund, King of Poland and for a short time also of Sweden (1592–1598), was a Catholic.

In contrast to the two other countries, there was little trace of Protestant influence in Norway before 1536. In the following year, by Danish decree, Protestantism was instated, and Christian III fulfilled the promise in his election charter that Norway should be a part of Denmark forever, like Jutland, Funen, and the other Danish landscapes. Norway was incorporated into the Danish realm and ceased to be an independent kingdom.

The twelve years between 1524 and 1536 are full of drama and have been much discussed. So has also the interpretation of the paragraph in Christian's election charter, as well as its legal status. Admittedly, the status of Norway was not identical to that of the Danish landscapes. The king of Denmark always referred to himself as king of Norway and Denmark; there was a clear distinction between the two territories, and even during the most centralizing phase of the period of absolutism, the revision of the laws resulted in a separate law for Norway (1687). Nevertheless, a drastic change from equality or near equality to subjection took place in 1536–37, and its course was largely a consequence of the Reformation.

The Norwegian council of the realm was dominated by the bishops and chaired by the archbishop. The archbishop rebelled against Frederik in 1531–32 and actively sought an alternative to Christian III as his successor, although he accepted him in the end. By then, however, it was too late. Drastic administrative changes would in any case be necessary to introduce the Reformation in Norway, and there was not much point in upholding the council of the realm if there were no bishops. The members of the Norwegian high nobility were too few to uphold the council as an effective institution, or, from the king's point of view, to necessitate such a concession on his part. Nor could they expect much solidarity from their equals in Denmark who now got free access to *len* in Norway. It must also be added that the fall of the Catholic Church was probably a greater blow against national interests in Norway than the fall of the council of the realm; the Church was the most important path to a career for the lower nobility in Norway, either as bishops or canons, or as the numerous laymen in the bishops' service. From the point of view of the Danish aristocracy, the elimination of Norway as a separate kingdom also had the advantage that the king could not use the Norwegian tradition of hereditary kingship to weaken the Danish council's right to elect his successor.

What accounts for the different fates of Norway and Sweden? The most obvious explanation is the difference in wealth and population between the two countries. In the early sixteenth century, the population in all countries was still smaller than it had been before the Black Death, but their relative size was probably similar. However, as we have seen, the economic decline hit the upper classes considerably harder in Norway than in the other countries. Moreover, it seems that Norway lost its independence at the time when its economic weakness relative to the neighboring countries was greatest. While Denmark and Sweden were on their way to recovering from the crisis by about 1450, it would last nearly a hundred years longer in Norway. In the following period, however, from around 1550, Norway experienced rapid growth, demographically, agriculturally, and economically, through the export of new commodities like timber and metals. Thus, Norway was more vulnerable in the period between 1450 and 1550 than ever before or after.

Not only did Norway succumb to Denmark, but the process also took place easily and without much violence. Although there had been rebellions against Danish rule during the union period, among the peasants as well as the aristocracy, they were significantly rarer and less serious than in Sweden. During the final stage, in 1536–37, the Danes already controlled the most important castles in the southern part of the country—Bohus, Akershus and Bergenhus—and a force of three hundred men was sufficient to conquer the rest without much fighting. This points to a strategic explanation, much the same as explains the ease with which the country was unified. During the later Middle Ages, Denmark had once again become the leading sea power in Scandinavia and could therefore easily control Norway from the coast. Once the Danes had taken the few important castles, which were all in reach of the coast, they had full control. When attempting to conquer Sweden, they usually managed to gain bridgeheads along the coast, notably Stockholm and Kalmar, but this was insufficient for control of the whole country. Conquering the inland regions was considerably more difficult and was only achieved for brief periods of time and with the aid of Swedish allies. Thus, we have come back full circle: the same factor that explains the rise of the kingdom of Norway also serves to explain its decline. A Danish conquest of Norway in the Viking Age would have meant a piecemeal struggle against various power-holders along the coast, but the Norwegian dynasty had eliminated these long before the sixteenth century, so that the Danish king could now take over the country as their successor. Politically, the Danish king had become the legitimate successor to the strong Norwegian monarchy, and the status of the legitimate dynasty was considerably stronger in Norway than in Sweden. In addition, the Norwegian elite had become even more dependent on the king's service in the later Middle Ages than before, because they had lost other incomes with the economic crisis.

Danish economic and military superiority over Norway would probably have led to Norway's subordination even without the Reformation, but the process would have been more gradual and might not have been carried so far. It might even have been halted by Norway's economic revival in the following period. Thus, while long-term economic and political factors explain Norway's increasing dependence on Denmark, the form this dependence took can only be explained by the Reformation.

The Reformation changed the relationship between the three kingdoms by abolishing what remained of Norwegian independence. It also had far-reaching consequences for internal conditions in all three countries. There were no longer two independent organizations within each country; the king had taken full control of the Church and gained an enormous profit from con-fiscated church lands. Of equal importance was his ideological gain in having the priests now as loyal servants of the monarchy, preaching obedience to the lawful ruler and even—particularly in Sweden—mobilizing the population for a new kind of cru-sade, the defense of the true faith against the "Papists" during the Thirty Years War. Admittedly, the Church had served somewhat similar purposes in the past, but the king's control over it had never been so direct. The second winner from the suppression of the Church was the secular aristocracy, which got hold of a large part of the former ecclesiastical lands and increased its position in the king's administration, centrally as well as locally. In Den-mark, the period between 1536 and 1660 (the introduction of absolutism) is usually referred to as "Adelsvælden" (the Domi-nance of the Nobles). It has been debated who benefited more, the king or the aristocracy, but whatever the answer, there can be hardly any doubt that it was a considerable step forward in state formation. The conditions for holding *len* became stricter, and the courts of law and the central administration more centralized and efficient. The king had to share his power with the council of the realm, which, in the case of seventeenth-century Denmark-Norway led to considerable rivalry, as well as other problems, until a series of disasters resulted in the introduction of absolut-ism in 1660. By contrast, Sweden had the advantage of good co-operation between the two powers, which in part explains her military successes during the Thirty Years War and the following period.

⊹⟾ CONCLUSION ⟽⊹

Scandinavian State Formation 900–1537: Break and Continuity

ACCORDING TO SOME SCHOLARS, notably Charles Tilly, the European state was formed during the Early Modern Period rather than the Middle Ages, not only in the sense that the change from personal to impersonal rule took place in this period, but also because it was then that the territorial divisions themselves were formed. It was therefore still an open question around 1500 whether Europe would be divided into national states or petty principalities or would become one great empire. The preceding examination of the Scandinavian kingdoms has not confirmed this hypothesis. Although the three kingdoms were apparently the products of a series of struggles between individual warlords from the ninth to the mid-eleventh century, the units formed by the end of this period show remarkable stability over the course of the following centuries, and this despite a series of internal and external conflicts. Petty principalities formed within one kingdom as the result of dynastic divisions (or through other causes) did not develop into independent kingdoms, but either returned to their original units or remained in some kind of feudal subordination. Land conquered by one kingdom from another was returned to the original possessor relatively quickly.

Scania remained under the king of Sweden for thirty years in the fourteenth century (1332–1361) and the border regions for around half of this time in the sixteenth century. Only Gotland, conquered by Denmark in 1361, was transferred from one kingdom to another. However, Gotland was only nominally under Swedish suzerainty even before its conquest. It was contested during the struggles over the union in the fifteenth and early sixteenth century and recognized as Danish as part of the settlement between Gustaf Vasa and Christian III. It was ceded to Sweden in 1645, as a result of the major changes in the Scandinavian borders consequent to Sweden's rise to the status of a great power.

This stability is also evidence of internal consolidation, of the formation of political entities held together by something more than a ruler's personal charisma or the decision by a certain number of people to keep together as long as it serves their interests. The dynastic unions from 1319 onwards are a test of the achievements in the previous period. They had their origin in the ambitions of the kings, together with marriage patterns and rules of succession introduced during the twelfth and thirteenth centuries, which increased the likelihood that the same person would succeed to the throne in more than one country. The union of the three countries in 1397 might seem to have opened the possibility of obliterating the eleventh-century borders and creating a Nordic super-state. That possibility might, in fact, have been entertained by the king and the circle around him, but there is little evidence that it was ever a realistic alternative. As expressed in its contemporary name, "the three kingdoms," the union consisted of three realms governed by one king. Moreover, the unions accelerated the movement towards an impersonal government by making an institution, the council of the realm, the bearer of its sovereignty and responsible for appointing its king. When Sweden ceded from the union in the 1520s, the old borders between this country and the two others were quickly reestablished after a short period of Swedish occupation of Danish and Norwegian territory. By contrast, the extinction of Norway as an independent country was a drastic change from the Middle Ages. However, Norway was never eliminated as a separate entity. Nor was it conquered in the real sense; the king of Denmark could claim a legitimate right as the successor of the ancient line of Norwegian kings. Finally, the Danish takeover in 1536–37 would hardly have assumed such a drastic shape if it had not been for the Reformation, which eliminated the strongest segment of the Norwegian political elite in order to introduce religious reform. Characteristically, the period of the Reformation and Counter-Reformation also saw the most drastic changes that would occur in the relationship between the European states before the French revolution. The state system that had developed during the Middle Ages was not resistant to any change, but quite substantial forces were needed to shake it.

The Historiography of the Scandinavian Countries

There is a continuous tradition of historical writing from the Middle Ages to the present day in all three of the Scandinavian kingdoms, as well as in Iceland, though admittedly it began later (not until the early fourteenth century) in Sweden than in the other countries. The works dating from the Middle Ages have already been discussed. Those of the Early Modern Period are of interest as evidence of learning and for an understanding of how "history" was viewed at the time, and also because they contain a number of documents from the Middle Ages whose originals have been lost. However, the beginning of modern scholarly historical writing is usually dated to the early nineteenth century, in Scandinavia as in the rest of Europe. The professionalization of history, which started in Germany, quickly spread to Scandinavia. Throughout Europe, this professionalization was related to a national revival that typically placed great emphasis on a nation's medieval past.

In all three Scandinavian kingdoms, this resulted in more university positions devoted to history, particularly national history; in the publication of scholarly editions of the sources; the inauguration of professional historical journals; and the appearance of a considerable volume of books and articles on national history based on the study of original sources. Throughout the nineteenth century, there was some tension between the use of history for national purposes and objective history, based on close examination of the sources. Erik Gustaf Geijer (1783–1847) in Sweden and J. E. Sars (1835–1917) in Norway are examples of the former, while the Danish historian Kristian Erslev (1852–1930) represents the latter. As in the rest of Europe, this latter approach gained ground towards the end of the century, which in Scandinavia led to important changes in the attitude of historians to the narrative sources.

Throughout the nineteenth century, extensive work was carried out to ensure that all available sources were used when confronting historical problems, in particular the oldest sources. Nevertheless, there were widely differing opinions on how to deal with these sources, notably with the narrative ones. The main sources for the early histories of Denmark and Norway were Latin chronicles, the most important of which was Saxo Grammaticus's *Gesta Danorum* and the Old Norse sagas, which date largely from the late twelfth or thirteenth centuries. In the mid-nineteenth century, these sources were regarded as derived from an oral tradition going back to the events themselves and thus as largely reliable. Consequently, the Norwegian historian P. A. Munch could write several large volumes on the earliest history of the Norwegian kingdom and even discuss in detail the political conditions of the country before the reign of Harald Finehair (c. 900), according to the sagas the first ruler of the whole of Norway. In the following period, a more critical attitude to the sagas gradually gained ground.

Then, in 1911, the Swedish historian Lauritz Weibull published his *Kritiska undersökningar i Nordens historia omkring år 1000* (Critical Examinations of Nordic History around the Year 1000), in which he rejected most of the information in the sagas about this period. The book was regarded as revolutionary and gave rise to a heated debate and much opposition. Theoretically, the novelty of Weibull's approach was his demand for absolute certainty, while his predecessors had been content with probability. However, this hardly explains the importance of his contribution; few historians will claim certainty for their results. Weibull's main importance therefore lies on the empirical level. His method as such was not new; it can be found in earlier European scholarship, as well as in handbooks of historical method, but up to now it had not been applied to the sagas, either because of their deceptively realistic appearance or because of continued belief in the reliability of the oral tradition.

By systematically examining the literary tradition that formed the basis of the later sagas, notably Snorri's *Heimskringla,* Weibull could show that what in many cases had been believed to be independent oral evidence was actually a transformation of earlier extant written statements. Thus, by examining the sources for the Battle of Svolder, he showed how new elements were gradually added to the original narrative, which in the end gave it an entirely different context and placed its site off Rügen, instead of Øresund, its location in the earlier sources. Later, his younger brother Curt Weibull did the same for Saxo's account of St. Knud of Denmark, showing that Saxo's changes and additions to the previous sources were not based on new evidence, but on a transformation of the previous sources to better fit a new purpose.

The Weibull revolution also had consequences for the link between historiography and the nation. The ideal of absolute certainty and objectivity was, not infrequently, at odds with the role of history in the nation building. Besides, without being political radicals, the Weibulls were not in sympathy with the conservative trend and the cult of the state in Swedish historiography. Their methods were developed further by Curt Weibull's pupil Erik Lönnroth in his rejection of the national interpretation of the Kalmar Union (Chapter 5 above). Discontent with national interpretations was also expressed in Erik Arup's *History of Denmark* (1925), in which the kings were mostly regarded as insignificant, whereas the important figures in history were the common people, the aristocracy, and the Church.

Norway differed somewhat from its neighbors during the first half of the twentieth century. Although influenced by the Weibulls, Norwegian historians were generally less critical of their narrative sources. They were also politically more radical; the most influential of them were even Marxists. Nevertheless, with one exception, Edvard Bull (1881–1932), they had fewer reservations about nationalism. This applied particularly to Halvdan Koht (1873–1965), a leading Social Democrat, who attempted a synthesis between Marxism and a national interpretation, in many ways continuing in the tradition of Sars. In practice, the Marxist historians paid more attention to social and economic history. In particular, Andreas Holmsen (1906–1989) did groundbreaking work in the areas of settlement, landownership, and demography. He was also one of the founders of the great Nordic project that studied deserted farms (1964–1981).

The period of Norwegian historiography from the end of the Second World War to around 1970 has often been labeled "critical empiricism," which meant a continuation of trends from the previous period in Denmark and Sweden, to which Norwegian historians had adapted. An important step in this direction was Jens Arup Seip's (1905–1992) article of 1940, which considerably modified the Marxist interpretation. Seip remained true to the basic idea that material conditions and interests explain political conflicts, but he now attributed greater importance to individuals and short-term trends and showed greater interest in institutions, political history, and the history of ideas. In harmony with then-current trends, Seip also underlined the importance of studying local conditions and attributed little importance to influence from abroad.

Finally, the 1970s and the following period brought a Marxist revival as well as—partly combined with the revival and partly in reaction to it—increased emphasis on the influence from international trends such as the history of mentality and social anthropology. This led to greater interest in the early Middle Ages and its historiography, particularly the sagas. This latter trend can to some extent be regarded as a continuation of the Weibull revolution, leading to the use of the sagas as evidence, not for the period with which they dealt but for their authors' understanding of their own society. However, an important aspect was also the attempt to use the sagas as sources for the history of mentality, norms, and social structure in the early period, based on comparison with stateless societies in other parts of the world, as studied by social anthropologists. This also led to a similar reaction against the focus on state formation, which also made itself felt in the rest of Europe. As the present book belongs to this period, however, and is at least partly influenced by these trends, I shall venture no further here, but instead refer the reader to the preceding chapters.

The Sources for Scandinavian History

There is little written evidence of Scandinavian history before the introduction of Christianity in the tenth and eleventh centuries, only some runic inscriptions and references in foreign chronicles. Consequently, archaeological excavations and place names are important evidence for the history of this period. For the following period, up to and including the thirteenth century, there is a considerable volume of narrative sources from Norway, Iceland, and Denmark, but little from Sweden. As we have seen, these sources present considerable problems. Although there may be some objections to the Weibull's interpretation, there is no way back to the nineteenth century view of the sagas and Saxo as valid sources for the period before the twelfth century. There are better reasons to trust the narrative sources for the following period, which are contemporary or almost contemporary with the events, although they too raise issues of bias, selectivity, and the individual authors' variable access to information. However, the narrative sources have a value apart from their factual information. They form an important part of the cultural heritage of the Scandinavian countries and can give information about ideas and attitudes at the time of their writing. They can also to some extent be used retrospectively as information about norms and social practices, including gift exchange, revenge, kinship, and alliances, phenomena that still occurred at the time of writing, but are unlikely to have been new in the twelfth and thirteenth centuries.

Whereas the Weibulls for the most part rejected the sagas as sources for the earliest Scandinavian history, they accepted the skaldic poems quoted in them. The sagas, notably Snorri's *Heimskringla,* contain a large number of such poems, the oldest allegedly dating from the time of Harald Finehair in the late ninth and early tenth centuries. Most of them are addressed to kings and praise them for their generosity—notably for their generosity to the skalds themselves—and for their achievements in war. We know that such poems were composed at the time, as there are traces of them on rune stones, but can we really trust the sagas when they tell us that they have been transmitted orally from the time of their composition? The arguments in favor of this are their complicated meter, which would tend to discourage the kinds of changes that often infect prose narratives, and the fact that they were highly regarded by contemporary society and thus likely to be remembered. Then too, it would seem a more likely hypothesis that the saga writers transmitted genuine poems than that they composed all of them themselves, while attributing them to various poets in the past. However, this does not necessarily mean that all of the poems are genuine, or that the saga writers' interpretations of them and their context is correct. The value of the poems will therefore be a challenge for the modern historian in each particular case.

Eventually, the narrative sources were replaced by documentary ones. There are some charters and correspondence with the papacy and foreign monarchs from the late eleventh century onwards, but no great increase in material of this kind until the thirteenth century. Even then, we have mainly to deal with scattered remains; only during the last centuries of the Middle Ages do we find some instances of continuous records and various kinds of cameral material. Nevertheless, the amount of written material is considerably less than in the following period and less than what survives from this period in many other countries, notably England. There were also great changes over time. Despite a considerable increase in the number of documentary sources during the thirteenth century, they represent only a small percentage of what once existed. By contrast, a very high percentage of the extant material dates from the end of the Middle Ages, the period between 1500 and 1550. Particularly in Norway, but to some extent also in Denmark and Sweden, the vast majority of the material concerns land transactions. By contrast, political history is often difficult to trace, particularly in Norway, but also in the other countries, at least in the beginning of the period. In many cases, this leads to highly diverse scholarly interpretations of the same events or phenomena and even to extensive debates over a few documents, the most famous of which concerns the interpretation of the two foundational documents of the 1397 Kalmar Union.

⤜⊶ REFERENCES AND GUIDE TO ⊷⤛ FURTHER READING

General

Most accounts of medieval Scandinavia deal with a single country rather than with the region as a whole. The main exception is Birgit and Peter Sawyer's *Medieval Scandinavia: From Conversion to Reformation* (Minneapolis, MN: The University of Minnesota Press, 1993), which is the closest parallel to the present book. It is organized thematically in ten chapters, each covering one subject from the beginning of the period until the end. It contains much information in a concentrated form but is less concerned with the relationship between the various themes. It also focuses more strongly on the early than on the later period. A more recent account is David Nicholas, *The Northern Lands 1-3* (Chichester: Wiley, 2009). Knut Helle (ed.), *The Cambridge History of Scandinavia* ([=CHS], vol. 1 [Cambridge: Cambridge University Press, 2003, 872 pp.) is an anthology in which a number of authors give extensive accounts of most aspects of Scandinavian history, dealing partly with the area as a whole and partly with the individual countries. There are also brief chapters in *The Cambridge Medieval History* (=CMH), by Niels Lund (vol. 2, pp. 202–27), Peter Sawyer (vol. 4.2, pp. 290–303), Sverre Bagge (vol. 5, pp. 720–42), and Thomas Riis (vol. 7, pp. 671–706). A brief survey in Swedish is Harald Gustafsson, *Nordens historia: en europeisk region under 1200 år* (Lund: Studentlitteratur, 2007).

On Norway, see most recently Sverre Bagge, *From Viking Stronghold to Christian Kingdom: State Formation in Norway, c. 900–1350* (Copenhagen: Museum Tusculanum Press, 2010). Nils Hybel and Bjørn Poulsen, *The Danish Resources, c. 1000–1550*

(Leiden: Brill, 2007) covers important aspects of Danish social and economic history, including royal finances and administration. Nils Blomkvist, *The Discovery of the Baltic* (Leiden: Brill, 2005) is an ambitious attempt to discuss the Europeanization of the countries around the Baltic Sea, up to the early thirteenth century. Within Scandinavia, its focus is particularly on Sweden. Reference works include Philip Pulsiano (ed.), *Medieval Scandinavia: An Encyclopedia* (New York: Garland, 1993) in one volume, and the far more detailed *Kulturhistorisk leksikon for nordisk middelalder* (Copenhagen: Rosenkilde og Bagger, 1956–78, repr. 1980–82), 22 vols., in the Scandinavian languages.

There are a number of general histories of each country in the Scandinavian languages. Knut Helle, *Norge blir en stat* (Oslo, etc.: Universitetsforlaget, 1974, 2nd ed.); Inge Skovgaard-Petersen et al., *Danmarks historie,* vol. 1: *Tiden indtil 1340* (Copenhagen: Gyldendal, 1977); Kai Hørby and Michael Venge, vol. 2.1, 1340–1559 (*ibid.,* 1980), and Gottfried Carlsson and Jerker Rosén, *Sveriges historia till 1718* (Stockholm: Bonnier, 1962) are all good surveys. On Iceland, see Jesse Byock, *Viking Age Iceland* (London: Penguin, 2001). There are also several series of national histories intended for a general audience, the most recent of which are *Gyldendals og Politikens Danmarks historie,* 16 vols. (Copenhagen: Gyldendal and Politiken, 1988–91); *Aschehougs Norges historie* (Oslo: Aschehoug, 1994–98); and *Norvegr,* 4 vols. (Oslo: Aschehoug, 2011).

Most of the documentary material for Scandinavian history is published in the series *Diplomatarium Danicum/Danmark riges breve* in Denmark (Copenhagen: Det danske Sprog- og Litteraturselskab, 1932–); *Diplomatarium Norvegicum* in Norway (Christiania/Oslo: Riksarkivet, 1849–) and *Diplomatarium Svecanum/Svensk diplomatarium in Sweden* (Stockholm: Riksarkivet, 1829–), all still incomplete.

Introduction

The quotation from *Ljosvetninga Saga* is taken from *Law and Literature in Medieval Iceland: Ljósvetninga Saga and Valla-Ljóts Saga,* trans. Theodore M. Andersson and William Ian Miller (Stanford: Stanford University Press, 1989), pp. 198–99. On the general discussion of medieval state formation, see Joseph Strayer, *On the Medieval Origins of the Modern State* (Princeton: Princeton University Press, 1970); R. W. Southern, *The Making of the Middle Ages* (London: Hutchinson, 1953); Charles Tilly (ed.), *The Formation of National States in Western Europe* (Princeton: Princeton University Press, 1975); and *Coercion, Capital and European States, AD 990–1990* (Cambridge, MA: Blackwell, 1990); Susan Reynolds, *Kingdoms and Communities* (Oxford: Blackwell, 1984) and *Fiefs and Vassals* (Oxford: Clarendon Press, 1994); Michael Mann, *The Sources of Social Power,* vol 1: *A History of Power from the Beginning to AD 1760* (Cambridge: Cambridge University Press, 1986); R. I. Moore, *The First European Revolution* (Oxford: Blackwell, 2000); and Gerd Althoff, *Spielregeln der Politik im Mittelalter* (Darmstadt: Wissenschaftliche Buchgesellschaft, 1997). On Scandinavia from this point of view, see the works listed above. Robert Bartlett, *The Making of Europe* (London: Penguin, 1993) discusses the expansion of Europe in the High Middle Ages, including the Europeanization of Scandinavia, although its main focus is on military expansion in Eastern Europe and the Mediterranean.

Chapter 1: The Origins of the Scandinavian Kingdoms

There are chapters on the development of settlement, early political organization, and the Viking expeditions in *CHS,* pp. 15–234. See also Peter Sawyer, *Kings and Vikings: Scandinavia and*

Europe, A.D. 700–1100 (London: Routledge, 1998). The examples of connections with The Roman Empire are derived from Michael Bregnsbo and Kurt V. Jensen, *Det danske imperium. Storhed og fald* (Copenhagen: Aschehoug, 2004). The publications of the recent excavations in Kaupang in southeastern Norway contain much information about Viking Age society; see Dagfinn Skre (ed.), *Kaupang in Skiringssal* (Århus: Aarhus University Press, 2007). For discussions of early Norwegian and Icelandic society based on the sagas, see William Ian Miller, *Bloodtaking and Peacemaking* (Chicago: University of Chicago Press, 1990) and Sverre Bagge, *Society and Politics in Snorri Sturluson's Heimskringla*, (Berkeley, etc.: University of California Press, 1991). Feuds and patronage during the internal conflicts in Denmark are dealt with in Lars Hermanson, *Släkt, vänner och makt. En studie av elitens politiska kultur i 1100-talets Danmark* (Gothenburg: Gothenburg University, 2000). On later Scandinavian foreign policy: Erik Christiansen, *The Northern Crusades: The Baltic and the Catholic Frontier, 1100–1525* (London: Macmillan, 1980); Espen Albrectsen, "700–1523," *Konger og krige. Dansk udenrigspolitiks historie,* vol. 1 (Copenhagen: Danmarks nationalleksikon, 2001); Narve Bjørgo et al., *Selvstendighet og union. Fra middelalderen til 1905. Norsk utenrikspolitikks historie,* vol. 1 (Oslo: Universitetsforlaget, 1995), pp. 19–132; Steinar Imsen (ed.), *The Norwegian Domination and the Norse World, c. 1100–1400* (Trondheim: Tapir, 2010); and Ane Bysted, et al. (eds.), *Jerusalem in the North: Denmark and the Baltic Crusades, 1100–1522* (Turnhout: Brepols, 2012).

Chapter 2: The Consolidation of the Scandinavian Kingdoms, c. 1050–1350

The development of the Scandinavian kingdoms is dealt with in a series of chapters in the *CHS,* pp. 345–462. There are different interpretations of the process. The interpretation offered in this volume is presented in greater detail for Norway in Bagge, *From Viking Stronghold;* whereas Hans-Jacob Orning, *Unpredictability and Presence: Norwegian Kingship in the High Middle Ages* (Leiden: Brill, 2008) emphasizes more strongly the continuity from the early Middle Ages. S. Bagge et al., *Statsutvikling i Skandinavia i middelalderen* (Oslo: Dreyer, 2012) contains various interpretations of the process in the Scandinavian languages. On Iceland, see Jon Vidar Sigurdsson, *Chieftains and Power in the Icelandic Commonwealth* (Odense: Odense University Press, 1999) and Sverrir Jakobsson, "The Process of State-formation in Medieval Iceland," *Viator* 40:2 (2009), 151–70.

Early state formation and national identities are discussed in Patrick Geary et al. (eds.), *Franks, Northmen and Slavs: Identities and State Formation in Early Medieval Europe* (Turnhout: Brepols, 2007).

On the royalist ideology in the High Middle Ages, see Sverre Bagge, *The Political Thought of "The King's Mirror"* (Odense: Odense University Press, 1987) and Nanna Damsholt, "Kingship in the Arengas of Danish Royal Diplomas, 1170–1223," *Medieval Scandinavia* 3 (1970), pp. 66–108.

There are several recent accounts of the conversion of Scandinavia. Richard Fletcher, *The Conversion of Europe: From Paganism to Christianity, 371–1386 AD* (London: Fontana, 1998) is a general survey which also includes Scandinavia. Nora Berend (ed.), *Christianization and the Rise of Christian Monarchy: Scandinavia, Central Europe and Rus, c. 900–1200* (Cambridge: Cambridge University Press, 2007) contains separate articles on the three Scandinavian kingdoms. See also Anders Winroth, *The Conversion of Scandinavia* (New Haven: Yale University Press, 2012) and Sæbjørg W. Nordeide, *The Viking Age as a Period of Religious Transformation: The Christianization of Norway from AD 560–1150/1200* (Turnhout: Brepols, 2011). On Archbishop

Eystein and the Norwegian Church in the twelfth century, see Tore Iversen (ed.), *Archbishop Eystein as Legislator: The European Connection* (Trondheim: Tapir, 2011).

The *CHS* has no separate chapter on law but deals with it in some of the general chapters on state formation. Otherwise, there has been great interest in legal history in Scandinavia recently. An important problem has been the relationship between Scandinavian and European law. Elsa Sjöholm, *Sveriges medeltidslagar. Europeisk rättstradition i politisk omvandling* (Lund, 1988) rejects any suggestion of an original Scandinavian law, explaining the existing laws partly by foreign influence and partly by royal decisions. Although much criticism has been directed against Sjöholm's method, the main trend in recent years has been to point to the European background of Scandinavian laws. See Helle Vogt, *The Function of Kinship in Medieval Nordic Legislation* (Leiden: Brill, 2010). The series *Medieval Legal History*, papers from the Carlsberg conferences on legal history, contains many valuable articles in English on Scandinavian law and its relationship to Europe; see in particular, Ditlev Tamm and Helle Vogt, *How Nordic Are the Nordic Medieval Laws?* (Copenhagen: University of Copenhagen Press, 2005); Per Andersen et al., *Law and Power in the Middle Ages* (Copenhagen: DJØF Publishing, 2008); and *Law and Private Life* (Copenhagen: DJØF Publishing, 2011). A different point of view is represented by Stefan Brink, "Law and Legal Customs in Viking Age Scandinavia," in Judith Jesch (ed.), *The Scandinavians from the Vendel Period to the Tenth Century: An Ethnographic Perspective* (San Marino: The Boydell Press, 2002), pp. 87–117, who points to runic evidence of similar rules as in the Swedish provincial laws. Sverre Bagge, "Law and Justice in Norway in the Middle Ages: A Case Study," in Lars Bisgaard et al. (ed.), *Medieval Spirituality in Scandinavia and Europe: A Collection of Essays in Honour of Tore Nyberg* (Odense: Odense University Press, 2001), pp. 73–85, is an attempt to use later narrative sources to trace early-medieval legal practice.

The military changes resulting from European influence are discussed briefly in Robert Bartlett, *The Making of Europe,* pp. 70–76. On the new administrative system, based on *len,* see Erik Lönnroth, *Statsmakt och statsfinans i det medeltida Sverige* (Gothenburg: Acta Universitatis Gothoburgensis, 1984 [orig. 1940] and Dag Retsö, *Länsförvaltningen i Sverige, 1434–1520* (Stockholm: Stockholms universitet, 2009). On the parallel development in East Central Europe, see Pál Engel, *The Realm of St. Stephen: A History of Medieval Hungary* (London: I.B. Tauris, 2001) and S. C. Rowell, "The Central European Kingdoms", CMH, vol. 5, pp. 754–68.

Chapter 3: State Formation, Social Change, and the Division of Power

The information in the text about Danish royal finances is based largely on Hybel and Poulsen, *The Danish Resources,* pp. 314–22. For Norway, see Bagge, *From Viking Stronghold,* pp. 110–21. The passage on coinage is based on Svein Gullbekk, *Pengevesenets fremvekst og fall i Norge i middelalderen* (Copenhagen: Museum Tusculanum Press, 2009). On the general European background for Scandinavian state formation, see Wolfgang Reinhard, "Introduction: Power Elites, State Servants, Ruling Classes, and the Growth of the State," in Wolfgang Reinhard (ed.), *Power Elites and State Building* (Oxford: Clarendon Press, 1996), pp. 1–18, and W. Mark Ormrod, "The West European Monarchies in the Later Middle Ages," in Richard Bonney (ed.), *Economic Systems and State Finance* (Oxford: Oxford University Press, 1995), pp. 123–60. See also Bjørn Poulsen, "Kingdoms on the Periphery of Europe: The Case of Medieval and Early Modern Scandinavia," *ibid.,* pp. 101–22.

The examples from England are taken from Michael Clanchy, *From Memory to Written Record: England, 1066–1307* (London: Edward Arnold, 1979). Slavica Rancovic et al., *Along the Oral-Written Continuum: Types of Texts, Relations and Their Implications* (Turnhout: Brepols, 2010) deals with various aspects of orality and literacy in Scandinavia, including administrative literacy, as does also Arnved Nedkvitne, *The Social Consequences of Literacy in Medieval Scandinavia* (Turnhout: Brepols, 2004).

The observations on the importance of the court and the relationship between the king and the aristocracy are partly inspired by Jacob Tullberg, *Beyond Feudalism: Comparative Perspectives on the European Middle Ages*, PhD thesis, The Saxo Institute, University of Copenhagen, 2012. On the relationship between the king and individual nobles and their way of addressing one another, see Lars Bisgaard, *Tjenesteideal og fromhetsideal. Studier i adelens tænkemåde i dansk senmiddelalder* (Århus: Arusia, 1988).

On contemporary social theories, see Sverre Bagge, "Old Norse Theories of Society: From *Rígsþula* to *Konungs skuggsiá*," Jens Eike Schnall and Rudolf Simek (eds.), *Speculum regale. Der altnorwegische Königsspiegel (Konungs skuggsiá) in der europäischen Tradition* (Vienna: Fassbinder, 2000), pp. 7–45. On slavery and its abolition, see Tore Iversen, *Knechtschaft im mittelalterlichen Norwegen* (Ebelsbach: Aktiv, 2004).

The question of feudalism in Scandinavia is discussed by Michael H. Gelting and Erik Opsahl in Sverre Bagge (ed.), *Feudalism: New Landscapes of Debate* (Turnhout: Brepols, 2011), pp. 159–201.

There has been considerable discussion on whether nationalism is essentially a modern phenomenon, originating in the late eighteenth and early nineteenth century, or whether it can also be found earlier. For the former point of view, see e.g., Ernest Gellner, *Nations and Nationalism* (Oxford: Blackwell 1983); for the latter, A. Smith, *Nationalism: Theory, Ideology, History* (Cambridge: Polity, 2001). The Scandinavian discussion includes Sverre Bagge, "Nationalism in Norway in the Middle Ages," *Scandinavian Journal of History* 20 (1995), pp. 1–18; Kåre Lunden, "Was there a Norwegian National Identity in the Middle Ages?" ibid. pp. 19–33; and Troels Dahlerup, "Omkring en dansk identitsfølelse i middelalderen," Per Ingesman og Bjørn Poulsen (eds.), *Danmark og Europa i middelalderen* (Århus: Aarhus Universitetsforlag, 2000), pp. 30–38. See also Brian McGuire (ed.), *The Birth of Identities: Denmark and Europe in the Middle Ages* (Copenhagen: Reitzel, 1996).

Chapter 4: Royal, Aristocratic, and Ecclesiastical Culture

For a survey of the various expressions of Scandinavian culture: religion, literature, art, and music, see *CHS*, pp. 465–555.

The European influences on various aspects of Scandinavian culture are discussed in Gerd Wolfgang Weber (ed.), *Structure and Meaning in Old Norse Literature: New Approaches to Textual Analysis and Literary Criticism* (Odense: Odense University Press, 1986) and J. Adams and K. Holman (eds.), *Scandinavia and Europe, 800–1350: Contact, Conflict, and Coexistence* (Turnhout: Brepols, 2004).

On books and libraries, see Alf Härdelin and Monika Hedlund, "The Monastic Library of Vadstena," *Acta Bibl. Reg. Universitatis Upsaliensis* 29 (Uppsala: Almqvist och Wiksell, 1990) and Mia Korpiola, "Literary Legacies and Canonical Book Collections: Possession of Canon Law Books in Medieval Sweden," *Law and Learning,* pp. 79–103. On the Norwegian fragments, see Åslaug Ommundsen, *Books, Scribes and Sequences in Medieval Norway* (Bergen: University of Bergen, 2007). On Scandinavian students abroad, see Sverre Bagge, "Nordic Students at Foreign Universities", *Scandinavian Journal of History* 9 (1984), pp. 1–29.

On Scandinavian Christianity, see Bisgaard, *Tjenesteideal*; Anders Fröjmark, *Mirakler och helgonkult: Linköpings biskopsdöme under senmedeltiden* (Uppsala: Uppsala University, 1992); Christian Krötzl, *Pilger, Mirakel und Alltag: Formen des Verhaltens im skandinavischen Mittelalter* (Helsinki: Helsinki University, 1994); Anne Riising, *Danmarks middelalderlige prædigen* (Copenhagen: Gad, 1969); and Arnved Nedkvitne, *Lay Belief in Norse Society, 1000–1350* (Copenhagen: Museum Tusculanum Press, 2009). Haki Antonsson, *St. Magnús of Orkney: A Scandinavian Martyr-Cult in Context* (Leiden: Brill, 2007) contains much information on the cult of Scandinavian princely saints in general. For the distinction between "hot" and "cold" regions, see André Vauchez, *Sainthood in the Later Middle Ages* (Cambridge: Cambridge University Press, 1997).

For an introduction to Old Norse literature, see Jonas Kristjánsson, *Eddas and Sagas: Iceland's Medieval Literature* (Reykjavík: Íslendska bókmentafélag, 1997, repr. 2007). On the use and interpretation of Old Norse mythology, see Margaret Clunies Ross, *Prolonged Echoes: Old Norse Myths in Medieval Northern Society*, vol 1: *The Myths, The Viking Collection* 7 (Odense: Odense University Press, 1994).

Scandinavian historiography is discussed in the following works: Sverre Bagge, "Scandinavian Historical Writing, 1100–1400," in Sarah Foot and Chase F. Robinson (eds.), *The Oxford History of Historical Writing*, vol. 2 (Oxford: Oxford University Press, 2012), pp. 414–27; Karen Skovgaard-Petersen, "Historical Writing in Scandinavia," ibid., vol. 3, pp. 449–72; Ildar H. Garipzanov (ed.), *Historical Narratives and Christian Identities on a European Periphery* (Turnhout: Brepols, 2011); and Lars Boje Mortensen (ed.), *The Making of Christian Myths in the Periphery of Latin Christendom (c. 1000–1300)* (Copenhagen: Museum Tusculanum Press, 2006). On the Old Norse saga literature, see Sverre Bagge, *Society and Politics* and *From Gang Leader to the Lord's Anointed: Kingship in Sverris Saga and Hákonar Saga*

Hákonarsonar, *The Viking Collection*, (Odense: Odense University Press, 1996); Theodore M. Andersson, *The Growth of the Medieval Icelandic Sagas (1180–1280)* (Ithaca: Cornell University Press, 2006); and *The Partisan Muse in the Early Icelandic Saga (1200–1250)* (Ithaca: Cornell University Press, 2012). Generally on historiography in the Middle Ages, including the term "civil service historiography," see Beryl Smalley, *Historians in the Middle Ages* (London: Thames and Hudson, 1974).

Most of the literature on Saxo is in the Scandinavian languages, including Inge Skovgaard-Petersen, *Da tidernes Herre var nær* (Copenhagen: Den danske historiske forening, 1987) and Kurt Johannesson, *Saxo Grammaticus: Komposition och världsbild i Gesta Danorum* (Stockholm: Almqvist och Wiksell, 1978). A classic analysis is Curt Weibull, "Saxo Grammaticus" in his *Källkritik och historia* (Stockholm: Aldus/Bonnier, 1964), pp. 153–240. However, there are several excellent studies in English by the editor of *Gesta Danorum*, Karsten Friis-Jensen, including *Saxo as Latin Poet: Studies in the Verse Passages of the Gesta Danorum* (Rome: Bretschneider, 1987) and "Saxo Grammaticus's Study of the Roman Historiographers and His Vision of History," in Carlo Santini (ed.), *Saxo Grammaticus: tra storiografia e letteratura* (Rome: Ed. Il Calamo, 1992), pp. 61–81. See also Karsten Friis-Jensen (ed.), *Saxo Grammaticus: A Medieval Author between Norse and Latin Culture* (Copenhagen: Museum Tusculanum Press, 1981).

Select Works from the Scandinavian Middle Ages in Translation

Egils Saga, translated from the Old Icelandic, with introduction and notes by Gwyn Jones (New York: Syracuse University Press, 1960).

Erikskrönikan: The Chronicle of Duke Erik, a Verse Epic from Medieval Sweden, translated by Erik Carlquist and Peter C. Hogg, introduction by Eva Österberg (Lund: Nordic Academic Press, 2012).

The First Grammatical Treatise, ed. and trans. by Hreinn Benediktsson (Reykjavík: Institute of Nordic Linguistics, 2002).

Heimskringla, trans. by Lee M. Hollander (Austin: The University of Texas Press, 1964, repr. 2005).

The King's Mirror, translated into English by Laurence M. Larson (New York: Twayne, 1917).

The Prose Edda: Norse Mythology, translated with an introduction and notes by Jesse L. Byock (London: Penguin Books, 2005).

The Revelations of St. Birgitta of Vadstena, trans. by Denis Searby, introduction and notes by Bridget Morris (Oxford: Oxford University Press, 2006).

The Saga of Hakon and a Fragment of the Saga of Magnus with Appendices, trans. G. W. Dasent, *Rerum Britannicarum Medii Ævi Scriptores* vol. 88.4 (London 1894, repr. 1964).

The Saga of King Sverri of Norway, trans. J. Sephton (London: David Nuff, 1899).

Saxo, *Gesta Danorum: The History of the Danes,* trans. by Peter Fisher, ed. by Hilda Ellis Davidson vols. 1–2 (Cambridge: Brewer, 1979).

Strengleikar: An Old Norse Translation of Twenty-One Old French Lais, ed. and trans. by Robert Cook and Mattias Tveitane (Oslo: Norsk historisk kjeldeskriftinstitutt, 1979).

Chapter 5: The Later Middle Ages: Agrarian Crisis, Constitutional Conflicts, and Scandinavian Unions

On the Black Death, the late medieval desertion, and late medieval society, see *CHS,* pp. 559–675. Svend Gissel et al., *Desertion and Land Colonization in the Nordic Countries, ca. 1300–1600: Comparative Report from the Scandinavian Research Project on Deserted Farms and Villages* (Stockholm: Almqvist & Wiksell, 1981) presents the main results of the Scandinavian project on the agrarian crisis.

The unions and conflicts in the Later Middle Ages are dealt with in *CHS,* pp. 679–770. Most of the more specialist literature is in the Scandinavian languages: Kristian Erslev, *Danmarks Historie under Dronning Margrethe og hendes nærmeste Efterfølgere,* vols. 1–2 (Copenhagen: Jacob Erslev, 1882–1901); Erik Lönnroth, *Sverige och Kalmarunionen 1397–1457* (Gothenburg: Akademiförlaget, 1969 [orig. 1934]); Lars-Olof Larsson, *Kalmarunionens tid: Från drottning Margareta till Kristian II* (Stockholm: Rabén Prisma, 1997), who differs from Lönnroth on several important points; and, most recently, Harald Gustafsson, *Gamla riken, nya stater. Statsbildning, politisk kultur och identiteter under Kalmarunionens upplösningsskede, 1512–1541* (Stockholm: Atlantis, 2000). On the explanation of the decline of Hungary in the early sixteenth century as a result of the strength of the aristocracy, see Engel, *The Realm of St. Stephen,* pp. 345–71.

Unless otherwise indicated, all translations of the sources are my own.

⤛ INDEX ⤜